Public Relations Strategy, Theory, and Cases

This book is part of the Peter Lang Media and Communication list.
Every volume is peer reviewed and meets
the highest quality standards for content and production.

PETER LANG
New York • Bern • Berlin
Brussels • Vienna • Oxford • Warsaw

Tricia Hansen-Horn and Adam E. Horn

Public Relations Strategy, Theory, and Cases

Praxis at Its Best

PETER LANG
New York • Bern • Berlin
Brussels • Vienna • Oxford • Warsaw

Library of Congress Cataloging-in-Publication Data

Names: Hansen-Horn, Tricia L., author. | Horn, Adam E., author.
Title: Public relations strategy, theory, and cases: praxis at its best /
Tricia Hansen-Horn and Adam E. Horn.
Description: New York: Peter Lang, 2018.
Includes index.
Identifiers: LCCN 2017047845 | ISBN 978-1-4331-2079-4 (hardback: alk. paper)
ISBN 978-1-4331-2080-0 (paperback: alk. paper) | ISBN 978-1-4539-1908-8 (ebook pdf)
ISBN 978-1-4331-3938-3 (epub) | ISBN 978-1-4331-3939-0 (mobi)
Subjects: LCSH: Public relations—Case studies.
Strategic planning—Case studies.
Classification: LCC HD59 .H2678 2018 | DDC 659.2—dc23
LC record available at https://lccn.loc.gov/2017047845
DOI 10.3726/978-1-4539-1908-8

Bibliographic information published by **Die Deutsche Nationalbibliothek.**
Die Deutsche Nationalbibliothek lists this publication in the "Deutsche
Nationalbibliografie"; detailed bibliographic data are available
on the Internet at http://dnb.d-nb.de/.

Table of Contents

Figures

Preface

You can do all kinds of things in a public relations career. It's full of exciting options for skill development, new ways of thinking, community impact, and self-actualization. Conversations abound about why and how public relations "takes" place; ongoing discussions highlight the many roles it does, can or, some argue, should play anywhere and in any culture. As a means to an end, most of us who spend our professional lives introducing others to public relations point to specific public-relations-in-action cases as examples, as, "for instances" instances. When we do, we usually have three objectives: (1) to introduce others to the many traditionally recognized areas in, and for which, public relations is and can be practiced, (2) to acquaint others with public relations cases so that they get an idea of what has been done before and with what effects, and (3) to acquaint readers with "best practices." When we classify what has gone on in recognized areas we label public relations activities. When we provide examples of what's gone on before we provide action-oriented ideas as learning opportunities. We do a lot of both through the printed word and, to a lesser degree, video and face-to-face settings.

When we read case studies for the purpose of understanding more about public relations, we can find ourselves hard-pressed to figure out just why a particular case is presented as an example of one kind of public relations or another. Similarly, we can find it hard to figure out how public relations actions relate to what else is going on in the organization. Sometimes it's hard to understand how public relations initiatives affect and are affected by other forms of professional communication (like employee training or procurement legalese), and business operations (such as legal counsel or buying practices), or how culture can or does facilitate or limit what takes place. Additionally, it's easy to assume that the public relations implications of one particular case begin and end under an author-labeled umbrella (such as media relations or investor relations or public affairs and so on). Thus, it becomes really easy to miss other important parts of the situation and the corresponding opportunity to learn more. In addition, we may not recognize the many other relevant orders of business, public relations strategies and initiatives, and relationships that do, could or even should be and, in the process, miss more strategic insights and options.

Unfortunately, when we learn from a case study approach we don't always think to ask the why and how questions leading to alternaquences (possible alternatives linked to possible consequences). We forgo them, meaning we don't critically analyze the case. We simply take what is written at face value and move on without completely understanding why and how something occurred, we can't explain what really went on in the case or, at least, was likely going on in it.

In addition, it's easy to assume that relevant public relations implications begin and end under a label such as media relations, community relations, public affairs, or investor relations, and, thus, be unprepared for the complex reality that really does define what we do. Public relations graduate preparation for the complexity of reality was a topic of discussion at a recent International Public Relations Research Conference.[1] For instance, we may label something a community relations case, but to reach our public relations objectives, we also have to engage in media relations and public affairs initiatives. This means, for example, that if we work in the media relations department of a professional football team, what we do still has to line up with the interests of the community relations department, the team's public affairs initiatives, ticket sales, security, marketing, legal counsel, and the like. We can't act in a vacuum. Nothing would get done or, if it did, chaos would reign. The intent of this book is to help its readers more clearly understand that complexity and interconnectedness.

The prequel to this book is *Strategic Planning for Public Relations: Beginning the Journey*. The 2014 book's purpose is to transform the next generation of public relations colleagues-in-training to "strategists first and tacticians second"[2] who are comfortable asking why and how, and asking these questions a lot. It encourages all public relations professionals to be SRC strategists (aka self-reflexive contextualizing public relations strategists), making sure that we are careful of our assumptions, choices, interpretations and intentions and of how we construct reality through our communication of or about them. The purpose of the present book, *Public Relations Strategy, Theory and Cases* is to keep the conversation going about what, how and why something is happening and who we are as participants in it. A primary goal is to introduce readers to the good and bad associated with learning from case studies. Following that, the discussion of what it means to a SRC public relations strategist is revisited, and different perspectives of strategy that might or can guide your public relations efforts are reviewed. Practical, easy-to-apply questions and exercises are provided to help readers recognize assumptions about and operative definitions of strategy; as well as what kind of economic business areas (B2B, B2C, B2G) and organizational environments (for-profit, non-profit, government) structure public relations initiatives; as well as which public relations situations and contexts (from advancement to sustainability) and specializations (from agency to volunteer) are involved. Finally, in the spirit of new perspective taking, four theories are introduced as lenses through which the questions of how and why can be asked with the expectation of new understandings. Embedded in the idea of perspective taking through theory is the notion of ethical imperative, a reality that no public relations professional can ignore. We explore excellence theory, contingency theory, rhetorical theory, and social capital theory from a public relations perspective.

The really good thing about all of the new ideas and theories introduced to you in chapters one through seven, is that we develop easy-to-use keys (found in Appendix A) to help you apply what you learn. And, in Appendix B, we included some great cases of current and ongoing public relations that you can use with those keys. We provide case insight into the following 11 cases: March of Dimes Rebrand Update; Inside Pediatrics Children's Mercy Kansas City; Vanity Fair Women Who Do LiftTOUR; TouchNet + Heartland; WeatherTech Super Bowl Ad Buy; ZF Fan Reporter/Race Reporter; Pinnacle Not So Silent Night; Lee Jeans—Influencer Relations: Fight CRC One Million Strong; Tips for Kids—Seventeen Years Later and DQ's Fan Food, Not Fast Food. At the end of Appendix A, we even included a Case Rubric Master. You can use it as a sort of hub for recording the analyses you do of the cases chapter by chapter. And, remember, this is a process that is to take place over a course of time, not in one sitting. You can apply the keys we provide and develop an understanding of each of the 11 cases from four different perspectives, or from four different theoretical lenses. Then, you can pull all of your observations together on the Case Rubric Master for the purposes of comparison.

Learning to feel comfortable with complexity and recognizing interconnectedness and guiding assumptions is more important now than ever before. The Pew Center for Research has clearly identified that today's generation, especially younger people, have a "thirst for instant gratification, settle for quick choices, and lack patience."[3]

While it's true that great public relations professionals must have a sense of urgency, remembering in the words of General George Patton "that a good plan today is better than a perfect plan tomorrow," they must also work for best practices that come from patience, delayed results, and careful choice-making. The great public relations strategists of the future will be those whose visions go beyond the immediate (and who voluntarily silence rss feeds, texts, tweets, pins, email notices, Facebook and Instagram posts, etc.) and, in fact, who pause long enough to be strategically passionate about telling others' stories (and helping others live them); embrace short- and long-term consequential thinking; and are willing to live with ambiguity, making sure what they do brings respect, honor and success to those they represent and to the public relations profession. They won't settle for satisficing, which means taking the first option they recognize; instead, they will optimize, which means doing what it takes to engage best practices and capitalize on sustainable desirable results.

Notes

1. University of Missouri Synor Fellow D. Myers, personal communication, March 4, 2016.
2. Hansen-Horn, T. & Horn, A. (2014). *Strategic planning for public relations: Beginning the journey.* New York: Peter Lang, p. xi.
3. Anderson, J. & Rainie, J. (February 29, 2012). Millennials will benefit and suffer due to their hyperconnected lives. *Pew Research Internet Study.* Retrieved from www.pewinternet.org/2012//02/29/millenials-will-benefit-and-suffer-due-to-their-hyperconnected-lives.

CHAPTER ONE

The Good and the Bad of Teaching Public Relations Through Case Studies

One of the tried and true methods of teaching something new is to point to examples of what we want others to learn about and understand. In public relations that's known as teaching and learning through case studies. In fact, academic and professional case study books abound and their place in the classroom and training room is well documented. In addition, the Public Relations Society of America makes available its Silver Anvil Award case winners (see http://www.prsa.org/Awards/SilverAnvil/Search); these are also used by many of us as we teach and learn about what's new, innovative, pure genius, and the like. Additionally, a large number of organizations, especially agencies, regularly publish case studies as examples of their work, of what they have done, and can do (see, for instance, "our work" at Crossroads www.crossroads.us, Weber Shandwick www.webershandwick.com or MSL GROUP North America www.northamerica.mslgroup.com). This chapter highlights the power for learning behind the use of public relations cases, some of the limitations set by traditional approaches to case study education (including a discussion of historical and grounded approaches to case study records), and the potential to bring new ways of thinking and perspective taking to case use.

Case Study Value

Learning through cases really can provide all of us with a lot of value; we can take away new information, understanding, and ideas. Take, for instance, the three cases presented in *Strategic Planning for Public Relations: Beginning the Journey* (Hansen-Horn & Horn, 2014). Much like all case studies intend, the best practices of the University of Central Missouri's Innovative PR firm's #teamUCM Social Media Night sponsorship, Parsons Brinckerhoff's Huey P. Long Bridge Widening campaign, and Crossroads' March of Dimes Rebrand are profiled.[1] In addition to showcasing best practices, the intent was to help readers understand how background information drove the "in a nut shell" situation analysis, how the situation drove the recognized problem or opportunity, the recognized statement of the problem or opportunity accounted for target publics while driving objectives, the objectives determined strategy, strategy drove each tactic, and evaluation started when objectives were decided. A widely-approved formula for planning, implementing, and reporting public relations campaigns is illustrated step by step in each case. The authors assume that their model is a best practice so they showcase it through the way they record their cases for reader consumption.

Another intent of the three cases is to give readers organizational insights to business operations that they might not encounter in any other way. We can't visit all of the organizations that we want to learn about, nor can we be involved with every team of professionals from which we want to learn. So, the case study is our alternative to travel, time, and opportunity. The convenient, easily accessible, and static nature of the case invites students to reflect on what they read and attempt to apply what they learn to their own public relations efforts. The case offers simulation heuristic (idea generating power when faced with similar appearing situations) potential. And finally, evidence of public relations professionals at work is made a permanent part of history; cases can be returned to and referenced time and time again. Hyperlinks to many of them are even presented when a web search is initiated by an enterprising individual.

Case Study Kinds and Limitations

Most case studies fulfill all of the intentions outlined above. They also come with inherent limitations that most of us don't recognize. For instance, very few case studies are intentionally developed to take the student down the how and why question-asking pathways. Their structure keeps us away from being truly self-reflexive contextualizing (SRC) strategists in a way that we keep the following top of mind:

Our ability to communicate is predicated on a lot of assumptions. Being able to communicate well and strategically is dependent on self-reflexive willingness and ability, as well as an ability to remember that the map is not the territory, a map does not represent all the territory, and a map is self-reflexive. Communication in the public relations world includes marketplace wrangle and contested terrains of meaning and interpretation. Finally, all communicative choices and initiatives are contextual and rhetorical. The SRC public relations strategist needs to be sensitive to the many factors of any communicative opportunity.[2]

For instance, we may find ourselves in the following situation. We're halfway through a meeting about a possible community relations crisis. Ten people are meeting in the small conference room containing 10 chairs. An additional person enters the room just as the meeting facilitator says, "we need to find the chair." Your first thought may be that an extra chair has to be found to seat the 11th person to join the meeting. However, because of your self-reflexive read of the situation itself and the cues in what the facilitator says, you will most likely realize (almost instantly) that while a physical chair is needed so the 11th person has somewhere to sit, the chair that needs to be found is the chairman of the board. You realize that the "map" represented in the words uttered by the facilitator is clearly not representative of the physical territory (the room that seats 10). In addition, as the meeting participants discuss getting the attention of the chair of the board, you will likely come up with strategies to get her vested attention in spite of the many demands of the marketplace wrangle (other problems she has to address "right now" in the course of facilitating business). When you do you will use tactics that can cut through the many messages she receives every hour so she gives you her attention and interprets the issue, given the rhetorical and contextual situational cues, as the potential crisis that it is.

Though simplistic, the meeting scenario above represents the way a SRC strategist thinks at multiple levels simultaneously and works to comprehend what is going on and can go on. As formal case studies students we can apply similar kinds of thinking. SRC strategist thinking helps us move beyond the obvious, beyond labels and surface understandings to levels of complexity and interconnectedness representing the rich nature of situations we encounter. Our world is not a simple one, and the success of our public relations efforts is predicated on clearly understanding that.

Interestingly, scholar Andrew Cutler (2004) argues in *Public Relations Review* that, "case studies make up as much as a third of the research in public relations journals, are widely used in textbooks and form the basis for industry awards. Despite their widespread use there has been limited discussion in the public relations literature of their methodological advantages or shortcomings."[3] He sets out to start correcting that lack of discussion and concludes that generalizability (the ability to use what was noted or discovered in one instance is not necessarily going to be true of any other instance) is a significant limitation of most case studies. What is represented in one case study is not necessarily applicable to what is going on (WIGO) today, tomorrow, in the future, or in a similar appearing situation. That said, he argues that the case study is still highly valuable as a venue for four activities: teaching, record keeping, case work in medical fields, and professional practice. It's valuable as long as we recognize its limitations and are careful to remember them as we learn.

The easiest access to case studies in the classroom is through books first and electronic sources second; it's much the same for boardroom trainers. In light of the case study's popularity, Cutler makes a potentially troubling claim about classroom case instruction. Quoting case study expert R. K. Yin he suggests that "'for teaching purposes, a case need not contain a complete or accurate rendition of actual events; rather its purpose is to establish a framework for discussion and debate among students'."[4] This is disturbing if the cases are taught as fact by unsuspecting individuals. However, given that public relations textbook, Silver Anvil, and agency cases clearly identify the organizations represented in them and are open to review by those named organizations, it's probably fair to say that for published cases derived from real activity, accuracy is not an urgent issue. While it's true that cases may suffer from incomplete representation because of publisher word count or reader attention span limits, they are generally accurate in representing major situational contributors, publics, objectives, strategies, courses of action, and outcomes. What they don't do is represent all that is going on or all whose interests are involved.

While Cutler correctly encourages us to think more carefully about the limitations set by most case studies, he doesn't encourage us to stop using them. We should use them, whether derived from actual or hypothetical situations, as best practice examples and, when we can get access, as examples of not-so-good practices. Ironically, the idea of best practices sans not-so-good practices limits the richness of the learning opportunity. PRSA and agency websites host professional practice cases as examples of what was done and done well. Rarely do you find examples of public relations initiatives gone wrong. The organizations that "own" those cases don't allow it; it's considered bad PR to do such a thing!

It's unfortunate that while we know we often learn best from what went wrong, we are usually only given insider access to what went right. The risk of organizational vulnerability keeps us on the outside looking in. Rarely do organizations of interest open their doors and invite us to conversations about what went wrong.

When we do find a case study of what public relations ideas went wrong, the perspective almost always comes from the outsider looking in. The case study author has to search high and low for third party evidence of what went wrong and do her best to represent what went on, how it went on, and the lessons her readers can derive from her assessment. Perhaps the reality of how this takes place is part of what Cutler means in claiming that "for teaching purposes a case need not contain a complete or accurate rendition of actual events."

Historical and Grounded–Business Cases

In the spirit of Cutler's admonitions to proceed carefully are Professor Don Stacks' (2011) distinctions in his *Primer of Public Relations Research* book. He defines the case study while discussing its advantages and disadvantages. He highlights two kinds of prominent case studies, the historical and the grounded—business.

In what he calls a "*historical case study,*"[5] under which #teamUCM, the Huey P. Long Bridge Widening and the MOD Rebrand could be classified, the "obvious advantage … is that what is being studied has already occurred. The case study looks back in an attempt to explain…what and why something occurred and, in the case of public relations, how the outcome was managed …[and it] provides detail only found in hindsight."[6] For our teaching and learning purposes,

> The historical case study in public relations can examine the way the problem is stated and the initial research-gathering stages based on environmental scanning and monitoring; the strategic communication planning based on stated objectives; the communications themselves; the actual outputs; and the evaluation of the entire program or campaign.[7]

The historical case study models a best practices formula while chronicling what did happen or was happening, at least on the surface. It does this in one of two ways, identified by Stacks as linear and process. The *linear approach* starts with an analysis of the case background and moves systematically to an evaluation of the impact made or not made. "This approach suggests that each case is independent of all other cases and provides an analysis of the case from a historical perspective … as the reader is introduced to the problem and then walked through what is being analyzed from the advantage of hindsight."[8] The situation is presented as static from beginning to end, which is not necessarily a good thing. It suggests to the reader that what was planned at the beginning was never changed or tweaked because of changes in the context, that what was going on never changed even across time. It gives us hindsight certainty.

In comparison, a *process approach* frames public relations as an ongoing process and introduces the elements of feedback and accommodation, or response, into case study development. It makes sure the authors and readers anticipate "the strategic decisions made based on changes in the case's timeline."[9] The process case study introduces us to the importance of "in process" or "in progress" evaluation with the idea that adjustments likely occurred as the situation changed through time. The case author highlights the adjustments and identifies the points in time at which they were made. Therefore, the reader gets a sense of change and response instead of simply assuming a static and unchanging case situation. This approach introduces us to processural possibilities.

Hansen-Horn & Horn's in-text chapter questions and end chapter exercises contain the essence of the process approach. General question structures like, "If this variable had changed, how do you think the public relations initiatives would have changed or would they?" encourage students to think in processural possibilities instead of only hindsight certainty. Hansen-Horn & Horn also introduce process into how we think about other things. "What is considered noise in today's conversations that you think will become important parts of your future [at the book's writing, perhaps, the idea of flying cars meant for the consumer]... How do you suppose your parameters of what is considered noise change as you learn new jargon, ideas, and ways of doing things?"[10] The questions posed by Hansen-Horn & Horn ask students to reflect on their assumptions about what noise is (from unwanted sound to unwanted thought to unwanted possibilities, at least in the present) and recognize how that same noise may be redefined as "not-noise" at another time. An individual's realm of knowledge may have changed, his ways of thinking been adjusted, or the situation changed with time to accommodate the noise.

We can further illustrate the difference between linear and process historical approaches with a brief review of the 2003 Krispy Kreme promotional Dozen for A Dozen partnership with the Kansas City Royals. Krispy Kreme worked a cross-promotion deal with the Royals which let fans redeem a game ticket stub for a dozen doughnuts when the Royals got a dozen or more hits. It was an excellent tactic to generate doughnut buzz and please Royal fans cum Krispy Kreme customers (of course, a SRC strategist would know that we could invert our labels and have Krispy Creme fans and Royals customers). It was especially excellent because the Royals was not a winning team at that time and it had a really young-to-the-team player roster. It was unlikely that there would be many 12-hit games in 2003, which would limit the amount of cost associated with the redemption of qualified ticket stubs. From a hindsight certainty view, the cross-promotion between the doughnut maker and the Royals was a total success. Royals fans who were also open to eating, or were loyal customers of, Krispy Kreme loved the free doughnut possibility and redemption reality. From the linear historical perspective, the partnership was a win-win and the evolving situation did not demand any adjustments to the plan. However, from the process perspective, the partnership could not have been a win-win unless Krispy Kreme corporate listened to the promotion feedback [indicators of 12-hit game frequency, fan response, store manager concerns about redemption rates] and made adjustments in its local store support.

According to then Krispy Kreme Director of Marketing for Missouri and Kansas Kelly Lehman, the doughnut maker "had no idea the Royals would end up being so successful this year ... It's been like a real wildfire—it's caught on more than we could have ever imagined."[11] It sounds great, but if the projections had been that the Royals would net 12 or more hits for less than three games when in reality the team netted 12 or more hits for significantly more than three games, the store owners had a lot more doughnuts to give away, even with the reported 1% redemption rate. Let's pause here to note that by May 1, 2003 the Royals already had three 12-hit games on its record and those 12-hit games kept on coming. Someone had to pay for those unanticipated free doughnuts, be it corporate or local stores. An adjustment to what Krispy Kreme initially planned for had to be made somewhere during the 2003 season to continue to call the cross-promotion a success. If not, fans would have lost because their freebies would be denied, or stores would have lost because of staggering costs associated with unanticipated expenses, or corporate (and therefore all stores) would have lost because of negative buzz from fans (frustration about unredeemed freebies) and stores (disgust over loss of money).

The process approach to case studies is more in line than the linear approach with the SRC strategist way of thinking. Still, much like the linear case, the process case provides the hindsight (after the fact) advantage. Many details are clearer when we've had time to consider them, at least we think they are clearer. Both historical approaches, however, still frame the cases as what went on from case background to evaluation without exploring additional complex and interconnected realities that contributed to or limited what took place.

Finally, Stacks identifies a very different kind of case as a "grounded—or business case study."[12] For simplicity's sake, let's refer to it as a *grounded* case study. Its purpose is to offer case background in the form of "some history, some financial data, some communication data in the form of a narrative—then asks [sic] the reader to make decisions based on their [sic] analysis of the narrative."[13] Common examples of the grounded case study are those hypothetical situations professors use to test student ability, and summative case assessment challenges in the agency employment process. They almost always encourage the participant to "imagine this" or get involved through "let's say we have." The very short meeting about a potential community relations crisis example offered earlier fits here. And, in the SRC strategist spirit Hansen-Horn and Horn[14] weave grounded cases into multiple pages to allow students to apply what they learn as they read to WIGO in a case with which they have some familiarity. The hypothetical nature of the cases, such as the one in which a client desires "to reach today's teen men for the purpose of inviting their interest in their financial futures,"[15] allows Hansen-Horn and Horn to change case components to facilitate the application of new student insights. For our purposes in the current discussion, the teen men target could first be identified as 13-year-olds. At another time in the grounded case discussion, the target could be changed to 18- to 19-year-old teen men. Two thoughts should come to mind immediately: mobility and income. US federal law prohibits 13-year-olds from working outside the home, while 18- to 19-year-olds can work unlimited hours in any type of job. The older group is likely to have more income and, therefore, different interests than the 13-year-olds. In addition, 13-year-old males are not allowed to drive. Eighteen- to 19-year-olds are. The mobility of the 13-year-old age group is likely much more restricted than that of the older group. From just these two changes to WIGO, many questions must be asked, whys and how answered, and adjustments made to thinking and ideas.

It's important to note, as does Stacks, that the grounded case study almost always comes with a teaching note, which is an analysis providing a critical look at the case purpose. It includes "a case synopsis, relevant study questions, an analysis of the events and decision-making processes ... made (or not made) and their potential impacts, and how the case should be attacked according to sequence and potential problems that the reader might face."[16] It concludes by asking the reader to make decisions and predict outcomes under the conditions of which the case is discussed. It is not tied to real people, etc., but is, instead, illustrative. Questions asking how planning should change based on changes to the situation are easy to ask, as illustrated above in the teen men case.

Generalization and Labeling for Classification

Just like Cutler, Stacks highlights the prominent goal of most case studies as to describe WIGO and illustrate it through real or hypothetical examples. He, too, views the inability to easily generalize findings and conclusions from one case to anything else as its major disadvantage.

For the purpose of learning through case study, Cutler puts the generalizability problem in perspective when quoting Hoaglin, Light, McPeek, Mosteller and Stoto (1982). "Most people feel they can prepare a case study, and nearly all of us believe we can understand one. Since neither view is well founded, the case study receives a good deal of approbation it does not deserve."[17] Approbation means approval or praise.

It's easy to praise the assumed and make unchecked assumptions. We all do it, but when we do we limit our understanding. For instance, it's easy for a case study author to assume that what he writes is all there is to the case. And, it's easy for those studying a case to assume that the public relations initiatives under review actually started when the case began in print and stopped when the case ended on the printed page. Because of the nature of the printed page, it starts and stops, we don't ask valuable questions such as: "What was important to this organization before this case? What is still important to it? What was going on in the case that I did not read about? Where did the organization go from here? What were the outcomes? What is going on today? Has the situation re-presented itself in some form?" The assuming reader can all too easily miss the opportunity to explore possibilities, generate new understanding, and become aware of complex interconnectedness.

For instance, our limited understanding can start with something as simple as our desire to be organized. When you think about your ability to and, many times, the felt need to classify ideas by naming them or giving them labels, you begin to get the picture. Labeling file folders and alphabetizing them in a file drawer is an example. Similarly, most public relations case studies are labeled, for classification and filing purposes as one type or another, such as media relations, community relations, public affairs, investor relations, and the like. Classification through labeling makes things digestible, easy to order and discuss, and easy to remember. But it's not all good.

The process of labeling keeps us from knowing and thinking about some of the things we should. First of all, we often assume that what's at the top of our list or in the front of our drawer is more important that what comes later. Political candidates know this well. Getting one's name listed first on a ballot nets many more votes than getting one's name on the list in fifth place. Even if voters don't know the candidate, they tend to vote for the person whose name appears first. In addition, it's rare that anything that we do involves only one form of public relations, or that we can act independently of other organizational participants. It almost always involves a multitude of other kinds of public relations practices, all the while under the advisement of legal counsel or suggestions from the market research department. For instance, an investor relations case probably also involves some sort of conference and convention relations, consumer relations, employee relations, and government relations. And, it might also involve maturing relations or relations with special publics. It's the sage public relations professional who understands this complexity and interconnectedness.

Case Study Value through New Ways of Thinking

Maintaining a SRC mindset leads to new ways of thinking. So, too, does recognizing three things: (1) the artificiality of the boundaries with which we generally organize case studies, (2) the limits labeling can put on the power of thinking outside the boxes, and (3) the power of applied theory to help us think and understand in new ways.

Anytime we resort to labeling WIGO for the purposes of classification we begin to limit potential; we impose artificial boundaries on what we see, know, and communicate. For instance, if we classify all dogs by the labels of big or little, we have only two types of dogs. We don't even recognize medium sized, giant or tea cup dogs. In addition, unless we connect our large or small classification system to color, we miss out on the richness of fuller understanding. So, we can add the labels of white or brown, but leave out black. Additionally, we can add more options and change our classification system to include the labels of white, brown, black, or brown and black. Our understanding gets richer but we still miss out on gray dogs. And, then, there is the classification of dogs by hair type. We could have a giant brown dog with wavy hair, or is that with short wavy hair or long wavy hair? And, we can give additional recognition to these dogs by whether they are attackers, hunters, or lovers. ... or maybe all three. If one dog is energetic and one is reserved we miss that. Furthermore, if the reserved dog is acting out-of-character because he was dewormed that morning and feels nauseous, we miss that enriching detail as well.

You get the drift. Classification through labeling brings order, recognition and organizational ease, but it also prevents a lot.

Conclusion

Studying public relations strategy, implementation, and impact from case studies is an important part of how we learn. As we learn from them, it's important to understand the heuristic potential and limits brought to us by the kinds of case studies we reference, whether they be linear historical, process historical, or grounded—business in approach. They help us "imagine" what went on, changed, or was adjusted, as well as what worked and why. We can generalize in our minds and imagine WIGO, etc., but we must be careful to situate the realities we face as professionals in the actual contexts, and cues available to us. And, we are free to label and classify as means to organizing and sharing, but as we do we are smart to keep in mind that we can miss important issues, developments and clues if we assume our labels and classification systems encompass everything that should be important to us.

Chapter two frames the strategic thinking mindset. It revisits the power and limits in assuming a definition of public relations, discusses public relations as communication and business, and highlights strategy and the strategic thinking that can come from a SRC strategist perspective.

Chapter Exercises

1. Develop a list of the benefits that can come with learning from case study analysis.
2. Develop a list of the disadvantages that can come with learning from case study analysis.
3. As you read a case study, ask yourself if it is written from a historical linear, process linear, or grounded–business approach.
   a. Write a summary of the heuristic potential and limits set by the approach taken.
   b. If you were to re-write the case from a different approach, what questions would you need to answer? What additional information would you need to include?
4. If you were teaching a beginning public relations student about the benefits and disadvantages of labeling and classifying cases, what would you tell her? Develop at an outline of at least four talking points you would use with the student.

Opportunity for Praxis

To apply this chapter's information to the cases in Appendix B, see Appendix A:
____ Case Kind Key
____ Case Rubric Master

Notes

1. Hansen-Horn, T. & Horn, A. (2014). *Strategic planning for public relations: Beginning the journey*. New York: Peter Lang, pp. 205–230.
2. Ibid., pp. 67–68. For a review of the SRC strategist idea, refer to the third chapter in Hansen-Horn & Horn, 2014. Communication Complexity: Self-reflexivity in the marketplace of ideas: Becoming an SRC Public Relations Strategist, pp. 45–71.
3. Cutler, A. (2004). Methodical failure: The use of case study method by public relations researchers. *Public Relations Review, 30*, p. 366.
4. Ibid., p. 367.
5. Stacks, D. (2011). *Primer of public relations research* (2nd ed.). New York: The Guilford Press, p. 158.
6. Ibid., p. 158.
7. Ibid., p. 158.
8. Ibid., p. 160.

9. Ibid., p. 160.
10. Hansen-Horn & Horn, 2014, p. 41.
11. Krispy Kreme Rises to the Top. (2003, May 1). *Sports Business Daily, 151*. Retrieved February 20, 2015 from http://www.sportsbusinessdaily.com/Daily/Issues/2003/05/Issue-151/Sponsorships-Advertising-Marketing/Krispy-Kreme-Rises-To-Top-With-Royals-In-Stadium-Promotion.aspx.
12. Ibid., p. 158.
13. Ibid., p. 158.
14. Hansen-Horn & Horn, 2014.
15. Ibid., p. 97.
16. Stacks, 2011, p. 163.
17. Cutler, 2004, p. 369.

Approaches to Public Relations and Strategy

Taking Our Place

Understanding strategy assumes we willingly engage in perspective taking and reflective thought simultaneously. A successful public relations strategist understands clearly that public relations is a communication and business function, that decision making is inseparable from consequences, the nature of strategy is really a complex kind of thing, and to be a SRC strategist is not easy but it is fruitful. Chapter two is dedicated to framing all of this for you, but first, it's important to visit the definition of public relations that drives this book. Public relations is "planned and strategic results-driven communicative effort with the publics in mind."[1] In the spirit of complexity and interconnectedness, let's unpack the definition.

Public Relations Definition Examined

Planned indicates that public relations is characterized by intention—always—even if the plan is to plan to change plans as WIGO changes or, simply, to plan to let the plan emerge across WIGO, as WIGO changes and across time. Even crises communication strategy is planned, whether it be in the form of a pre-existing crisis plan or a quick 15-minute phone call among those most equipped to deal with a crisis in a proactive manner. *Strategic* reminds us that in planning and anticipating we ask how and why questions, and we readily look for and accept complex and interconnected responses to our questions. For instance, a financial services client may have just been named "best in the business" by WealthManagement.com. It's important to communicate that to specific publics. As public relations counsel, you realize that award announcement coincides with the coming announcement of your client's title sponsorship of the local AAA baseball team. Therefore, you alter the title sponsorship announcement to include the "best in the business award" message because you know third party endorsements such as this are regarded by your client's target publics as highly credible. The situation changed and so did your message strategy.

Results-driven attests to the fact that we measure or evaluate the impact of what we undertake, making sure cost-benefit analyses are second nature. And, in fact, we build our evaluation process into the initial or emergent plan from the beginning. We include the cost of evaluation right along with everything else in our budget, and we attribute as much importance to in-progress or in-process evaluation as end evaluation. As strategic planners we change things if in-progress results show that our anticipated impact is not going as planned. In addition, to be results-driven is to remember that all initiatives, even those to do nothing, have impact. If a client needs to announce that it is expanding its air passenger services to the New England states, a media pitch to relevant journalists may be in order (given that we are in the twenty-first century, please define journalists very broadly here). If the pitch is planned for Tuesday, but on Monday the FAA grounds two of your client's largest passenger planes because of inspection violations, you will need to rethink your media pitch plan. Your intended publics for the New England announcement just received an unintended message about your client's perceived service record about grounded planes (maybe even be perceived as a safety message), and that unintended message will mitigate Tuesday's hoped for results. If you can, you suspend the client service extension announcement until the FAA grounding conversation clears. In another example, you may be running an integrated effort involving coupon redemption. If you are half-way through the campaign and less than 50% of the projected coupon redemptions have been made, you and your client's promotions people may get together and alter your planned course of action, which will include a closer look at your communication strategy.

The term *communicative* reminds us of the vast number of communication contact points possible in every public relations situation. It reminds us that every contact point has the power to communicate something, whether we want it to or not. Publics can assume messaging (even inanimate objects are often "assumed" to say something) consciously or subconsciously. All words, gestures, logos, client buildings, meeting locations, employees, employee habits, modes of dress, media mentions, story line-ups, etc., are potential message contributors or purveyors. Take, for instance, Domino's® pizza stores. You probably aren't surprised when you see a Domino's pizza store with bars on its windows in certain parts of the town you are visiting, but you would be surprised if you saw a Papa John's pizza store in the same area with bars on its windows. The physical location and structure of the stores communicate something about the company. Papa John's does not view bars on its store windows as fitting in with its message of quality in everything. But, as strategists we know that even if we carefully orchestrate everything we can think of to communicate an intended message, we never assume that the message someone is aware of, receives, interprets, and retains or discards is necessarily the exact one we want him or her to get. We know there are too many influencing factors beyond our control. So we construct many messages designed to say the same thing, plan multiple times and modes of delivery, and plan for responsive feedback. If a drug search just happens to go down in a Papa John's parking lot, the intended message for that store at least, is impacted. The quality image has been disrupted, but if there are multiple continuing quality messages in place already, and they continue, Papa John's will not enter a crisis situation of any kind. The messages of quality will redress the drug-bust-in-the-parking-lot one. Some might call this image equity; you bank positive perceptions for such a time as this.

The challenge of message intended, equaling message received and retained, is why Hansen-Horn & Horn advanced the term communicative as more appropriately used in the definition of public relations than is communication. It reminds us of the power of communicative potential, be it desirable or undesirable, of our efforts and all contact points. In addition, it helps us remember that humans tend to assume that communication is separate from most of WIGO and from things like buildings, meeting locations, and modes of dress. It's not. Finally, we know that successful strategic public relations only takes place in light of public perspective-taking—with the publics in mind. And, we clearly recognize that there really is no such thing as a general public.[2]

Keeping *the* (anticipated and intended) *publics in mind* keeps us remindful of three truths: (1) successful public relations strategy is developed with the self-interests of priority publics in mind. Without them we have no reason to do anything, nor can we accomplish our purposes. For example, US presidential election hopefuls can campaign all they want, but without voters, delegates, media members, and the electoral college they can't be elected President of the United States. (2) Talking about specific publics for which we have identified clear-cut parameters is an artificial process. It's nearly impossible to include all those who are relevant to our purposes; and public composition, preferences, knowledge levels, self-interests, and changes in WIGO happen from one point in time to another. Therefore, we analyze our publics often, making sure to build some sort of public monitoring check points and accommodation processes into our ideas. And, (3) as we represent the interests of a client, keeping the publics in mind honors the ethical imperative inherent in all successful public relations. We know that if what we achieve is not somehow positively correlated to the interests of the publics we have in mind, the sustainability of those relationships is endangered. A client who pursues her interests without the ethical consideration of "what's in it" for the publics she is affecting is destined for a short run in the business. For instance, a public relations strategist can work tirelessly to communicate the attractiveness of his client real estate group to chambers of commerce, rotary clubs, and potential first time home owners. But, if that same strategist is not allowed to counsel his client about the need to stay involved in legislation that keeps first time home ownership afford-able and feasible, the client (and his public relations professional) will eventually go out of business.

Public Relations as Communication and Business

Puzzlement over where public relations programs fit in a university setting is noth-ing new. It illustrates the tug-of-war that takes places because people want to label and classify public relations as all one thing or another. We are comfortable will all encompassing labels and classification systems. But, maybe public relations does not need to be classified as one kind or another. Perhaps it is both? Or more? Or also?

Public relations degree programs are commonly found in communication schools and departments, journalism schools, journalism and media departments, and as part of advertising programs. In addition, some public relations programs are in business schools or departments and, interestingly, master's level public rela-tions courses are becoming more frequent in MBA programs, especially in light of the current Public Relations Society of America (PRSA) partnership with leading business schools. PRSA recently published a white paper, *PRSA MBA Program: Bridging the Gap between Strategic Communications Education and Master of Busi-ness Administration (MBA) Curriculum,* "providing an overview of the successful assimilation of strategic communications content into Master of Business Admin-istration (MBA) programs nationwide."[3]

The varying placement of public relations programs and curriculum is not surprising given the increasing recognition of public relations as an important organizational function and its professionals as important organizational decision makers. And, the PRSA/MBA programs recent partnership illustrates the fact that business leaders across the US are attributing more and more importance to public relations cum strategic communications at the policy setting and decision making tables. It should come as no surprise to any reader, then, that the US Bureau of Labor routinely provides a report for public relations, advertising, and marketing in the same category in its Occupational Employment Statistics report marketing.[4] The US Bureau of Labor gets the business value of public relations.

In non-academic settings, public relations is also found in a variety of departments and under many titles. One organization may house it under corporate communication, another under public affairs, a third under public relations, and a fourth under marketing communications. And, some house public relations under more than one department such as internal communication and external communication, or media relations and community relations. Indeed, for organizations with a heavily vested interest in it, investor relations itself is often housed in its own department apart from other public relations departments.

The existing variety of labels under which public relations may be found and/or operate is a discussion taken up again later in the chapter. That discussion points to the many situations, contexts, and specializations involved in public relations. The complexity this discussion illustrates is a key theme in this book. Before the anticipated discussion commences, however, we need to spend some time framing the conversation of how public relations is both a communication and business function.

Public relations clearly involves ideas, messages, words, visions, channels of communication, inferences, perceptions, images, and people (their moods, skills, knowledge levels, beliefs and value systems, and frames of reference). It also involves getting things done with a view to a return on investment (ROI) that can facilitate long-term organizational survival. It involves budgets, expenditures, investments, projections, profit and loss statements, employees, and boards. Its definition is predicated on the "business of reaching desired results" through "strategic means and modes of communication."[5]

Getting things done automatically engages the professional in a business practice. So, too, does attaining results that help secure an organization's future. All business goings on necessarily involve alternative choice making and a myriad of possible and realized consequences. The strategic public relations professional recognizes this truth and is careful to keep it in mind.

Think for a moment. As a reader of this book you can't make a decision separated from some kind of impact, effect, or consequence. Sometimes, decision making nets multiple impacts, effects, or consequences. Even your decision to read this book chapter brings consequences, be that perspective-taking that comes into play 10 years from now in your then-director position, immediate time away from taking a nap, a good test result next week, impact on the way you manage your co-worker relationships now and in the future, etc. Choosing to not read the chapter is also an alternative that you have. It, too, is inherently tied to consequences. You might not advance to director in 10 years, you get to take a nap right now, next week's test result is not so good, you don't think twice about managing your co-workers now or in the future, etc. As an aside, note that general semanticists (scholars who study how language use constructs our world view) are famous for using the "etc."

symbol. It stands for consequential thinking, more alternatives, changes among meanings, and revised perspective thinking, etc. It keeps us from assuming that life and the business endeavors we undertake are unchanging and static ... *etc.*

Consequential thinking, when considering options for action, has long been called "alternaquence thinking"[6] by general semanticists. Unfortunately, the dualistic nature of the English language, most clearly illustrated by the concept of "either-or," makes it easy to assume that choices come without impact, costs, effects, or consequences. Nothing is further from the truth. Remember the dog classification example provided in chapter one? The one asking whether the dog is big or small, black or white, or something much more? The dog example illustrates the consequences of the either-or thinking alternative. We miss out on what is really going on, or can go on and why. We don't even realize the richness of a situation, person, personality, opportunity, problem, or ... dog. For instance, either-or thinking can keep us from recognizing a gray dog.

Sage public relations professionals routinely engage in alternaquence thinking. We don't separate alternatives from consequences when we imagine the future or envision the past. We make decisions with them in mind. We're always anticipating action cum reactions, choices cum consequences, and decisions cum impacts. And, we are sure to engage in in-process monitoring to observe those that do or start to take place as deciding and decision implementation get underway. We make accommodations for those we anticipate even if they don't happen, etc.

Understanding public relations as communication and business, as well as populated with alternatives inherently tied to consequences, helps the public relations professional feel at ease with the rich and complex nature of strategy. Let's address that next. Hansen-Horn and Horn dedicate an entire chapter to unpacking the ideas of strategy, being strategic, and strategic planning.[7] The highlights of that chapter are reviewed here.

Strategy Highlights

As we undertake a discussion of what strategy is or may be, it's important to note that the idea of strategy is problematic much like the idea of a general public is. We can imagine it but not provide definitive parameters of what it is. We often assume it, but we shouldn't. Take for instance a college student public. Do we intend a group enrolled full time or part time? Is the public in mind graduate or undergraduate level or both? Do the public members attend four-year or two-year colleges? Additionally, we remember that the college student public, even if narrowed to full-time undergraduates at all four-year universities in Missouri, will not be the same across time. It can change very quickly because of dropouts, transfers, graduation, and the like. And, the public's interests or perceptions may change as WIGO changes, especially if a particular issue is suddenly magnified in their life.

Just as there really is not one general public, but instead there are as many publics as there are issues, causes, objectives and more, there really is no one general idea of strategy. We can image it, but not provide definitive parameters of it. Strategy is relevant to the strategist's predisposition, assumptions, and intentions. And, it can change across persons, time, organization, and WIGO.

Tied to the Greek word *strategos*, the idea of strategy is linked to the art of serving as a recognized wartime leader. Its historical context ties strategy to the idea of war, but that's not the only context in which strategy is derived and put into play. While it's true that public relations initiatives can be part of warfare, that idea is not, by any stretch of the imagination, the biggest portion of what public relations can do. Of course, we can also speak metaphorically of waging war with competitors, against lack of awareness, against falling stock prices, and the like. But, that's certainly not all we do, nor does this idea provide evidence of the many approaches to strategy behind doing these types of things.

Scholar Ellen Chaffee does a great job of describing the "what is strategy" conundrum. She argues that "those who refer to strategy generally believe that they are all working with the same mental model. No controversy surrounds the question of its existence; no debate has arisen regarding the nature of its anchoring concept. Yet virtually everyone writing on strategy agrees that no consensus on its definition exists."[8] Additionally, scholar and consultant Henry Mintzberg and his coauthor James Quinn point out that, "it is important to remember that no one has ever seen a strategy or touched one; every strategy is an invention, a figment of someone's imagination."[9]

So, what's the key takeaway from all this? It's to encourage you to explore the different recognized perspectives on strategy that do and can come into play, and to recognize that the kind of strategy one assumes or chooses brings with it consequential impact. Strategy sets the course for public relations intent and initiative. Furthermore, "as intent, it can be prescriptive, descriptive, or transformative; linear, adaptive, or interpretive; deliberate or emergent; a plan, ploy, pattern, position and/or perspective."[10] We can imagine all kinds of strategy but when we decide to put our imagined strategy into words, drawings, or notes Mintzberg argues that we necessarily (because of our communicative nature) start to put parameters on it.[11] We do this through what Hansen-Horn & Horn term the Mintzberg *codification-elaboration-conversion process.*

As we recognize and give voice to our imagined strategy (tell it to ourselves and others, for instance) we do so through a commonly recognized and used coding or *codification* process (labels and words, known systems of distribution, and so on). Much like the either-or dog example in chapter one, our coding of

WIGO in our head necessarily reduces or limits our imagined strategy. We can't say everything about it for at least four reasons. First, we'd never get done communicating. Second, those we are communicating to would tune us out after a while because of boredom or being overwhelmed. Third, there aren't enough words in the English language (or any language for that matter) to describe all of WIGO in our thoughts. And, fourth, we have to put it into some recognized (or commonly shared) system of symbolic representation (a code or language or flow chart) so others can be aware of and understand it, and put it into play.

Let's say we have an extreme sports client. Our client's objective is to communicate to people living in Florida who are aged 60 years and older that engaging in extreme sports is something that's a real option for them. Our background analysis of the target public's demographics and psychographics, as well as relevant issue-driven secondary research and our own primary research from focus groups conducted with members of this public, tells us that the majority members of this group cannot imagine themselves participating in this sport at all. They feel they are too old and it's not safe. We also find, though, that many of them would like to be able to imagine participating in this sport because it is new and exciting, and it looks like fun … for someone else. Our client's objective calls for awareness of feasibility because the data indicates this group assumes extreme sports is not for it; those kinds of things are out of its reach. (Of course, our research is, itself, a result of codification and represents what "we" find generally to be true and most useful to our purposes.) Our client knows differently. Our team recommends a visual strategy through which our target public's members can "easily envision themselves engaging in extreme sports and having fun doing it." This means that we know the public needs to actually see people just like them doing and enjoying these sports, and be able to imagine actually doing these things, before they will consider extreme sports part of their possibilities. How we put our strategy into play is tactical.

Because of the codification process, our extreme sports strategy prioritizes two things: (1) visual imagery and (2) enjoyment. It does not, however, allow for serious athleticism, which could be the key to awareness for some subset of our target public. The codification process, by nature, sets limits to or pares down our imagined strategy. Furthermore, when the strategist puts the strategy into action, *elaboration* takes place. The essence of the strategy is altered into sub-strategies related to best practices for resourcing, best plans for timing, best practices for message sequencing, etc. For instance, if our ideal launch date is June 1 because of complementary things going on at the national and state levels, but our client's fiscal year ends June 30, we may have to revise our strategic start date to account for fiscal year stop and start dates. Finally, the *conversion* of the strategy takes place because of the understood impact its implementation will have on organizational operations and plans already in place. Mintzberg describes this as crossing the great divide from optimal to doable, to accommodate for "hierarchies of strategies and programs (action planning) to those of budgets and objectives."[12] What this means is that our optimal imagined strategy will necessarily be constrained, controlled or re-imagined by available funds (not necessarily fiscal year start and end dates), our creative team's skill and abilities, the organization's internal and external communication networks, and the like. Some might argue that this is when strategy meets organizational reality and, in so doing, is necessarily altered accordingly. Our ability to raise awareness among our target public will be significantly impacted by the funds made available for our efforts. There is a vast difference among $5,000, $500,000, and $5,000,000 budgets. And, though the ideal budget is determined by strategy and tactical need to maximize results, that's not always what the client can offer. In our extreme sports example we might use the visual push medium of standing billboards. Large billboards in strategic places along public-frequented routes are quick to communicate images that are essentially "pushed" in the faces of passersby (as long as they get looked at by those passing by). Hence, billboards are within the tactical choices we might make. If running a six-month campaign is optimal, and each billboard on which we want to purchase time leases for $400 a month, to rent one for six months will cost us $2,400. The average design and vinyl production work of the billboard is $300 per board if we produce at least 10 of them. With $5,000 we can produce the 10 billboard vinyls but only lease one billboard, and at that we can only rent it for five months. However, if we get to work with a $5,000,000 budget it is clear that the $3,000 production cost for 10 vinyls is not an issue; neither is leasing 10 boards for six months. You get the idea.

A general exploration of how the nature of strategy can be prescriptive, descriptive, or transformative; linear, adaptive, or interpretive; deliberate or emergent; a plan, ploy, pattern, position and/or perspective can set the stage for recognizing our own assumptions about what strategy is or can be, opening our minds to the array of strategy choices available to us, and imagining the consequences that are inherently tied to strategy choices. As you embark on this journey, it should move you away from the assumption that strategy is a clearly defined thing that can only be used in one way. The multiple approaches to strategy present in academic discussions, while not mutually exclusive, are different enough in their descriptions to illustrate that no one approaches strategy the same way, nor is there one universal definition for what strategy is or can be.

The highly interested reader can read Hansen-Horn and Horn (2014) to grasp the many nuances of difference among identified approaches to strategy.[13] However, for the purpose of this book, the list below represents the approaches identified and discussed by Hansen-Horn and Horn following their in-depth survey of academic and professional literature about strategy. One of the most prolific students of and authors about strategy is Henry Mintzberg.[14] His classifications of strategy, along with those he offered in cooperation with J. Quinn,[15] as well as the perspectives of Elizabeth Chaffee[16] and Michael Porter[17] are represented.

Mintzberg: Prescriptive, Descriptive, Transformative

- Prescriptive—Just like a medicine can be prescribed to cure a bacterial infection, some professionals assume that they have a good handle, perhaps the best handle, on what strategy is. They assume that they key to success is that they simply need to find the best way to put their strategy into action.
- Descriptive—PR professionals who work with strategy from a descriptive perspective are not as interested in prescribing best practices as they are in being able to identify and describe (tell stories) how strategy unfolds as it is "imagined" and communicated by himself and/or others. From this perspective, a strategy could be described from one's assumption that a leader necessarily provides his or her own vision for what needs to be done, or has access to the power needed to get something accomplished. The involved strategist describes what transpires as strategy.
- Transformative—The individual who operates with a transformative understanding of strategy assumes that significant organizational change will take place across time (change is inevitable) even apart from the strategist's intervention. As a result, he imagines strategy as something that will necessarily be reconfigured itself or the implementation of it reconfigured to accommodate inevitable changes correlating to changes in internal and external WIGO.
- Emergent—The emergent public relations strategist recognizes strategy as it happens or emerges across time. It's recognized by organizational players as what is intended meets a changing reality so that the intended strategy is modified accordingly. It's plan based but only in so far as the public relations strategist plans to plan and re-plan as well as re-plan what was re-planned and so on.

Chaffee: Linear, Adaptive, Interpretive

- Linear—A linear understanding is similar to prescriptive and is plan based. Public relations strategists adhering to this understanding of strategy view themselves as agents of power and change and, therefore, it is their job to plan, implement, and change strategy relevant to WIGO across time.
- Adaptive—Also prioritizing organizational objectives but instead of assuming strategists can simply act upon the organization and its environment, this strategist understands that an organization does not act or exist in a vacuum. As such, organizations and strategies have to adjust and change relevant to the environment or WIGO on a continual basis.

- Interpretive—The interpretive strategist does not hold a linear or adaptive approach to strategy. Instead, she believes all public relations action is only possible in cooperation with consenting individuals and organizations other than her client. In other words, this strategist believes an organization can only exist at the permission of those whom it impacts so, thusly, those individuals are part of strategy.

Porter: Deliberate

- Deliberate—A deliberate approach to strategy always involves the assumption of planned strategy. It presupposes organizational profitability and sustainability. It's all about organizational position and goal achievement.

Mintzberg and Quinn: Plan, Ploy, Pattern, Position, Perspective

- Plan—Referred to by Mintzberg as one of the five Ps of strategy, a plan strategy is a consciously intended course of action or set of guidelines to deal with a situation.
- Ploy—Referred to by Mintzberg as one of the five Ps of strategy, a ploy is still a plan but it is simply a strategic maneuver to outclass, outperform, get the jump on something, capitalize on an unanticipated endorsement, or counteract undesirable publicity. It is often embedded within a planned strategy as an "in case this happens" we can "do this."
- Pattern—Referred to by Mintzberg as one of the five Ps of strategy, this kind of approach to strategy gives credence to plan and ploy but focuses on how strategy is defined by patterns in a stream of actions. It does not assume strategy is imposed prescription, but instead recognizes a pattern of intended or untended action across time that limits or facilitates strategy.
- Position—Referred to by Mintzberg as one of the five Ps of strategy, when someone operates with an assumption of strategy as position, he focuses on WIGO external to the organization as more important that WIGO internal to the organization. He does this with the intent of situating or positioning the organization within its environment for short- and long-term success. This public relations professional may seek to position a client through the use of plan, ploy, and position while making modifications because of pattern.
- Perspective—Referred to by Mintzberg as one of the five Ps of strategy, the public relations professional with this approach is largely internally focused. She assumes that WIGO internally, and her ability to interpret it, are the most important contributors to strategy. She tries to imagine the organization from the perspectives of those who are committed to it. From here,

she tries to understand their perspectives of how to perceive the world from their shared understanding of what the organization is and does. This strategy is founded on the idea of collective perspective taking.

Two things are going on in the descriptions provided for you in the above strategy list. One is a set of labels generally applied to schools of thought about strategy. The second is a set of labels variously attributed to the intended codification and application of strategy. For our purposes, it's the systems of labels that make classification possible (something we like, right?) that are useful to us as we work to understand the complexity of strategy. We can work from the list and use each description as a lens through which we can try to identify the assumptions behind strategies used in particular cases. We can also try to identify alternative strategies that could be used instead and imagine the potential differing consequences.

The SRC Strategist

As Hansen-Horn and Horn put it, those who are the best in the public relations business are business-minded SRC strategists. These individuals are comfortable devising and revising strategy before tactics are on the table. In fact, to start, they clearly know the difference between a strategy and tactic. They are professionals who are:

> self-reflexive; acutely aware of short- and long-term organizational aspirations; contextually grounded and sensitive to internal and external influences including larger socio-political-economic factors, organizational culture, and employee perceptions; committed to keeping short- and long-term ROI visions; aware of organizational performance control and sometimes willing to use influential means to overcome it; and comfortable with flux and change. Decisions are not separated from outcomes, initiatives from resources and responses, alternatives from consequences.[18]

Let's briefly unpack what this means. We'll start with differentiating between strategy and tactic. Strategy comes from the why and how. Tactics are the whats based on the why and how. Let's give this a try. Which is a strategy and which is a tactic? "To implement a 300-person gala" and "To appeal through face-to-face opportunities designed with the target public's social comfort in mind." The first is a tactic and the second is a strategy that could drive the 300-person gala. Let's try this again. Which is which? "To adhere to visual imagery that facilitates nostalgia" and "to use a prominent display of black and white photo images from the 1950s at AARP-sponsored events." The first is strategy and the second is a tactic that could be driven by the strategy. Now let's move on to describing (codifying) a SRC strategist.

A self-reflexive person asks himself why and how quite often. He epitomizes Simon Sinek's *Start with Why* admonition to be careful about making "decisions based on what we *think* we know"[19] and, instead, knows the why behind WIGO. He routinely asks himself why and how. He works to recognize his own biases, predispositions, expectations, attitudes, and aspirations. He works to understand how those can or do impact his decision making at home and work. He is an observer of others, viewing their habits, preferences, actions, etc., from a why and how position. He imagines alternatives while anticipating consequences. He is a student of his own language and personal language habits. His is open to change. He realizes his words shape his reality and that different words can alter that reality. He's willing to do his best to separate emotion from his thought processes, especially as he considers the communicative implications of his words and actions. He understands that meaning is contested terrain, meaning consensus is not permanent nor even complete. Meanings change across time, with changes in WIGO, with a different set of participants. He is aware of the short- and long-term goals of his organization. He also recognizes their absence. He separates stated (formally codified) goals from unarticulated yet expected goals. He has a vision of the future and can imagine what it will take to sustain the organization into that future.

Additionally, he understands his place in the formal organizational structure and follows it appropriately; but he is also sensitive to the informal system (the organic one that forms on its own among the people populating the organization) and works with it as well. He is sensitive to organizational politics and interpersonal relationships that impact him, WIGO, and what can go on. He keeps his eye on legislative changes, grassroots activism, social pressures, stock performances, etc., as they have potential to impact what he needs to accomplish. He's immersed in and a student of the unique culture operating within or structuring his organization as well as other organizations with which his client must act. He's a student of employee feelings, behaviors, and belief systems. He even understands that directors, managers and VPs are employees and, as such, he gets the idea of perceptual boundaries that are both useful and restrictive to organizational purposes. He understands that building relationships of trust is necessary to ethical sustainability. He understands that transparency is key. He predicates his words, actions, and intent on the idea that ROI is not bad and, in fact, it's necessary. He knows that short- and long-term ROI are not always complementary and, he's an advocate for doing what's right in the long-term over what works in the short-term. He does not erupt in anger nor act in panic when things don't go as planned. In fact, he is comfortable planning to plan to re-plan. He readily participates in frank discussions about decisions and possible outcomes, habits and impacts, resources and responses, expectations and possibilities, and alternatives and consequences.

The SRC strategist has a mirror of behavior and communication as a constant companion. He consistently thinks about his own word choices and behavior; he is his own chief analyst. He is comfortable directing the reflective mirror to others, the organization, and the socio-economic-political environment in which the organization exists. He asks, "What am I doing?" "Why am I doing what I am doing?" "Should I be doing something differently?" "What is my vision?" "What are my assumptions and should or can they be different?" He asks himself the same reflective questions of those around him. He is comfortable with why and how question-asking. He is comfortable with ambiguity. He is comfortable with decision-making in spite of uncertainty. He makes choices from alternaquence thinking.

While it's not hard to impose the SRC strategist label on the idea of a successful public relations strategist, it is pretty difficult to provide a succinct description of who this professional is and how he is. But, really, that's okay. The desirability of succinct descriptions is a product of a cultural assumption that short and concise is better. While it may be more memorable, the limits often set by it help us miss the richness of what is really going on. So, we should be content with our complex description of the SRC strategist because it represents the complexity of the public relations professional's world. In fact, a real SRC strategist is comfortable pulling out and referencing the Strategic Planning Checklist (see Figure 2.1) time and time again throughout his professional career.

☐ What are your own assumptions about communication?
☐ What communicative methods do you prefer?
☐ What kinds of communicative strengths do you have?
☐ Are you able to think for yourself or are you thinking what you think someone else wants you to?
☐ Who or what is your client?
☐ What makes your client unique?
☐ What do you know of your client's assumptions about communication?
☐ What do you know of your client's communicative preferences?
☐ What kinds of communicative strengths does your client have?
☐ What frames of reference to you share with your client?
☐ How would you describe the situation that calls for formation of public relations strategy?
☐ How does your client describe the situation that calls for formation of public relations strategy?
☐ What do you not know that you should know?
☐ What kinds of research need to be pursued to answer your questions?

(Continued)

- □ What objectives are most relevant to the situation?
- □ Do the objectives you identify correspond with those your client identifies?
- □ Does your client seem to have any unarticulated expectations?
- □ What does your client propose that you do in light of the situation?
- □ What do you propose that you do in light of the situation?
- □ What kind of overlap exists between your client's proposed ideas and your own?
- □ What are the alternaquences the client faces?
- □ What type of ethics seems to be guiding your own and your client's proposed ideas?
- □ Is there any situational noise that should not necessarily be discarded?
- □ What kind of culture exists within your client's organization?
- □ Which of your client's long-standing stakeholders and stakeseekers are relevant to the situation?
- □ Can you identify any stakeseekers relevant to the current situation that have not been relevant to this client before?
- □ Among the stakeholders and stakeseekers you can identify, which would be the primary publics?
- □ What are the communicative assumptions help by the identified primary publics?
- □ What communicative preferences are held by the primary publics?
- □ What kinds of words and messages appear to resonate best with the primary publics?
- □ Can your client provide those kinds of messages?
- □ What demographic and psychographic information about the primary publics is most relevant to this situation?
- □ What socio-political-environmental factors that contextualize the situation have the ability to redefine it?
- □ What marketplace wrangle contextualizes the situation?
- □ What terrain is being contested in the situation?
- □ What additional research do you need to conduct?
- □ What kinds of organizational structure define your client's organization?
- □ What kinds of organizational structure and relationships exist to help you execute strategy?
- □ What elements of conversion are influencing the situation in desirable and undesirable ways?
- □ What elements of integration are influencing the situation in desirable and undesirable ways?
- □ What kind of ROI-vision do you have?
- □ What kind of ROI-vision is held by your client?

(*Continued*)

(*Continued*)

- ☐ How is success defined by your client in light of the situation?
- ☐ Does the way the client defines success in light of the situation seem to resonate with organizational history?
- ☐ How does that resonate with your definitions of personal and professional success?
- ☐ Do you think the formulated strategy should be prescriptive, descriptive, or transformative in character?
- ☐ Does your client think the strategy should be prescriptive, descriptive, or transformative in character?
- ☐ Do you think the strategy should be linear, adaptive, or interpretive?
- ☐ Does your client think the strategy should be linear, adaptive, or interpretive?
- ☐ Will the situation context allow the choice of strategy?
- ☐ Do the situation and client expectations call for strategy to be a plan, ploy, pattern, position, and/or prescription?
- ☐ Does the situation call for deliberate or emergent strategy?
- ☐ What kinds of communicative choices in terms of print, audio, video, face-to-face, experiential, and digital best fit the situation and the kinds of messages that will best reach the primary publics?
- ☐ How will the choice of communication mediums massage the message?
- ☐ Is it possible to remain silent?
- ☐ Have you given strategy formation a chance before invoking long-standing rules?
- ☐ As a strategy is formed, what is getting lost in the codification process?
- ☐ As a strategy is elaborated to the client as action and implementation planning, what resources, sequencing, and timing factors influence it and even re-codify it?
- ☐ As the strategy is converted to actual implementation what budgetary considerations, policies, and procedures will support or limit it?

Figure 2.1. Strategic Planning Checklist.

Figure 2.1. is a strategic planning checklist developed from T. Hansen-Horn and Horn's book: *Strategic Planning: Beginning the Journey* (2014). Its purpose is to help public relations strategists in training become SRC public relations strategists.

Conclusion

As public relations professionals like us take our place in the strategy conversation, we remember that to be strategic requires us to plan, be results-driven, contemplate the impact of the nature of communication, and keep in mind relevant publics. We are careful to keep the fluidity and porous nature of publics top-of-mind. We know fully that public relations involves both communication and business imperatives. As we proceed we keep consequential, or alternaquence thinking, in mind because we don't separate choices from impact, or alternatives from consequences. Sage public relations professionals remember that there's not one best practice or understanding of strategy because strategy can be prescriptive, descriptive, emergent, or transformative; linear, adaptive, or interpretive; deliberate; and/or a plan, ploy, pattern, position, and/or prescription in intent. And, as professionals we realize that the only way to let others know what is being imagined (thought about and planned) is through a process of codification, elaboration, and conversion (codification-elaboration-conversion process) which, in itself, impacts what goes on or gets said.

In an effort to make sense of the increasingly complex world in which public relations professionals do business, and to position themselves to succeed in making strategic decisions, many public relations professionals find themselves referring often to something like the Strategic Planning Checklist. In fact, asking the many questions found on the checklist becomes almost second nature.

As a move to make further sense of the complexity in which we do public relations business, chapter three presents an overview of the B2B, B2C, and B2G economic areas that characterize public relations initiatives; as well as the for-profit, non-profit, social enterprise non-profit, and government macro-environments that structure organizational existence and purpose. The discussions of economic areas and organization type are followed by a review of prominent public relations situations and contexts, and role specializations that exist within the widely varied public relations industry. The discussions in chapter three serve as launch pads for developing readers' abilities to imagine and work through increasingly complex public relations situations and the interconnectedness that characterizes them.

Chapter Exercises

1. How would you define public relations? What explanatory power for successfully engaging in public relations does your definition have? How does your definition compare with the one in this book?
2. Describe how you view public relations as a communication and business function? How does your view color what you imagine as your public relations career? How does it color the power public relations has to engage in organizational strategy?

3. How much of an alternaquence thinker are you? Are you satisfied with that? How do you think it will affect your professional success?

4. How do see the codification-elaboration-conversion process taking place in your own lived experience? How important is it, do you think, to be aware of this process and the effects it has on all communicative experiences? How does awareness impact strategic choice-making in the public relations profession? How does lack of awareness of it limit strategic choice-making in the profession?

5. Reflect on your own experiences and behaviors. What kind of strategist (from the choices provided on this chapter's strategy list) do you generally tend to be? Why? If there is no one choice that seems to represent you most of the time, why do you think that's the case?

6. Peruse the Strategic Planning Checklist provided in this chapter and choose at least 10–15 questions that you think are most important to illuminating the kind of SRC strategist you plan to be.

Opportunity for Praxis

To apply this chapter's information to the cases in Appendix B, see Appendix A:
_____ Strategy Key
_____ Case Rubric Master

Notes

1. Hansen-Horn, T. & Horn, A. (2014). *Strategic planning for public relations: Beginning the journey.* New York: Peter Lang, p. 19.
2. Ibid., pp. 32–34.
3. Byrum, K. (n.d.). *White Paper:* PRSA MBA program: Bridging the gap between strategic communications education and master of business administration (MBA) curriculum. Retrieved March 11, 2016 from http://www.prsa.org/Learning/MBA/documents/White-Paper-MBA.pdf.
4. US Bureau of Labor. (n.d.). Retrieved March 11, 2016 from http://www.bls.gov/oes/current/naics4_541800.htm.
5. See Hansen-Horn & Horn, 2014, chapters 2–4 for a detailed discussion.
6. Hansen-Horn & Horn, 2014, p. 111 and MacNeal, E. (1983). Semantics and decision-making. *Etc., 40*(2), p. 163.
7. Hansen-Horn & Horn, 2014, pp. 95–120.
8. Chaffee, E. (1985). Three models of strategy. *Academy of Management Review, 10*(1), p. 89.
9. Mintzberg, H. & Quinn, J. (1996). *The strategy process: Concepts, contexts, cases* (3rd ed.). Upper Saddle River, NJ: Prentice Hall, p. 15.

10. Hansen-Horn & Horn, 2014, p. 114.
11. Mintzberg, H. (1994). *The rise and fall of strategic planning: Reconceiving roles for planning, plans, and planners.* New York: Free Press.
12. Ibid., p. 340.
13. Hansen-Horn & Horn, 2014, pp. 100–110.
14. Mintzberg, 1994.
15. Mintzberg & Quinn, 1996.
16. Chaffee, 1985.
17. Porter, M. (1998). *On competition.* Boston, MA: Harvard Business School.
18. Hansen-Horn & Horn, 2014, p. 111.
19. Sinek, S. (2009). *Start with why: How great leaders inspire everyone to take action.* New York: Penguin Books, p. 1.

CHAPTER THREE

Public Relations Complexity and Interconnectedness

Economic Area, Organization Type, Situations and Contexts, and Specializations

This chapter presents an overview of the B2B, B2C and B2G economic environments that characterize public relations activities; as well as the for-profit, non-profit, social-enterprise non-profit, and government macro-environments that structure organizational existence and purpose. It's followed by a review of prominent public relations situations and contexts, and role specializations that exist within the widely varied public relations industry. This chapter's discussions should serve as a launch pad for your professional ability to imagine and work through increasingly complex public relations situations and the interconnectedness that characterizes them.

Economic Area: B2B, B2C, and B2G

B2B stands for business-to-business, B2C stands for business-to-consumer, and B2G stands for business-to-government. *Business-to-business* activity serves the needs of businesses (of all kinds, non-profits included) and not individuals. In involves purchases, requests for qualifications (rfqs), requests for proposals (rfps), contracts, etc., designed to facilitate business as usual. It generally consists of large-scale transactions between manufacturers and retailers, manufacturers and wholesalers, or wholesalers and retailers. In addition, it includes contractual public relations services to a manufacturer, wholesaler, retailer, or organized group. Note, the contract can be for organizational communications needs, products, services, or even idea generation. In terms of products, a B2B transaction can be the purchase of commercial toilet paper for a Coca-Cola bottling plant. Toilet paper is a large US commodity. In 2008, .858 million tons of toilet paper was sold in the United States for away-from-home purposes, which means for general commercial use.[1] In terms of services, a B2B contract can exist between a small retailer like Terra Health & Wellness Market in Independence, MO and a credit card merchant account provider (a company that processes credit card transactions on behalf of its clients). If Terra hired a public relations agency to help with its brand image directed at environmental activist groups, that would also be a B2B arrangement. In addition, a B2B arrangement for the purposes of promoting an "idea" is the partnership between March of Dimes (MOD) and the Kansas City-based Crossroads agency. One of the partnership objectives is to convince all relevant publics that any kind of premature birth is risky. The MOD Healthy Babies are Worth the Wait campaign focuses on the idea that elective deliveries before 39 weeks gestation is dangerous and that waiting longer, regardless of circumstances, are worth it for the baby's health.

B2C stands for *business-to-consumer* relationships. It involves meeting the needs and wants of individuals, who consume something, with products, services, or ideas. The transactions are generally less formalized, smaller in amount and cost, and less complex than those associated with B2B or B2G transactions. In the instance of toilet paper, this would involve a purchase of toilet paper for at-home use. If we go back to Terra, we know that the store exists as a business-to-consumer enterprise. Its purpose is to sell products to individuals who enter its store or eat at its small dine-in restaurant. Its sales of organic chocolate milk to customers are B2C transactions. So, too, are its sales of gluten free items and organic toilet paper. If it diversifies into event catering for local companies, that will take it into the B2B world as well. At present, however, should Terra hire a public relations agency to help it generate store and restaurant awareness among potential customers through its sponsorship of special events, the hired agency will provide B2C services on Terra's behalf through a B2B contract. If we continue with the earlier MOD example, the idea that all premature births are risky (even elective ones at 38 weeks) is being "sold," if you will, to consumers who can make the choice to suggest elective delivery.

More likely than not, you are getting a glimpse by now of the complexity and interconnectedness of the public relations industry. Complex thinking like this really is valuable to your future. A recent announcement by the Association to Advance Collegiate Schools of Business (AACSB) urges business schools to get more practical with what really goes on. AACSB board of director member Michael Arena, who is the chief talent and development officer for General

Motors Co., framed the move in a way relevant to our current discussion. He said, "Business graduates must be fluent in the 'practice of theory in a less-than-ideal context.'"[2] The real world is complex and public relations professionals need to be ready to handle that complexity in strategic ways.

It's quite likely that you are probably familiar with the B2C environment because you are a frequent and, many times, enthusiastic consumer of products and services. Because many college students are attracted to working for what they know, such as well-known brands in their market like Nike, Under Armour, PINK, and Sonic they are often uncomfortable with the idea of exploring non-B2C brands as an excellent employment opportunity. They are afraid of what they don't know. Brands such as Dolby Laboratories, MailChimp, and WeWork consume public relations services as well as offer excellent long-term career options. All three B2B brands provide excellent employment options but you've likely never heard of them, much less dreamed of working for one of them. You don't knowingly consume their products and services, so they aren't on your radar, but they should be. The B2B industry is big business.

Adding complexity to the B2C discussion is our ability to label organizations like Children's Mercy Kansas City, Make-A-Wish, and the Pediatric Brain Tumor Foundation as B2C organizations. Each one of these charitable organizations is really about serving the consumer and, as such, its services are consumed by the consumer. However, because we don't usually pair non-profits with business of any kind, you may be a bit uncomfortable thinking of these three as B2C kinds of organizations. In addition, we can classify a cooperative organization such as CureSearch, because it exists to facilitate and fund pediatric cancer research among children's hospitals and leading researchers, as a B2B organization. It exists to promote transactions among those in the business of searching for a pediatric cancer cure. Labeling CureSearch as a B2B organization might make you uncomfortable, but that is generally where its mission places it.

Finally, B2G stands for *business-to-government*. It involves non-government organizations doing business directly with government offices and enterprises at local, state, national, and international levels. In fact, the US government is the biggest contractor of goods and services in the United States. It's imperative that public relations professionals know how to work with it, understanding that it works within its own prescribed guidelines and requires prospective business partners to submit contract proposals and make bids through a formal rfp or procurement process. It's important to note that the government does not use the term public relations, but instead uses the term public affairs. It also widens the scope of priority publics. And, public affairs is viewed as a less persuasive term in its intent than is public relations. The US government is tasked with engaging in public service and not public persuasion.

At this point in the chapter you should have a more comprehensive understanding of B2B, B2C, and B2G economic environments. A grasp of for-profit, non-profit, social-enterprise non-profit and government macro-economic environments is also essential to your professional future.

For-profit, Non-profit, Social-enterprise Non-profit and Government

A *for-profit* organization exists for the purpose of making money. A non-profit's business is not conducted solely for making a profit but, instead, is undertaken for a cause or special interest. A *non-profit* must return all of its revenues beyond operating expenses to itself. A for-profit is not under any such restrictions. Nike, Under Armour, PINK, Sonic, Dolby Laboratories, MailChimp, and WeWork are all for-profit organizations. Children's Mercy Kansas City, Make-A-Wish, the Pediatric Brain Tumor Foundation, and CureSearch are non-profit organizations.

A for-profit organization can operate under the control of a private owner, a group of entrepreneurs or private investors, or a board, among other unique arrangements for oversight. If it is publicly traded, it also answers to its shareholders and to the Securities and Exchange Commission (SEC), especially in the use of resources, decision making, and ROI. A non-profit can operate under the control of its founder or founders, its board, or the direction of another non-profit. It must meet many guidelines enforced by the US government if it has attained any sort of official non-profit status such as 501(c)(3), the most common, and the status held by Children's Mercy Kansas City, Make-A-Wish, the PBTF, Cure-Search, and many others. Non-profit examples holding a different type of status are organizations with 501(c)(4) status that exist as politically active non-profits. Examples are Crossroads GPS and Progress Florida.

Interestingly, if a non-profit operates at the international level and is not part of the US government (though it can be a government grant recipient) it might be referred to as a *non-government-organization* or NGO. The major distinction between a non-profit and a NGO is level of operation. According to GrantSpace, an online resource for non-profits, NGO is typically reserved for non-domestic organizations[3] such as Greenpeace, World Vision, and Care International because of the scope of their operations.

Finally, there's even more non-profit complexity to add to the mix. Given the demand for non-profits to sustain themselves, meaning to have enough money to guarantee continuing operations, it's imperative to clearly understand the difference between non-profit organizations that are funded philanthropically and those organized as social enterprises. Of course, there are organizations dependent on a mix of the two models as well. For the purpose of understanding, the two are treated as mutually exclusive here.

A *philanthropically funded* organization relies on donor giving and grants as its main sources of operating revenue. It asks for and collects money to back its charitable initiatives. Philanthropic non-profits are not self-funded, which keeps them scrambling for market share in the charitable giving arena. Giving USA: The Annual Report on Philanthropy is an excellent source for understanding the charitable giving mix.[4]

A *social enterprise* (SE) non-profit, however, has as its main mission the ability to self-fund while it does good. The Social Enterprise Alliance defines a SE as "an organization or initiative that marries the social mission of a non-profit or government program with the market-driven approach of a [for-profit] business."[5] In other words, it exists for the purpose of doing good but its intent is to fund much or all of its own do-good initiatives. This means it operates for the purpose of profit-making so it can re-invest those profits into its social mission. Its objective is the *double bottom line* (DBL), which is to perform well financially while also making a sizable social impact. Social enterprise examples are the Nehemiah Social Enterprise and Better World Books.

For many of you, the non-profitable (philanthropic) vs. profitable (SE) distinction is a totally new idea. You may question its feasibility and advisability. In fact, you may buy into the idea that a charitable organization that focuses on profit-making is unethical or, at least, going to compromise its mission. If this is true of you, you are not alone. Harvard Business Review's Gregory Dees put it well in 1998 writing, "When nonprofits become more businesslike, they may run afoul of public values and meet with political resistance ... but the point is that nonprofits are not expected to behave like businesses. When they do, critics are ready to pounce."[6]

Your likely surprise at the idea of making a profit to do well, coupled with the resistance Dees described, align well with the challenges many SE leaders find themselves facing. SE leadership authors Y. Tian and W. Smith (2015) argue that, "Striving to fulfill a social mission is associated with goals, missions, and stakeholders that can be inconsistent with seeking profit, creating strategic paradoxes, and fostering distinct challenges for social entrepreneurs."[7] Prioritizing a social mission to do good can get difficult under the demands of making a profit, especially when the stakeholders are wide and varied. A SE necessarily serves stakeholders vested in its social mission as well as those vested in its profit making mission. The tensions heighten if it works with outside investors who are more concerned with earning a profit (and that is not necessarily a bad thing) more than doing good.

SE expert Yves Mombeleur, former managing director of the Nehemiah Community Reinvestment Fund (a member of the Nehemiah Social Enterprise), suggests a third tension when he refers to the recent redevelopment of downtown Los Angeles while he describes the end result of many SE business initiatives.

> Recently, the mayor remarked on how vibrant the downtown is and how good it is that millennials are rushing to live there. Development has been great but it was really not social enterprise engagement because the developers created wonderful new living quarters, shops, and public use areas while not addressing the purported 50,000 homeless who call downtown their home. Real social enterprise, in my eyes, addresses how to help those at the lowest economic strata rather than just displace them. We can't grow and prosper as a country when doing good means only a very selected and often privileged few prosper. So, essentially, SE is doing well while doing good in a way that all those who will be impacted get a positive piece of the pie.[8]

In essence, the real spirit of SE is to make sure all parties involved in a particular situation or context do well and do good, leaving no one behind or pushed out to make room for a favored few.

Government organizations, then, are much more highly regulated as a general rule. They operate totally under the purview of national, states or local governments. They answer to "the public" because their funds come from tax dollars. Their sole purpose is public service. As such, all of their activity (and communication) is highly restricted by prescriptive laws and rules. All government employee communications (internal and external) are permanent records and open to scrutiny at any time. Like non-profits, all revenue generated by government organizations must be returned to the organization. In the spirit of public affairs, strategic planning and communication is a vital part of all government operations. Regularly communicating what it is doing, why it is doing something, and making available accountability statements are mandatory activities. Government organizations have their own prescribed rules governing what and how things can be communicated. The same holds true for government decision making and contracting.

The real world, as students so often refer to it, truly is complex. Now that we've briefly distinguished among B2B, B2C, and B2G economic environments; and established a framework for understanding organizations as for-profits, non-profits (charity or cause driven at the domestic level, NGOs at the international level, and philanthropic vs. SE), or government entities, let's move on to a brief exploration of the many situations and contexts in which a public relations professional can find herself working. The rich variety of situations and contexts defining career paths available to its professionals, as well as the array of specializations one might choose, make public relations an exciting pursuit. Together they illustrate the complexity in the field and of engaging in public relations business.

Nineteen Public Relations Situations and Contexts

Hansen-Horn and Horn (2014) identified 19 situation and context defined career paths, and 22 specializations in the field. The lists are not necessarily exhaustive, nor are the career paths and specializations necessarily mutually-exclusive, but they do represent the vastness of the public relations field. The 19 career paths are advancement, campaigning and debating, cause marketing and branding, community relations, corporate communications, corporate social responsibility, crisis communication (and/or management), development, image and reputation management, integrated marketing communications, issues management, lobbying, marketing communications, media relations, public affairs, risk communication, special event planning, strategic communication, and sustainability. Each of the 19 is briefly described in the list below.[9]

PR Situations & Contexts	Descriptions
Advancement	Fundraising and political representation for academic organizations. Sometimes used interchangeably with "development."
Campaigning and debating	Relating to local, state and federal level activity for the purposes of elections, voting, and/or legislation.
Cause marketing and branding	Matching a for-profit organization's marketing efforts with a charitable organization's cause/goals for the purpose of favorable perception building
Community relations	Usually geographically designated, but can also occur in digital communities. For the purpose of relationship building and/or maintenance between operating organizations and the people of the communities in which they exist.
Corporate Communications	Generally referring to internal public relations activities at large for-profit organizations, although some government offices are similarly named.
Corporate Social Responsibility	Referring to organizational vision and activity designed to act ethically and make a positive impact in areas from which it benefits or serves.
Crisis Communication and/or management	Predates actual organizational crises; can preempt crises, purpose during crises is to provide factual, timely, and situation-relevant information to all vested parties while working for a timely return to "regular" operations.
Development	Referring to fundraising and resourcing efforts for all non-profit organizations; sometimes used interchangeably with "advancement."

PR Situations & Contexts	Descriptions
Image and reputation management	Referring to efforts to build and/or maintain an organization's multifaceted collection of public perceptions into a desirable end result. Reputation refers more than image to perceptions of past actions and intents.
Integrated marketing communications	Referring to initiatives undertaken with the understanding that every possible vehicle of organizational communication is perceived by recipients as coming from one indistinguishable source, therefore, all communicative efforts should be complementary in some way.
Issues management	The address of emerging issues for the sake or organizational pursuits or before they can negatively impact doing business as usual.
Lobbying	Involves formal and informal efforts. Paid lobbyists represent the interests of employers and advocate at local, state, and federal levels. Grassroots activism takes place from the efforts of non-paid advocates in attempts to drive public activism.
Marketing communications	Referring to communication initiatives supporting consumer and/or trade promotions. Not to be confused with IMC.
Media relations	Referring to long- and short-term relationship development with, as well as strategic communication efforts directed at, media members relevant to your organization's goals.
Public affairs	Referring to efforts to interpret and impact political and/or social issue regulation as they have potential to impact business as usual.
Risk communication	Involves strategic messaging designed to reduce perceptions of and/or the reality of conditions that can bring harm to publics. Often able to preempt crisis.
Special event planning	Referring to the planning and execution of meetings, conventions, tradeshows, ceremonies, team building activities, and the like; designed for public relations purposes.
Strategic communication	Some times used interchangeably with public relations, referring to coordinated communication efforts to net desirable organizational impact.
Sustainability	Referring to efforts to insure long-term organizational livelihood. Sometimes used interchangeably with corporate social responsibility.

With at least 19 situation and context defined career paths open to public relations professionals, you wouldn't think there would be room for even more variety, but there is. There are at least 22 specializations that can be pursued.

Twenty-two Public Relations Specializations

Twenty-two specialization areas are also available to public relations professionals. Traditional case study classifications categorize cases by these labels. They are agency public relations, aviation relations, conference and convention relations, consumer relations, digital communications, education relations, entertainment public relations, environmental or conservation relations, employee relations, fashion relations, fundraising, government relations, healthcare communication, international relations, investor and financial relations, member relations, maturing publics relations, relations with special publics, sports public relations, travel and tourism relations, university relations, and volunteer relations. Each of the 22 identified specializations is briefly described in the list below.[10]

Public Relations Specializations	Description
Agency Public Relations	Services provided for a fee at client request; can consist of any of the other specializations.
Aviation Relations	Initiatives to represent the interests of all level of airports, travelers and cargo systems, aircraft manufacturers, and service providers.
Conference and convention relations	Special event services, relationship building among businesses, and professional services representation.
Consumer relations	Services to build iconic brands and brand reputation for loyal consumption.
Digital communications	Social media strategies and tactics, among others, as used to provide relevant messages and representation to consumers of electronic media.
Education relations	Efforts on behalf of elementary, middle, high school, and post-high-school organizations in cooperation with the Department of Education.
Employee relations	Often neglected, this includes treating employees as a valued public, recognizing them as brand ambassadors and word-of-mouth sources. Sometimes called corporate communications.

Public Relations Specializations	Description
Entertainment public relations	A catchall for strategic work with television, movie, music, fashion, radio, athletic, and event-related celebrities.
Environmental or conservation relations	Involving efforts to preserve the environment, natural resources, animal life and/or gain permission to do business in protected areas. Generally an area of robust activism.
Fashion relations	Truly a global industry, it involves efforts to define latest trends, follow celebrities, and communicate beauty.
Fundraising	Services to elicit voluntary financial contributions from relevant publics, largely a responsibility of the not-profit arena.
Government relations	Efforts to work within laws and regulations enforced by the US government (or any government), influence legislation and leaders, or change policy.
Healthcare communications	A growing area in light of the US-push for preventative measures and a rapidly aging public, it involves work on behalf of hospitals, insurance companies, special interest groups, and the like.
International relations	Involves building and negotiating relationships with nondomestic governments, etc., and working with groups such as the IMF. It often involves questions of policy.
Investor and financial relations	Highly regulated by the federal agencies, this involves initiatives to communicate financial statuses in ways beneficial to all vested parties.
Maturing publics relations	A rapidly growing public, it involves issues of health care, geriatric care, palliative care, and long-term support, as well as vested interests in retirement, travel, and the like.
Member relations	Like employee relations, this involves working with an external public. However, the voluntary nature of members is a significant differentiator. Services include making sure members retain their membership through satisfaction brought about by communication to them and of their interests.
Relations with special publics	Identified as specific groups clustered around special interests determined by demographics and psychographics.
Sports public relations	As a valuable source of entertainment and international unity, efforts to represent the interests of sports-related publics is key.

(Continued)

(*Continued*)

Public Relations Specializations	Description
Travel and tourism relations	Image and reputation are the foundation of the health of this industry, as are vital sources of state and national income. This generally relates to hospitality as well.
University relations	Services to tell a university's story and its promise to those holding a real or potential vested interest in it.
Volunteer relations	Directed at members and non-members, these are a defining part of allegiance to causes, activist activities, and so on. Also a source of employee relations activities.

Conclusion

Any public relations professional who has a solid grasp of the intricacies of the B2B, B2C, and B2G economic areas; as well as the for-profit, non-profit, social enterprise non-profit, and government organization types is sure to find himself ahead of the competition (aka marketplace wrangle or contested terrain—see chapter six for more on this). In addition, recognizing the 19 situations and contexts that define public relations career paths and action, as well as the 22 specializations that currently exist in the US industry as we know it, will help him successfully negotiate the complex interconnectedness that characterizes and contextualizes public relations.

Opportunity for Praxis

To apply this chapter's information to the cases in Appendix B, see Appendix A:
____ Economic Area Key
____ Organization Type Key
____ PR Specializations Key
____ PR Situations and Contexts Key
____ Case Rubric Master

Notes

1. Kalil, B. (October 31, 2008). *Tissue market continues to grow.* Retrieved March 28, 2016 from http://www.risiinfo.com/magazines/October/2008/PP/PPMagOctober-Tissue-market-continues-to-grow.html.
2. Gellman, L. (April 6, 2016). A new push for real-world lessons at business schools. *The Wall Street Journal.* Retrieved from http://www.wsj.com/articles/a-new-push-for-real-world-lessons-at-business-schools-1459972295.
3. GrantSpace. (n.d.). Retrieved April 2, 2016 from http://grantspace.org/tools/knowledge-base/Resources-for-Non-U.S.-Grantseekers/ngo-definition-and-role.
4. Giving USA. (n.d.). Retrieved April 8, 2015 from http://www.givinginstitute.org/?page=GUSAAnnualReport.
5. Social Enterprise Alliance. (n.d.). Retrieved April 2, 2016 from https://socialenterprise.us/about/social-enterprise.
6. Dees, G. (January-February, 1998). Enterprising nonprofits. *Harvard Business Review,* Retrieved April 2, 2016 from https://hbr.org/1998/01/enterprising-nonprofits.
7. Tian, Y. & Smith, W. (2015). Entrepreneurial leadership of social enterprises: Challenges and skills for embracing paradoxes. *Journal of Leadership Studies, 8*(3), pp. 43–45.
8. Mombeleur, Y. (March 2016). Personal email communication.
9. Hansen-Horn, T. & Horn, A. (2014). *Strategic planning for public relations: The journey begins.* New York: Peter Lang, pp. 128–138.
10. Ibid., pp. 138–146.

CHAPTER FOUR

Value in Applied Theory

Writing and Reading Theory: Starting with Excellence Theory

Excellent SRC strategists apply theory to their understandings of what is going on (WIGO), what can go on, and what should go on. When you can do this yourself, the point in your professional journey will be reached at which you'll be a sought-after decision-maker and counselor. This chapter discusses the ins and outs of reading theory, introduces four theories judged as valuable to every public relations student, and ends by introducing you to excellence theory.

Writing and Reading Theory

If your first reaction to reading a chapter about theory was negative, as in "this is going to be boring," or "ugh, theory has nothing to do with what I want to do," or "I shouldn't have to learn theory because it has nothing to do with the real world," you've already limited your professional potential. So before you make your mind go blank, ask yourself this question. If your parents gave you $4,000 last weekend to pay your tuition and fees this week, but you (are 21 or older) lost it all at the casinos last night, what will you do? Will you immediately call your parents because you know they'll be happy to give you more money? Will you find it hard to breathe and panic at the thought of having to tell your parents because they'll be angry with you? Will you frantically look for another source of funds hoping to avoid the conversation? Will you drop out of school and not tell your parents what you did?

If you're like most students, the prediction is that you'll find it hard to breathe and panic at the thought of what you have to tell your parents. If this is the case, you just used your own "parent reaction theory" to predict their behavior. You can make your prediction because you have a clear idea of how they'll react to the fact that you gambled away your tuition money. You've gathered evidence before the event ... you've experienced them before. As such, you can invoke your own theory in your own life, based on what you have observed about parental expectations and responses, to make predictions about your future (what will happen when you confess). And, notice the prediction that was just made about you as a student anticipating your parents' reactions? The "hard to breathe" one? That, too, comes from the application of theory, from author-application. So, you see, using theory to explain and make predictions is not bad at all and is actually commonplace.

We (including students) use the power of theory all of the time; we just don't realize it. If we go back to the strategy codification-elaboration-conversion process described in chapter two, we can argue that it applies to our ability to share theory, as well as strategy, with each other. Remember, codification refers to the process through which we do our best to use labels and words, voice inflections, known systems of distribution, availability of resources, and so on to represent and communicate the strategy we intend to follow. It's a process that necessarily leaves out some of what we intend and, in turn, is vulnerable to unintended interpretations. As we put strategy into action, the process then turns to elaboration, which involves the alteration of our strategy into pieces and parts relevant to best practices for resourcing, timing and so on. Finally, the conversion part of the strategy process is unavoidable because when our strategy is implemented in anyway, it will necessarily be impacted by what is already going on or known to be true, a best practice, or real. And, of course, our ability to engage in the codification-elaboration-conversion process depends on some shared of common frames of reference.

That's why reading someone else's descriptions of theory that they want to share can be so challenging. Trying to encode (symbolically represent) and decode (make sense of) a perspective of what is going on and what will go on in the future "because" (this is theory writing and reading), is tough. It has to be coded in such a way that it can be understood and shared with others. Imagine trying to tell someone who you just met exactly why you would predict your parents' behavior the way you do. It will likely take you awhile and, you may have to explain and illustrate, explain and illustrate before your prediction is clearly understood. If English is not your new friend's first language, it will take much longer.

To explain anything using any form of communication, the one doing the coding must assume that other people share some sort of common *frames of reference* (shared experiences, understandings, and systems of assigning meaning through which we filter everything) with him. He must try to build systems of thought, logical processing (a cultural expectation), metaphors, and the like, that help you imagine the theory and its parts, as well as the perspective-taking it can offer. And, when writing about theory he must account for the printed page, publisher word count limitations imposed on his efforts, anticipated reading levels, and reader attitudes. And, as the reader of theory, you must try to imagine and understand or assign author-intended meaning. You must share a common thought process, engage in an expected culturally-specific system of logical processing, and "get" the metaphors the author uses. It's a pretty complicated process, that's true, but we do it all the time whether we realize it or not.

While writing and reading theory are complex processes, they are still worth the effort. As T. Hansen-Horn and B. Dostal Neff (2008) argue so clearly in *Public Relations: From Theory to Practice*:

> There is nothing as practical as a good theory. However, for many students (academic and professional) of public relations, attaining the theory-practice connection can be tough. It is not always an easy matter to take theoretical constructs and predictions and apply them to practice.[1]

Much like reading and writing theory, the effort to apply theory to practice is challenging, but is a good thing; it's called *praxis*. Practicing praxis helps us see multiple possibilities and perspectives, and both are important to successful decision-making in our complex world. Chapter four sets the stage to help you develop this skill. Its intent is two-fold. The first is to begin introducing you to four theories (judged by prominent leaders in the field as valuable to all public relations students), starting with excellence theory. The second is to provide a theoretical framework (lens or key) that you can apply to view public relations situations from varying heuristic (idea generating) perspectives. This is praxis-in-the-classroom.

Four Theories to Benefit You: Selection Process

Four of the most active public relations scholars cum teachers cum professional consultants participated in a loosely-coupled omnibus-type survey for the purposes of this book. The four were Dr. Glen Cameron (CEO Treeple, LLC; Co-Investigator Center for Health & Policy; Director of the Health Communication Research Center; Professor of Strategic Communication @ the Missouri School of Journalism, and Gregory Chair in Journalism Research), Dr. Robert L. Heath (Professor Emeritus-University of Houston, editor of *The Sage Handbook for Public Relations* and the *Encyclopedia of Public Relations*, and industry consultant), Dr. Bonita Dostal Neff (Professor and Chair of Communication Department [recently launching the department's public relations program] at Indiana

University), and Dr. Maureen Taylor (Director of the School of Advertising and Public Relations at the University of Tennessee, prolific researcher and author, and international consultant). They undertook the task of recommending "four or five theories you would like every public relations student to learn intimately." The potential response invited at least 20 suggested theories. However, consistency among responses (something we would expect because the question was asked of experts in public relations education and practice) netted 16 suggested theories. Of those, the most often mentioned theories named were contingency theory (it got the most votes), excellence theory, rhetorical theory, and social capital theory. Though contingency theory received the most votes, excellence theory appears in most textbooks so it is addressed here first.

Chapter four provides an excellence theory overview, while chapter five is dedicated to the contrasting ideas found in contingency theory. Rhetorical theory is explored in chapter six, and chapter seven is dedicated to social capital theory. We invite you to make use of the content in all four chapters, paying special attention to the chapter exercises and opportunity for praxis found at each chapter's end. Furthermore, the opportunities for praxis direct your attention to *Appendix A*, with chapter relevant keys and rubrics for your use as you analyze the cases recorded in Appendix B. Your skill in adopting and applying multiple theoretical insights will lead to making well-reasoned inferences and predictions about WIGO, what may go on, or what should go on to best address or redress priority interests. Or, in short, to make sound strategic decisions.

Excellence Theory

Because excellence theory is dominant in a lot of public relations textbooks and as a model from which public relations is practiced and examined, we begin with it. Introduced first to the public relations field in James Grunig and Todd Hunt's 1984 book,[2] excellence theory proposed four models of public relations thought to chronicle the development of the field, and be representative of the approaches to public relations taken by organizations. The intent was to discover and articulate "best practices" in the field. Grunig and Hunt famously defined public relations as "the management of communication between an organization and its publics."[3] Well-known excellence model advocate J. Grunig believed that he and his colleagues had "produced the first general theory of public relations"[4] as one with four models. Characterized as the classic models of public relations, and stemming from the tradition of systems theory, excellence theory assumes that all public relations can be classified into one of four models: press agentry/publicity, public information, two-way asymmetrical, and two-way symmetrical. Noting that "all models are false—at least in part—because they cannot represent all of reality [but] the human mind must rely on models because it can only isolate and group key variables that can be abstracted from reality,"[5] the excellence theory proponents still found value in recognizing and classifying public relations activity as they did. It's important to explore each of the four models and the assumptions, or world views about public relations, embedded in them. Excellence theory advocates claim that we can understand and choose best practices for our own efforts after studying the models. But first, let's take at look at the basics of systems theory as it informs excellence theory. Becoming acquainted with the basic tenets of systems theory will help you more clearly understand many of the terms and assumptions found in excellence theory.

Excellence Foundation: Systems Theory

Systems theory originated in the study of living organisms. It was first formalized and introduced to the biology world by Ludwig Von Bertalanffy in 1950.[6] In 1966, industrial and organizational psychology scholars Daniel Katz and Robert Kahn adapted it to the study of organizations.[7] They developed a process model for interpreting organizational behavior in terms of input, throughput, and output while accounting for internal and external conditions that can mediate a system's behavior.

At its core, a systems approach to organizational functioning encourages us to understand all organizations as living organisms marked by birth, life and death, and comprised of interdependent parts, each with its own function and interrelated responsibilities. The input, throughput, and output process; as well as the concepts of environmental adaptation, feedback, homeostasis, equifinality, and open vs. closed systems are also central to the theory.

All organizations start sometime, somewhere and somehow, hence they have *birth*. Organizations have *life* as long as they can bring in (or *input*) the resources they need to operate, transform those resources somehow via their *throughput* process as *output* (products, graduates, produced services, etc.) that then have the power to solicit or bring in additional input. The system process is circular and facilitates organizational life. Organizational life ends in *death* if and when the input, throughput, output process is no longer sufficient and the organization goes out of existence.

In essence, a systems theorist believes that an organization's survivability depends on its input, throughput, output success. Its ability to acquire the resources or inputs it needs from its operating environment (which it affects and which affects it) in a way that it can transform those inputs into outputs (that then become inputs for other organizations operating in and making up its environment) are key to sustained life. An example is a university system. University students are one system input. The throughput process involves transforming minds and visions into critical thinkers and professional contributors to areas of expertise. The output then, is graduates. The cyclical process begins again, for example, when a graduate recommends his or her university to someone else and that student then becomes university input with the purpose of transformation and the end goal of graduation. This, of course, is just one of the many university input, throughput, output processes we can address; there are many more.

Further systems theory understanding comes from the exploration of *interdependence* and *interrelatedness*. As systems themselves, organizations are made up of other systems that operate within them, or in which they operate and/or overlap. For instance, a university is comprised of many systems, such as admissions offices, departments, colleges, academic programs, advising centers, financial aid offices, student activities, athletics, and so on. Each affects and is affected in some way by the others; the success of the university as a whole depends on their successful interaction with and effects on each other. That is interdependence through being interrelated in light of task and function.

In the same way, a university system must also exist in its larger environments (also viewable as systems) such as towns, states, larger university systems, public opinion, and the like. Again, each is affected by and affects the others in some way. The idea of *environmental adaptation* comes in here. Interdependence and adaptation are key to understanding system theory through *feedback* processes. Most systems can only adapt to and/or influence others if some sort of organizational measurement (stock reports and analyses, customer comments, market data, curriculum reviews, etc.) as feedback are part of their operations. The feedback allows organizations to reset or reaffirm goals, try new things, change policies, or stay the course.

As organizations account for feedback, systems theorists argue that a healthy future is governed by expectations of *homeostasis* or balance. Note that an individual's (we are systems ourselves) physical balance is not a rigid state but, instead, a process of correction and accommodation. It involves shifting one's weight or posture to accommodate uneven ground, wind, a stubbed toe, and so on. In the same way, the skyscrapers and large bridges most likely to remain standing over long periods of time are characterized by "firm flexibility;" they move and sway instead of being rigid. The same is true of a room's temperature. Say a thermostat (the device that triggers warmer or cooler air by gathering and evaluating feedback) is set to 75 degrees Fahrenheit. The actual room temperature is rarely exactly 75 degrees, instead, it fluctuates comfortably within a degree or two above or below the set point. It's a balancing act. Finally, if we return to our university example we can apply the same principle. At a very basic level, let's say the university is designed for optimal operation and educational excellence when it is host to an average of 10,000 students holding steady across five years. Those reviewing numbers will not panic if they discover the following data fluctuations. In year one, they count 9,500 students; in year two, they count 9,750 students; in year three, they count 10,250 students; in year four, they count 10, 300 students; and in year five, they count 10,250 students. The average is roughly 10,000 students per year. The optimal five-year goal is met because homeostasis is reality.

Systems theorists also introduce us to the ideas of equifinality and open vs. closed borders. *Equifinality* allows for difference in the pursuit of the same end. It means that a similar systems goal can be reached through a variety of paths. A great example of this is university students who seek graduation as an end goal. Ten thousand students can graduate, but each one can take different classes at different times from different programs and complete their degrees (graduate) at different times. Degree completion is their universal goal, but there are many ways students can get there. Equifinality is important to adaptation and accommodation.

Finally, is the notion of *openness vs. closed-ness*. This relates to how much an organization accommodates and/or adjusts to the demands of its environments or other systems upon which its sustained life depends. An organization that never accommodates customer feedback will likely have a significantly shortened lifespan. In the same way, if an organization is designed to accommodate all demands (from relevant internal and external systems) all the time, that will also result in a significantly reduced lifespan. In addition, open vs. closed refers to a system's need for input from external sources as well as the need to release output to external sources. Much of the open vs. closed balancing act (similar to the idea of homeostasis) depends on an organizational feedback process and how the feedback is used.

Hence, the input, throughput, output process is key to understanding organizations as systems. So, too, are birth, life and death, as well as interdependence, environmental adaptation, feedback, homeostasis, equifinality, and open vs. closed-ness. We now have a better foundation for examining the four models (press agentry/publicity, public information, two-way asymmetric, and two-way symmetric) proposed in excellence theory.

The Excellence Models

Press Agentry/Publicity

Press agentry/publicity involves the communication of messages from an organization to publics under the assumption that meaning is more important than truth. It's believed that the organization sending the messages knows what messages will get its publics to do what it wants them to do in order to attain desired organizational objectives. Propaganda is typically classified as coming from the press agentry/publicity model of public relations. Dictators, celebrity publicists, shock jocks, salespeople, radical-like activist groups, and some entertainment and sports representatives often use this model. For instance, the publicity surrounding the recent release of the Captain America and X-Men: Apocalypse movies is representative of the press agentry style of public relations. The objective is to create buzz leading to high volume ticket sales and profit. Producers, public relations professionals, and target publics aren't concerned with truth as much as entertainment value. In addition, while the production of the movies was likely predicated on market research about public consumption patterns, the publicity associated with the films is designed and released with the assumption that if the publics hear the messages they will attend the movie showings. In the case of a dictator, the communication process is different. He/She proclaims law, that proclamation is reproduced and communicated to the masses, and it's enforced. Critique or feedback is not invited, expected, or allowed in either situation. Communication is one-way with the sole intent of impacting a public in ways that cater to the issuing organization's self-interests, be they entertainment, control, or something else.

Public Information

The *public information* model is different in intent. It involves communication from the organization to intended publics with the assumption that the communicating organization has access to or understanding of information that the public needs to know. The efforts of the US government under the label public affairs (not public relations as the US government prides itself as not being in the business of persuasion) fit this model. When the Centers for Disease & Prevention Control (the CDC is an arm of the US government) issues a statement about the Zika virus, as well as steps to reducing the risk of contracting the virus, the assumption is that the CDC knows and has information in the best interests of its publics that needs to be dispensed or made available to its publics. Because the organization "knows best" its public relations goal is to get those around it to adapt to or cooperate with it. An April 23, 2016 visit to the CDC website found a page dedicated to the Zika virus at www.cdc.gov/zika. The existence of the page itself attests to the fact that the CDC has judged the threat as serious to the US population; because of preexisting attitudes, its readers will accept it as so. Furthermore, a ticker present on the page declared that same day that there had been 388 "travel-associated Zika cases reported." It's clear that the US public and government assume that the CDC should keep track of the virus, can keep track of it, and the information it provides is truthful and in the best interests of the public it serves. Communication takes place with one-way intent to provide information presumed to be in the best interests of publics. The communicative intent is to get the job done in a manner that invites no response or feedback because none is needed. Both the press agentry and public information models assume "no response needed." The two-way asymmetry model, however, counts on feedback.

Two-way Asymmetric

Two-way asymmetric public relations is different from press agentry/publicity and public information. Its users actually account for the knowledge, interests, and intents of target publics in the formation of the organization's messages, objectives, and strategies. Some sort of public research; looking for public understanding, perceptions, incentives, preferences, etc.; is conducted so that the organization can better accomplish its own pre-determined objectives. Unlike the assumption that accompanies practicing public relations according to the press agentry/publicity and public information models, two-way asymmetric public relations is predicated on the idea that a successful organization pays significant attention to its publics' idiosyncrasies and makes adaptations to best leverage those if it wants to accomplish its objectives. Public research is conducted by the organization, and public relations strategies and tactics are driven by the results of it in a scientific sort of way. The results of the organization-driven research or systems of organizational or public monitoring are considered feedback. The purpose is to find the best way to accomplish organizational objectives through research-driven public relations advocacy. Communication takes place in a two-way fashion controlled by the issuing organization, with the purpose of benefitting that organization as it maintains some kind of control or dominance in WIGO or what should/could go on. It's safe to say that the vast majority of public relations efforts in the US fall under this model. Very few, if any public relations efforts fall in to the final model. Most professionals argue that the reality of organizational survival, for all organizations, prevents a holistic two-way symmetric reality.

Two-way Symmetric

Finally, is the *two-way symmetric* model of public relations. Public relations professionals ascribing to this model do not assume that they (or their organizations) know best and, in fact, they believe that the best way to engage in public relations is to consider the target public's needs, wants, and desires to be as important as the organization's. Ideally, the organization and its target publics should cooperate in the co-creation of meaning and policy in ways that will maximize benefits for all involved in the particular situation. Public relations plays this mediating role; it facilitates give and take. The ultimate goal is dialogue between an organization and its publics with the intent of reaching organizational objectives (that have been co-negotiated with its publics) and its target publics' objectives in a win-win situation through balanced cooperation or adaptation to each other's interests. Communication is two-way with the intent of mutually beneficial meaning creation and outcomes.

While an attractive utopian idea, many scholars and practitioners alike view the two-way symmetrical model as idealistic and naive. If an organization is to please all of its publics all of the time, it will go out of business from revenue loss or a counter-productive focus on initiatives that are non-essential to the organization's livelihood. However, many argue that the ethical imperative underlying all public relations activity in the pursuit of relationships based on trust makes two-way symmetrical efforts really important. In fact, it's argued that the willingness to negotiate meaning together brings about trust. We might argue that nonprofits (they exist to serve specific sets of people) and employee-owned for-profits (employees own where they are and where the organization is going) are most likely to approximate this model. In addition, organizations committed to sustainability recognize their symbiotic, or dependent, relationships with publics. Forestry companies holding a long-term vision for their own survival often partner with Amazon rainforest activists to make sure the forests the companies depend on will be available in the future. The activists want to save the forests indefinitely. The two work together. And, organizations dedicated to corporate citizenry keep in mind the need to engage in public-approved community efforts. The US Postal Service's annual "stamp out hunger" campaign fits here. It works with its own customers to generate food and monetary donations. It expends its own resources to advertise the one-day event and transport customer donations. This USPS situation-specific campaign closely aligns with the two-way symmetric worldview.

Excellence Model Descriptors

In an effort to help us better understand them' the four models are commonly differentiated through seven descriptors: characteristic, purpose, organizational goal, public relations contribution to goal, nature of communication, communication model, and nature of research.[8] The differences can be and generally are represented through a simple matrix.

Ideally, the two-way symmetrical public relations model was proposed by Grunig and Hunt as the most excellent and ethical of the four. However, it could be that public relations mediated dialogue (two-way communication with all interests as a priority) will lead to nothing getting done because the discussions never end. Or, it could be that what the target public really wants. An example is the US population's psychological desire to consume high levels of fat-delicious

Characteristic	Press Agentry/ Publicity	Public Information	Two-way Asymmetric	Two-way Symmetric
Purpose	Propaganda	Dissemination of information	Scientific persuasion	Mutual understanding
Organizational goal	Environmental control/ Domination	Environmental Adaptation/ Cooperation	Environmental control/ Domination	Environmental adaptation/ Cooperation
PR contribution to goal	Advocacy	Dissemination of information	Advocacy	Mediation
Nature of communication	One-way, complete truth not essential	One-way, truth important	Two-way, imbalanced effects	Two-way, balanced effects
Communication model	Source to receiver	Source to receiver	Source to receiver accounting for feedback	Group to group
Nature of research (for success)	Very little, counting house	Little other than read-ability and readership	Formative, evaluative of attitudes	Formative, evaluative of understanding

Figure 4.1. Excellence Theory: Four Models and Descriptors.
*The first depiction of the models appeared in Grunig & Hunt[9] and Grunig.[10]

food. All that leads to is long-term health issues. Unchecked and long-term consumption of high fat food is not in anyone's best long-term interests. Unfortunately, the US population is dominated by a taste for fat and large consumptions of it. The truth is that this kind of diet leads to unwanted physical consequences such as high blood pressure, diabetes, heart disease, and high cholesterol. The same can be said of the almost US-universal desire to avoid disciplined physical exercise. While many want to avoid it because it hurts, is not fun, or makes them tired, total avoidance of disciplined exercise is not in their long-term best interests if they value health and life longevity. So what the public wants is not in its best health interests and giving it what it wants, say the National Institutes for Health (NIH) communicating that eating whatever feels or tastes good in the moment, is not in anyone's best interests either. It would not be in the best interests of the NIH itself as, over time and with increase in fat-related diseases, the NIH would lose its credibility and support.

Conclusion

Like any form of communication, reading and writing theory is a complex yet worthy undertaking. The same is true of praxis, which involves the actual application of theory to WIGO, what could go on, and what should go on. In the spirit of reading, writing, and applying theory this chapter highlights the process through which four theories were chosen for inclusion in this book as those that every public relations student should learn. The four are excellence theory, contingency theory, rhetorical theory, and social capital theory. Chapter four ends with an exploration of excellence theory basics as it provides a beginning exploration of the theory's four models of public relations.

Chapter Exercises

Case Application Lens: Excellence Theory

Public relations definition: Public relations is the management of communication between an organization and its publics.

Excellence theorist intent: To determine best practices for accomplishing organizational goals; best practices are differentiated by purpose, organizational goal, public relations contribution to goal, nature of communication, communication model, and nature of research for success.

Excellence theory questions:

1. Excellence theory suggests to us that a two-way symmetric model of public relations is the most ethical and sustainable way of doing business. Develop three talking points that illustrate your agreement or disagreement with this claim. Share your thoughts with someone else who understands excellence theory.

2. Of the four models of public relations presented by excellence theory (press agentry/publicity, public information, two-way asymmetric, two-way symmetric), with which are you most familiar? Why do you think that's the case? As a professional, with which are you must comfortable? Why do you think that's the case?

3. Pull a news release from the pressroom of your favorite organization. Do your best to answer the following questions: Which of the four models was used? Why do you say that? What were the results?

4. Pull a news release from the pressroom of your favorite organization. Do you best to answer the following questions: Which of the four models could have been used? Should have been used? Why do you say that?

5. Six descriptors help us distinguish among the four models and label examples of public relations in practice as one type of public relations or another. The six are purpose, organizational goal, public relations contribution to goal, nature of communication, communication model, and nature of research for success. Develop one statement for each descriptor that would help another colleague grasp the essence of that descriptor as she seeks to understand the excellence model.

Opportunity for Praxis

To apply this chapter's information to the cases in Appendix B, see Appendix A:
____ Excellence Theory Key
____ Case Rubric Master

Notes

1. Hansen-Horn, T. & Neff, B. (Eds.). (2008). *Public relations: From theory to practice.* Boston, MA: Allyn & Bacon, p. xvii.
2. Grunig, J. & Hunt, T. (1984). *Managing public relations.* New York: Holt, Rinehart, & Winston.
3. Ibid., p. 4.
4. Grunig, J. (1992). Communication, public relations, and effective organizations: An overview of the book. In J. Grunig, (Ed.). *Excellence in public relations and communication management.* Hillsdale, NJ: Lawrence Erlbaum, p. 2.
5. Grunig, J. (1984). Organizations, environments, and models of public relations. *Public Relations Research and Education, 1*(1), p. 8.
6. Von Bertalanffy, L. (1950). The theory of open systems in physics and biology. *Science, 111*(2872), pp. 23–29.
7. Katz, D. & Kahn, R. (1966). *The social psychology of organizations.* New York: John Wiley.
8. Ibid., p. 9.
9. Grunig & Hunt, 1984.
10. Gruning, 1984.

CHAPTER FIVE

Value in Applied Theory

Contingency Theory

Known widely as the "it depends" approach to public relations, contingency theory is presented as a more complex way of understanding and making predictions than excellence theory. In fact, it's all about explaining actions and predictions based on WIGO (remember that stands for what is going on, and reminds of what has gone on and should go on). It's rooted in the idea that conflict (not necessarily a good or bad thing, but simply something that exists in organizational functioning) is an inherent part of what we do whenever something is up for disagreement, acknowledging that disagreement comes in all ways and forms. Conflict can be linked to threats to organizational existence and functioning, as well as competition for limited resources. Chapter five examines the contingency theorists' perspectives of conflict, competition, and threat, as well as public relations stances as strategic responses that depend on more than 80 situational factors.

Contingency Theory

Contingency theory is all about conflict, competition, and threat appraisal. Conflict occurs when we present ideas different from those others assume to be true of WIGO, or when they present ideas different from those we assume to be true of WIGO. It involves disagreement over ideas or ways of sense making, as well as perceived threats (especially in crisis situations) to organizational functioning, meaning, sustainability, etc. In this sense, conflict is not necessarily good or bad; it just is. Threats are not good in light of the perceived organizational losses that may occur.

The ability to recognize threats to organizational functioning and goals, as well as evaluate the potential for recognized threats to affect the organization, is a key to success and survival. "Threat appraisal [perception of threat] consists of the interplay between demand and resource appraisals [ability to overcome or thwart the perceived threat]. More specifically, demand appraisals involve the perception or assessment of danger, uncertainty (situational versus task uncertainty), and required effort inherent in the situation."[1]

Additionally, it's important to understand that the way a professional engages conflict or assesses threat depends on our perceptions of WIGO, what can go on, and what should go on. Both can involve competition, but are almost always more than that. Because so many factors contribute to WIGO, what can go on, and what should go on, contingency theory has been aptly coined the it depends theory.

Competition, Conflict, and Threat

Most of us automatically pair the idea of competition with conflict. The threat of losing can also be perceived as conflict as in who should win. As a result, contingency theorists are careful to outline an essence of difference between competition and conflict while suggesting that the distinction is a matter of degree and focus.[2] They are careful to point out that conflict is not necessarily competition. Competition is an inherent part of life and of organizational existence, it "is inevitable and omnipresent. It occurs when two or more groups or organizations vie for the same resources."[3] It should come as no surprise to you that we compete for natural resources, human capital, news coverage, clients, grants, and the like. Public relations professionals are highly involved in competition. In contrast, conflict "occurs when two groups direct their efforts against each other, devising communication and actions that attack."[4] More clearly, while competition keeps those involved in it focused on the prize, be it sales, customers, donations, or market share; "conflict, in contrast, involves confrontations and attacks [about ideas, perceptions, interpretations, etc.] between organizations and various stakeholders or publics."[5] Competition involves who wins. Conflict addresses who or what should win. A perceived threat to ways of organizational sense-making, doing things, well-being, etc., can come from it. Importantly, confrontations and attacks involve contested meanings, not necessarily physical assaults or threatening behaviors.

We're involved in conflict as we seek to create meaning. When stakeholders heatedly question an organization's five-year business plan, activists charge our organization with ignoring environmental conservation norms, our employees ask for a more team-oriented workplace, or a client wants to sell beef products in a country where the culture pronounces beef as unclean, conflict is present. Ideas and perceptions actively collide or cause conflict in the negotiation of meaning.

Threat Appraisal

Crisis involves conflict and can involve competition. However, it's categorically different in the related perception of threat to the organization and its normalcy. Pang, Jin, and Cameron describe the process by which a public relations professional may perceive or appraise a threat in a crisis situation.

> The threat appraisal process in a crisis is composed by, firstly, a primary appraisal (*situational demands*) including *danger, uncertainty* (lack of prediction and control make it difficult for meeting adequately), *required effort*, and secondly, a secondary appraisal (*resources*) which includes *knowledge and skill, time, finance*, and *support from the dominant coalition* [decision- and policy-makers, or those in charge].[6]

So, the initial appraisal is the primary one during which the public relations professional is sensitive to WIGO in light of what he perceives should be going on. He assesses the situation in light of operative organizational goals and plans against dangers to them, uncertainty coloring his ability to accomplish them, and insufficiencies in available resources needed to accomplish them. Once this is done, he re-examines his primary appraisal at another secondary level. He conducts an evaluation in light of available knowledge and skills, time, budget or expenditures, and managerial or board support.

Threats occur in three dimensions. The first involves external and internal threats.[7] At the external level are: "*litigation, government regulation, potentially damaging publicity, scarring of organization's reputation in community,* and *legitimating activists claims.*"[8] Internal threats are qualitatively different. They include: "*economic loss or gain from implementing various stances, marring of employees' or stockholders' perception of the company,* and *marring of the personal reputations of the company decision makers (image in employees' perceptions and general public's perceptions).*"[9]

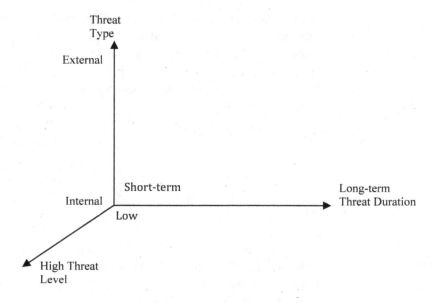

Figure 5.1. The Dimensionality of Threats.
The dimensionality of threats figure was discussed by Augustine Pang and Glen Cameron in their 2008 "Contingency Theory: Strategic Management of Conflict in Public Relations" contribution to the first edition of *Public Relations: From Theory to Practice*. It's re-presented here with permission.

The second dimension involves levels of threats,[10] which can be appraised as low, medium, and high. And, finally, the third dimension involves the duration of threats. "This dimension refers to the longitudinal [across time] facet of a threat, which means whether the threat is perceived as a short-term one or long-term one."[11] Pang, Jin, & Cameron propose a "dimensionality of threats" model for use in threat appraisal.

From their focus on conflict, competition and threats, contingency theorists' definition of public relations is different than the official one ascribed to by the Public Relations Society of America (PRSA), which is "a strategic communication process that builds mutually beneficial relationships between organizations and their publics."[12] Contingency theorists depart from the idea of mutually beneficial relationships, per se, to focus on the reality of the competition for limited resources, meanings, perspectives, and interpretations of all kinds. In this sense, "public relations can be defined as the 'strategic management of conflict and competition in the best interests of an organization and, when possible, also in the interests of key publics'."[13] It views public relations as leading the way in healthy and honest conflicts that organizations must work through and with, in their efforts to be successful (recognizing that no organization defines success in the same way). In that sense, it's not all that far removed from the definition of public relations held to in this book, "planned and strategic results-driven communicative effort with the publics in mind." Both prioritize results or best interests while keeping relevant publics in mind.

The Accommodation—Advocacy Continuum

Contingency theory's official debut to the academic world was published in a 1997 *Journal of Public Relations Research* article titled, "It Depends: A Contingency Theory of Accommodation in Public Relations."[14] The argument advanced by the authors is for a "theory of accommodation in public relations based on a continuum from pure accommodation to pure advocacy ...[suggesting] that antecedent, mediating and moderating variables lead to greater or lesser accommodation." [15]

At the pure accommodation end, the organization accepts full responsibility for the perceived conflict and moves to do whatever it takes to "fix" the problem

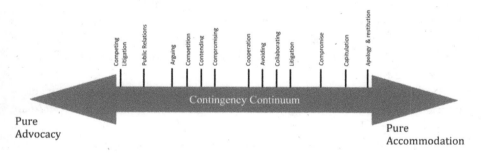

Figure 5.2. Contingency Continuum.
The contingency continuum helps us estimate the degree to which public relations may involve accommodation and/or advocacy. It is reproduced here with the permission of G. Cameron.

in the eyes of the public, or to make itself completely vulnerable to the threat as it makes "concessions to the other party exclusively."[16] At the pure advocacy point, the organization decision makers assume that the organization's interpretation of WIGO is correct to the degree that legal action must and can be taken to establish its authority; "they argue for their own interests exclusively."[17]

Stances and Stance Taking

Worthy of note is that when conflict is recognized, an organization takes a "stance" toward it. A stance is an attitude, sense-making position, or evaluative posture, if you will, to WIGO because "the stance we take is influenced by the situation we are in."[18] It's not static, which means it can and often does change as perceptions of the situation change. At its simplest form, a stance of pure *accommodation* means the organization will do and say everything called for by publics involved in the perceived conflict. A pure *advocacy* stance means the organization will engage in full out competition to win, be right, dominate, or control the conflict outcome. Moving along the continuum, then, in degrees of increasing advocacy are apology and restitution (accept blame, apologize to vested parties and make wrongs right), capitulation (give in to all accusations and demands), compromise (give something to get something in what is not a win-win situation), litigation (ask courts to mediate action), collaborating (working together to redefine WIGO and courses of action), avoiding (ignoring), cooperation (publicly cooperating through communicative action while working for organization's best interests), compromising (working together to define give and take in what is not a win-win situation), contending (publicly debating), competition (working against each other to win), arguing (debating to win), public relations (advocacy through strategic communicative initiatives in the interests of the organization), and competing litigation (appealing to the law or courts to determine all). It's important to note that the degrees of difference between these are not equal, but they do indicate some increase or decrease in degree along the scale.

Underpinning an organization's stance, and contributing to changes in it across time, are antecedent, mediating, and moderating variables. *Antecedent variables* are relevant situational factors that precede conflict and shape organizational stances. *Mediating variables* are those that influence how or why a stance is taken as the situation unfolds. *Moderating variables* influence the degree to which, or length of time, a particular stance is held by the organization. "Stance then determines strategy—what will be done and why."[19] The positions the organization takes influence its every perception, interpretation, and initiative.

When confronted with conflict all public relations professionals, consciously or subconsciously, adopt at least one stance and act accordingly. And, because the complexity of every situation we encounter is so varied, it is possible to adopt different stances to different parts of the situation or to different publics involved in the same conflict. In fact, "communication acts reflecting both extremes can actually occur simultaneously in dealing with one public."[20] For example, a publicly traded organization can engage in or be engaged in conflict over the issue of environmentalism. Environmental activists would, ideally, like all organizations to participate in every possible avenue of environmental preservation available to them. If we developed the actual "everything the organization can do to preserve the environment" list it would be really long. At a minimum, it would include things like paper recycling; plastic bottles recycling; card board recycling; aluminum can recycling; glass recycling; Styrofoam recycling; ink cartridge recycling; halogen lighting; motion detection lighting; the purchasing of environmentally safe office products that, ideally, are certifiably green; geothermal heating and cooling systems; and certifiable organic products in vending machines and the corporate kitchen. While lengthy, the list printed here only scratches the surface of what's possible. However, we can still work from it.

Because recycling products costs money in terms of appropriating needed recycling containers and service contracts, buying products made of recycled materials is generally more costly than the purchase of new materials products, and the installation of green lighting and HVAC systems is quite expensive, the organization will likely take at least two "it depends" stances to the environmentalism conflict. Its leaders may feel that it does not need to apologize for anything but that taking a *capitulation* stance to paper, plastic bottle, cardboard, aluminum can, and glass bottle recycling is in its short- and long-term best interests. As a matter of course, it will purchase and place appropriate bins throughout the organization and contract accordingly with a recycling vendor. It will do this because it estimates it can underwrite these without adversely affect its costs of doing business and negatively impact its bottom line goals. In fact, the positive effects the decision makers know will incur are the reduction of the organization's carbon imprint, and an increase in employee and public sense of goodwill. However, when it comes to halogen lighting, the organization may adopt a *compromise* instead of capitulation stance. Its decision makers may decide that the organization can replace in-use lights as they burn out, but to replace them all at once is wasteful and too costly. As a result, it may adopt a one to five year phase-in plan. The organization might also adopt a compromise stance toward motion detection lighting and set as an objective the accomplishment of this option through a five-year plan. Budget appropriations will be set aside for five years to allow for the reality of motion sensors installation throughout the organization in year six. Finally, at the more extreme end of the contingency continuum, the organization may simply *avoid cooperating* in any way with demands for geothermal HVAC systems, green office supplies purchases, etc., while citing budgetary limitations and the need to secure target quarterly earnings for its investors. Because it's been determined that it can accommodate most of the recycling expectations brought to it through the environmental conflict, and compromise in other areas like halogen lights, organizational decision-makers may also predict that these are enough to redress perceived conflict and satisfy activist publics without alienating its priority investor public. Only if it becomes the sole target of an activist environmental group making demands that will adversely affect its profits and sustainability, will the organization likely adopt something like a pure *advocacy* stance and consider any kind of *litigation* to protect its assets.

Contingency Factors Behind "It Depends"

The environmental situation described above is pretty complex, yet as printed here it is really a simplistic picture of WIGO or what should go on. The inherent complexity of conflict situations is most clearly represented in a review of the contingency theory factor matrix. More than 80 factors have been identified that contribute to the "it depends" choices public relations professionals must make as stances are chosen.

Internal Variables

Organizational Characteristics

- ☐ Open or closed culture
- ☐ Dispersed widely geographically or centralized
- ☐ Level of technology the organization uses to produce its product or service
- ☐ Homogeneity or heterogeneity of officials involved
- ☐ Age of the organization/value placed on tradition
- ☐ Speed of growth in the knowledge level of organization uses
- ☐ Economic stability of organization
- ☐ Existence or nonexistence of issues management official or programs
- ☐ Organization's past experiences with the public
- ☐ Distribution of decision-making power
- ☐ Formalization: number of roles or codes defining and limiting the job
- ☐ Stratification/hierarchy of positions
- ☐ Existence of influence of legal department
- ☐ Business exposure
- ☐ Corporate culture

Public Relations (PR) Department Characteristics

- ☐ Total number of practitioners and number of college degrees

(*Continued*)

☐ Type of past training: trained in PR or ex-journalists, marketing, etc.
☐ Location of PR department in hierarchy: independent or under marketing umbrella/experience encroachment of marketing/persuasive mentality
☐ Representation in the dominant coalition
☐ Experience level of PR practitioners in dealing with crisis
☐ General communication competency of department
☐ Autonomy of department
☐ Physical placement of department in building (near CEO and other decision makers or not)
☐ Staff trained in research methods
☐ Amount of funding available for dealing with external publics
☐ Amount of time allowed to use dealing with external publics
☐ Gender: percentage of female upper-level staff/managers
☐ Potential of department to practice various models of public relations

Characteristics of Dominant Coalition (Top Management)

☐ Political values: conservative or liberal/open or closed to change
☐ Management style: domineering or laid back
☐ General altruism level
☐ Support and understanding of PR
☐ Frequency of external contact with publics
☐ Departmental perception of the organization's external environment
☐ Calculation of potential rewards or losses using different strategies with external publics
☐ Degree of line manager involvement in external affairs

Internal Threats (How Much is at Stake in the Situation)

☐ Economic loss or gain from implementing various stances
☐ Marring of employees' or stockholders' perceptions of the company
☐ Marring of the personal reputations of the company's decision makers

Individual Characteristics (Public Relations Practitioners, Domestic Coalition, Line Managers)

☐ Training in diplomacy, marketing, journalism, engineering, etc.
☐ Personal ethics
☐ Tolerance or ability to deal with uncertainty
☐ Comfort level with conflict or dissonance
☐ Comfort level with change
☐ Ability to recognize potential and existing problems

(Continued)

- ☐ Extent of openness to innovation
- ☐ Personality: dogmatic, authoritarian
- ☐ Communication competency
- ☐ Cognitive complexity: ability to handle complex problems
- ☐ Predisposition toward negotiations
- ☐ Predisposition to altruism
- ☐ How individuals receive, process, and use information and influence
- ☐ Familiarity with external public or its representative
- ☐ Like external public or its representative
- ☐ Gender: female versus male

Relationship Characteristics

- ☐ Level of trust between organizations and external public
- ☐ Dependency of parties involved
- ☐ Ideological barriers between organizations and public

External Variables

Threats

- ☐ Litigation
- ☐ Government regulation
- ☐ Potentially damaging publicity
- ☐ Scarring of company's reputation in business community and in the general public
- ☐ Legitimizing activists' claims

Industry Environment

- ☐ Changing (dynamic) or static
- ☐ Number of competitors/level of competition
- ☐ Richness or leanness of resources in the environment

General Political/Social Environment/External Culture

- ☐ Degree of political support of business
- ☐ Degree of social support of business

The External Public (Group, Individual, etc.)

- ☐ Size and/or number of members

(Continued)

□ Degree of source credibility/powerful members or connections
□ Past successes or failures of groups to evoke change
□ Amount of advocacy practiced by the organization
□ Level of commitment/involvement of members
□ Whether the group has public relations counselors or not
□ Public's perception of the group: reasonable or radical
□ Level of media coverage the public has received in the past
□ Whether representatives of the public know or like representatives of the organization
□ Whether representatives of the organization know or like representatives from the public
□ Public's willingness to dilute its cause/request/claim
□ Relative power of the organization
□ Relative power of the public

Issue Under Question

□ Size
□ Stake
□ Complexity

Figure 5.3. Contingency Factors.
The list of contingency factors was designed to help professionals pinpoint the "it depends" factors that affect stance. It is used here with personal permission [email May 1, 2016] from Cameron, reproduced in 2010 Sage Handbook of Public Relations, Chapter 2, pp. 29–32.

It's very clear from this chapter's contingency theory discussion that two principles are key to understanding the theory's heuristic value for the public relations professional. The first is that, "many factors determine the stance or position of an organization when it comes to dealing with conflict and perceived threats against" it; and the second "is that the public relations stance for dealing with a particular audience or public is dynamic" and changes as events unfold.[21]

As the it depends model, contingency theory clearly departs from the excellence model in the way it helps us understand decision-making situations and courses of actions. "The practice of public relations is too complex, too fluid, and impinged by far too many variables for the academy to force it into the four boxes known as the four models of public relations."[22] As the contingency theorists clearly argue, and most public relations professionals today can confirm, when you ask a long-time professional whether the two-way symmetrical model posed by excellence theory is the "best," the answer is almost always "it depends." It depends on a whole lot of things such as what publics are involved, what resources are involved or possible, what the issue is, how the issue is impacted by things going on outside the organization, what the boss wants, what's coming down the pipe next year that is important right now, what the budget is, etc.

In fact, contingency theory is seen by some as a direct move away from the seemingly unrepresentative nature of public relations imposed by excellence theory, and a robust questioning of "symmetrical communication as normative theory on how organizations should be practicing public relations that was regarded as the most ethical and effective."[23] These proponents argue that you can't always, or even often, engage in symmetrical communication and conflict resolution. In fact, what you can and should do depends ... on many real and perceived factors that contribute to perceived conflict and threats. But, not all people agree with this assessment. They argue, instead, that contingency theory is just an extension or enhancement of the two-way symmetrical model. However, given the excellence model ideal of co-creation of meaning in the best interests of all parties involved, it seems that contingency theory introduces a degree of difference as "when possible" in the best interests of all.

Conclusion

Contingency theory sensitizes us to conflict, competition, and threat as part of organizational functioning and as important to understanding organizational goals and sustainability. Its proponents represent public relations complexity through the dimensionality of threats appraisal model and the contingency continuum ranging from pure accommodation to pure advocacy. Contingency theory also advances 13 stances an organization may assume in response to WIGO and as a result of professional understandings and assessments of more than 80 "it depends" factors.

Chapter Exercises

Case Application Lens: Contingency Theory

Public relations definition: The strategic management of conflict and competition in the best interests of an organization and, when possible, also in the interests of key publics.

Contingency theorist intent: To understand how public relations leads the way in the recognition of threats, and adopting stances to conflict and competition, in an "it depends" advocacy to accommodation manner that helps accomplish organizational goals.

Contingency theory questions

1. Is there competition? If so, describe it as you perceive it.
2. Is there conflict? If so, describe it as you perceive it
   a. How relevant is the conflict to the organization's stated objectives? How relevant should it be?
3. Was a threat (or threats) perceived? If so, describe the process by which you think the public relations professional appraised it via the primary and secondary appraisal processes.
   a. If a threat was appraised, where would you place the process on the "dimensionality of threats model"? Why?
4. What stance (or stances) on the contingency continuum appears to have been adopted?
   a. Why do you think the organization seems to have taken the stance it did?
   b. Does the stance seem to change over time?
5. How is the stance different relevant to each key public, or is it?
6. What factors (of the more than 80 identified as influential by contingency theorists) seem to have contributed the most to the stance/s the organization took in the case?
   a. What led to the "factors" conclusions you made?
7. When threats are perceived, contingency theorists predict that they can be appraised on the dimensionality of threats model along three dimensions: context (internal and external), threat-level (low, medium, high), and duration (short-term, long-term). Pull any public relations case (even one from Appendix B) and assess the situation for perceived threats on the dimensionality of threats model.
8. Contingency theorists have identified 13 stances on the accommodation—advocacy model that represent a wide variety of positions public relations professionals help organizations take. Working with the contingency factors list from this chapter, make a list of the factors from it that you think most clearly suggest that an organization assume each of the stances (apology and restitution, capitulation, compromise, negotiation, collaborating, cooperation, avoiding, compromising, contending, competition, arguing, public relations, competing litigation) in a crisis of confidence situation. Do this again for a situation whereby the organization faces a source credibility issue.

9. The contingency factors that influence perceptions of competition, conflict, and/or threat are classified under 11 general categories: organizational characteristics (internal), public relations department characteristics (internal), characteristics of dominant coalition (top management) (internal), internal threats (how much is at stake in the situation) (internal), individual characteristics (public relations practitioners, domestic coalition, line manager) (internal), relationship characteristics (internal), threats (external), industry environment (external), general political/social environment/external culture (external), the external public (group, individual, etc.) (external), and issue under question (external). What categories, if any, should be added to this classification system? Why do you feel this way?

    a. Can you imagine any "it depends" factors that are not accounted for that should be added? If so, what are they?

Opportunity for Praxis

To apply this chapter's information to the cases in Appendix B, see Appendix A:
    ____ Contingency Theory Key
    ____ Case Rubric Master

Notes

1. Pang, A., Jin, Y. & Cameron, G. (2006). Do we stand on common ground? A threat appraisal model for terror alerts issued by the Department of Homeland Security. *Journal of Contingencies and Crisis Management, 14*(2), p. 86.
2. Wilcox, D., Cameron, G. & Reber, B. (2011). *Public relations strategies and tactics* (11th ed.). Upper Saddle River, NJ: Pearson, p. 251.
3. Wilcox, Cameron & Reber, 2011, p. 250.
4. Ibid., p. 250.
5. Wilcox, D., Cameron, G., Reber, B. & Shin, J-H. (2010). *Think public relations*. Boston, MA: Allyn & Bacon, p. 45.
6. Pang, Jin & Cameron, 2006, p. 87.
7. Ibid.
8. Ibid.
9. Ibid.
10. Ibid.
11. Ibid.
12. What is public relations? (n.d.). Retrieved April 29, 2016 from https://www.prsa.org/AboutPRSA/PublicRelationsDefined#.VyOCjzbmrIU.

13. Ibid., p. 44.
14. Cancel, A., Cameron, G., Sallot, L. & Mitrook, M. (1997). It depends: A contingency theory of accommodation in public relations. *Journal of Public Relations Research*, *9*(1).
15. Ibid., p. 31.
16. Pang, A. & Cameron, G. (2008). Contingency theory: Strategic management of conflict in public relations. In T. Hansen-Horn & B. Neff (Eds.), *Public relations: From theory to practice* (pp. 134–157). New York: Allyn & Bacon, p. 136.
17. Ibid.
18. Ibid.
19. Wilcox, Cameron & Reber, 2011, p. 255.
20. Cancel, Cameron, Sallot & Mitrook, 1997, p. 37.
21. Ibid., p. 257.
22. Ibid., p. 32.
23. Pang, A., Jin, Y. & Cameron, G. (2010). Strategic management of communication: Insights from contingency theory of strategic conflict management. In R. Heath (Ed.), *The Sage handbook of public relations* (pp. 17–34). New York: Sage, p. 17

Value in Applied Theory

Rhetorical Theory

Don't forget from reading chapter four that a professional finds terrific value from reading and applying theory, if he just knows how to do it. Remember, too, that the discussions of excellence theory and contingency theory found in chapters four and five were the first steps in your ability to engage in praxis (the application of theory to your professional aspirations). Chapter six picks up where chapter four left off, and addresses rhetorical theory as a different perspective from which to approach public relations and case studies. From a rhetorical theory perspective, public relations serves as an organizational rhetor with a vested interest in meaning and message creation. It does this thorough a robust and interactive process of language and symbol use and misuse involving other relevant rhetors that may or may not have the same meaning and message goals. Seven rhetorical situations are explored, as are eight rhetorical factors important to understanding them. Finally, five rhetorical responses are discussed that may be adopted in the face of relevant rhetorical situations.

Rhetorical Theory

Instead of searching for one best way to accomplish organizational goals, or to understand how a public relations professional assumes stances to perceived conflict and threats, rhetorical theorists focus on the processes by which meaning is created and accepted by organizations. They argue that public relations professionals are influential rhetors[1] in the "message and meaning business."[2] In this sense, rhetoric can be defined as a "contest among multiple voices"[3] through which we use symbols and symbolic language to make our client's case. However, the focus is on the "how" we make organizationally desirable meaning rather than a search for the best practices in making meaning.

Rhetoricians view humans as unique in our ability to devise and use symbols in the creation and negotiation of meaning. So, to study rhetoric is to study the use and misuse of language and symbols by human beings. From the rhetorical theory perspective, a SRC strategist is a constant student of his own language and symbolic representation of WIGO; he is also a student of the language and symbolic representations of WIGO by others. For example, he is sensitive to the limitations placed by labeling something or someone as fat or skinny, big or small, or all or nothing. He knows that these classification systems leave no room for options like just right, medium, and some. The SRC strategist is also aware of and studies how his ability to use symbols for meaning creation and exchange is uniquely human and complex. For instance, he knows that using the word "chair" to refer to something he sits on has nothing to do with the chair he's thinking of, it's just a term we've assigned to it to represent it. He also knows that he can say the word chair without thinking of one particular piece of furniture; he can think of an abstract notion of chair instead. Additionally, he knows that the word "chair" can refer to the head of a committee (as chair), and as a verb like "to run or chair a meeting." And, he knows that meanings of symbols can change across contexts and time. The chair in the classroom is likely a hard non-moving chair; it might be bright red in color. The chair in the board room is likely made of soft leather and placed on wheels for easy movement; it's likely dark in color as a symbol of what professionalism is assumed to be. And, he knows that the chairs in the classroom and boardroom can change from one year to another through replacement schedules. Finally, he is sensitive to changes across context such as the favorable feelings he attributes to his committee meeting chair that are, at the same time, not reciprocated by his colleague who attributes feelings of ill will to the same committee chair. In fact, he may use his ability to engage in symbolic representation through language to persuade his colleague to think more favorably about the committee chair. He's a self-reflexive rhetorically sensitive communicator.

Public relations scholar and consultant Robert Heath was the first to vigorously support the application of rhetorical theory to public relations.[4] At this level, the idea of organizational voices replaces the notion of individual voices; the intent is to create collective/organizational action. Heath views public relations as an important player in the rhetorical processes that shape culture, businesses, interpersonal and intrapersonal organizational understandings, organizational management and positioning, etc. From his perspective, public relations is necessarily a participant in the rhetorical processes, and the rhetorical processes impact all things human. Heath points to the writings of the Greek philosopher Aristotle, who conceived of rhetoric as a good man speaking well (to represent his own interests to persuade others), while arguing that public relations professionals, as rhetors, are:

> vital to society. Society could not exist if people did not use words and visual symbols to share and evaluate information, shape beliefs, and establish norms for coordinated collective action. Through rhetoric, people—individually and on behalf of organizations—influence opinions, understanding, judgment, and actions ... Corporations, as well as other organizations have used rhetoric to help form our society.[5]

In line with Aristotelian thought, Heath urges us to define rhetoric as "the ability to observe in any given case the available means of persuasion—what needs to be said and how it should be said to achieve desired outcomes."[6]

Aristotle viewed dialogue as a noble goal, while also exploring the persuasiveness of one man to another, or of one to many. He claimed that those skilled in persuasion were able to use all the available means of persuasion and to appeal to a listener's senses or systems of *logos* (logic), *ethos* (emotions), and *pathos* (credibility). Famously known for his three-book volume called the *Rhetoric* dating from the fourth century BC, Aristotle compared rhetoric to *dialogic*, which was the then popular idea of communicating cooperatively together for the noble goal of arriving at truth. In contrast, rhetoric, he argued, was a counterpart to dialectic and involved the art of persuading others (not necessary to find truth, but only to convince others of one's perspective). Rhetoric was not simply the art of dialogue with noble intent.

Widely discussed and critiqued throughout history, Aristotle's work was heavily referenced by Kenneth Burke (who wrote between the 1930s and 1960s) as he explored rhetoric and humanity or what makes us uniquely human. Burke understood humans as symbol using and misusing animals and, in that, declared the symbolic capability of humans as what distinguished them from other animals. He also understood that the use of symbols for the purposes of communication was the means by which people could identify with each other (and fulfill an innate need to belong) or drive each other apart in separation. For Burke, rhetoric was the use of language as a symbolic means of inducing cooperation in beings that by nature respond to symbols.[7] He argued that rhetoric replaces dialectic (dialogue to find truth) with persuasion. Burke saw human ability to use and misuse symbols as a powerful productive and destructive component of humanity. From his perspective, man (he used the term generically) "is the symbol-using (symbol-making, symbol-misusing) animal, inventor of the negative (or moralized by the negative), separated from his natural condition by instruments of his own making, goaded by the spirit of hierarchy (or moved by the sense of order), and rotten with perfection."[8] Burke understood rhetoric as a powerful force in being human.

Aristotle defined rhetoric in terms of one individual influencing others through public speaking, and taking his cue from Burke's exploration of humans as symbol using and misusing animals, Heath argues that rhetoric is also applicable to the study of organizational influence if organizations themselves are viewed as rhetors. He envisions rhetoric as more than the spoken word, including use of written words, as well as nonverbal and visual tactics (any symbolic representations that *mean* something to someone). As Heath puts it so aptly in terms that public relations professionals can appreciate, rhetoric occurs in all media forms: "film, television, radio, painting, sculpture, and architecture. It is inseparable from corporate and product names, as well as nonverbal components of corporate image, including logos."[9]

Rhetoric exists because everyone perceives things differently and not everyone agrees as to what is or should be. The only way that we arrive at agreement in thought and definition, or cooperative behavior, is through some sense of togetherness or shared meaning (even if it means we reach a standoff, go to war, etc.). Heath argues that all public relations efforts result in created messages and meanings. Because they do, "doing" public relations well "requires a solid understanding of messages and the meaning[s] they can create—as well as how they can fail to adequately address rhetorical problems confronted by their employers, clients and others in society."[10] He advocates that public relations exists to address rhetorical problems and defines a problem as any situation inviting responsive meaning.

As we explore rhetorical theory, we must keep in mind that not every organization has the same interests, goals, or intents. Let's look at an example of this first developed by Hansen-Horn and Horn in 2014.

Two different organizations may operate in the *same* industry (say outdoor apparel and equipment), but they may *compete* with each other for brand equity and customer loyalty through repeat business. For instance, while a company like Patagonia wants you to buy its outdoor gear, so too does its competitor Columbia Sportswear Company. Columbia Sportswear is listed at Hoovers.com as one of Patagonia's primary competitors. Both companies want market share in the same industry; both want loyal customers. In response to customer feedback, and as a proactive step toward its own mission, Patagonia launched its Common Threads Partnership program in spring 2012. It partnered with ebay.com to help its customers sell their used Patagonia products as a way to reduce their environmental footprint; it continues as a corporate-assisted customer form of recycling. Patagonia's willingness to help its customers list and resell their used Patagonia products was a rhetorical act, a message with intended meaning in reaction to a rhetorical situation (a situation inviting meaningful messages). It was a rhetorical move to maintain or increase current customer loyalty, invite new customers to become interested in and loyal to Patagonia, and to further the company's long-time commitment to conserving the global environment. The Common Thread Partnership was part of Patagonia's ongoing conversation, its rhetorical exchanges, about environmentalism.

Columbia Sportswear Company has its own and very different customer loyalty program. The program follows a traditional customer loyalty structure. It is designed to let members accumulate purchase points, free-shipping qualifications, and member-only perks. It appeals to a different kind of customer base than does Patagonia's partnership recycling program. And in fact, its message (of buy more, get more) is not in line with Patagonia's mission statement. Also known as *our reason for being*, Patagonia's mission is to "build the best product, cause no unnecessary harm, use business to inspire and implement solutions to the environmental crisis."[11] Columbia Sportswear's mission is different. A clear mission statement is not readily available but a personal email request sent to the company received a February 18, 2013, reply that directed us to the company profile. It reads, "Columbia Sportswear Company is a leading innovator in the global outdoor apparel, footwear, accessories and equipment markets."[12] Columbia's FAQ section for prospective employees, its communications to investors, and its advertising and marketing materials are filled with the idea of leading in innovation. Innovation in the industry is the key to Columbia Sportswear's mission. Environmental conservation is the key to Patagonia's mission. Both companies are about selling products and making money. Both have products that appeal to outdoor enthusiasts. Their respective customer loyalty programs, however, have different rhetorical power. Those who are interested in buying more and getting more will gravitate toward Columbia's messaging. Those who want to limit their environmental footprint will gravitate toward Patagonia's. However, in an economic recession, some of Columbia's customers may turn to Patagonia, some of Patagonia's customers may turn to Columbia. It depends on the rhetorical messages involved and the customers' interpretations of them. A public relations strategist will help marketers keep abreast of change.[13]

From the Patagonia and Columbia example, it's clear that not all organizations share the same meaning or even desire the same meanings. As rhetors they compete in the same industry for much of the same market share. The rhetorical strategy each uses, however, frames the narrative or wrangle in the marketplace with a different perspective from which customers can choose as they place their loyalty to a brand.

The Rhetorical Process

Rhetorical theorists study rhetorical processes. Heath writes that, "rhetoric is the rationale for explaining how people and organizations strategically [or non-strategically, we might add] manage their relationships through words, interests, opinions, and action."[14] Rhetoric is used to address specific situations and associated problems that impact an organization's well-being.

Every situation invites at least one response. Variously addressed in the literature as wrangle in the marketplace, marketplace wrangle, or contested terrain, situations that invite the management of meaning are rhetorical problems (they're not good or bad; they just "are").

Heath[15] identifies for us seven kinds of rhetorical situations that generally need addressed: *natural disasters* like Hurricane Katrina; *concerns voiced by others* such as the possible disappearance of social security or public safety from the Zika virus; *recognition of problems that need to be addressed* such as the presentation of the Jitterbug cell phone touted as the answer to the problems some people have with over-complex phones and buttons too hard to see; *choices, such as products or services* like which hospital to use, which non-profit to support, which golf club to buy; a *matter of sound character* such as whether or not a utilities company price gouges or simply raises rates because it has to; *a matter of sound policy* such as the educational impact of the legalization of marijuana, or the financial and social impact of a university-mandated requirement that all freshmen and sophomore college students live in campus housing; and *crisis response* such as how an organization can respond to tragedy or significant interruption of business as normal in a way that meets federal guidelines for privacy and due process, but also indicates the organization's sympathy (not necessarily accepting blame) for those impacted and its willingness to do what it can to reduce the impact of the crisis. Rhetorical problems arise when agreement among organizations with a vested interest in a situation is not a reality or foregone conclusion.

Rhetorical Factors

Heath also points to eight rhetorical factors important to understanding rhetorical theory and the rhetorical process. All of them are involved in or invite a rhetorical response: "a *situation* [or communicative context] that requires or allows a strategic [or non-strategic] response, a *problem* [or perceived exigency] that arises from that situation"[16]; a *rhetor* (the one facing or engaging a situation calling for a response to a problem); *audiences or publics* (they change with the issues and across time; they hold a vested interest in the situation and organization and are perceived as relevant to the organization); *messages* (symbolic representations, including language and imagery, that elicit meanings); *message sources* (those from whom, what, or where the messages come); *images* (concepts or visual remembrances from language, symbols, experiences, and perceptions) or *opinions* (ideas driven by values, beliefs, attitudes, and frames of reference the participants in the event have of the sources); *channels* (modes and mediums through which messages can be sent, represented, received, or exchanged); and *the opinion environment surrounding each statement* [or call for a statement or statements] (social, political, economic, and cultural messages perceived by any or all parties as relevant to WIGO). The rhetorical factors are further explored in the situation and context section of this chapter in which they are applied to a hypothetical case study.

Rhetorical Responses

Because an invitation to respond goes nowhere without some kind of response, Heath provides further understanding of rhetorical theory and identifies five broad rhetorical responses[17] that public relations professionals might use as they work to help organizations successfully engage the situations they face. The first is *encouraging enlightened choice*, which is to "appeal to agree with one point of view, make one choice in preference to another—the rationale for rhetoric." In this instance, the organization as rhetor helps its publics make enlightened choices because it offers facts, reasons, and evaluative reports to the publics for use as they make their decisions. You might see this in a corporate wellness program appeal as employers invite employees to become committed participants to improve their personal health (and reduce costs to the organization from absences and insurance premium rate increases). The message is that it is better to participate than to not participate. The second is *adjusting organizations to people and people to organizations*, which involves appealing to those outside the organization to adjust their views of it or use their own appeal to get organizational leaders to adjust to their ways of thinking. Institutions of higher learning have adjusted to a very mobile student population and offered education through online courses and programs. At the same time, students have learned to adapt to online opportunities and pursue their education in a way that departs heavily from the traditional high school model. The third is *building a case based on good reason*, which involves using public relations initiatives to "appeal to virtue, fact, and sound reasoning that offers positive solutions to personal and collective problems." An example of this is when the organization above introduces a wellness program to its employees, filled with information about workplace and home health habits, with the promise of financial rewards to those who join and complete a six-month wellness team project. A fourth rhetorical response identified by Heath is *inviting people to use rhetoric as courtship: invitation and identification*, which involves using communicative appeals to help get a public to identify, or identify more closely, with an organization. Branded merchandise overtly representing the world records that a sports team has recently won is a simple example of this. Those who buy and wear the merchandise want to identify and be identified with the winner. Finally, Heath suggests that public relations professionals might get involved in *building identifications by shared perspectives, social construction of meaning, and connecting zones of meaning*, which simply put means to develop and execute an "appeal to share one point of view or perspective as opposed to another." This strategy promotes a shared sense of the world, such as that shared by members of People for the Ethical Treatment of Animals (PETA) or Home School Association for Military Families (HSAMF). PETA supporters are passionate about making the world a better place for animals while pressuring animal owners to adopt better standards of care for animals. Animals come before profit. PETA supporters likely identify with or feel connected to Humane Society for the Prevention of Cruelty to Animals (HSPCA) members through connected zones of meaning about animal rights and well-being. Members of the HSAMF communicate to organize around providing the best education possible for children who, as a matter of military life, must frequently move from school to school if they don't have a different, more consistent, option. It's likely that HSAMF members share perspectives with other US home school organizations.

Situation and Context: Illustration from Beginning the Journey

An organizational exigency (instance for which a response is needed) or invitation for a rhetorical response *contextualizes* your perceptions, understandings, and intentions. A perceived exigency of invitation involves a *contextualization* of situational dynamics. The situational dynamics involved in setting the stage for response, if you will, are the rhetorical factors. To *contextualize* means to embed or inscribe something, including words, gestures, presences, and symbols in a way that it is assumed others can recognize the structure, meaning, or symbolism.

> For example, if your client wants you to send to the city newspaper a news release about the fact that the office was being relocated to a different part of town, you would likely tell him, "That is not newsworthy," and encourage that the release not be sent. In fact, you wouldn't even want to write it. If your employer insisted anyway, you would likely contextualize the situation for him. You would remind him that unless the office relocation benefitted the town or clients in some significant way, the release would simply be advertising masquerading as news. It would end up on the editor's floor and the experience would most likely leave a negative impression with that editor. Once your client understands the context of the situation, he will agree that the release should not be written.[18]

The newsworthy discussion lends some insight into the power rhetorical theory has to inform public relations thinking. As thinking takes different shapes, strategy does as well.

For an even deeper understanding of Heath's ideas, and a direct attempt at praxis, read through the following hypothetical situation first published in *Strategic Planning for Public Relations: Beginning the Journey* (2014) to see if you can pinpoint the eight rhetorical factors. You need to look for: (1) a rhetor, (2) situation, (3) problem, (4) messages, (5) message sources, (6) images or opinions participants have of the sources, (7) channels, and (8) opinion event.

Let's say you are the agency of record for a global pub chain. Its social media efforts, however, are contracted to a marketing agency you have not worked with before and that is not obligated to work with you. So, there are two separate agencies on retainer, two separate budgets, with two separate charges both working for the same company. Seem weird? It happens. You are to work for the company on behalf of its media and investor relations. The social media marketing company is to maximize the use of the pub's social media sites to generate store traffic, sell product, and induce customer loyalty. The company has a Facebook fan page, a Twitter feed, and a YouTube channel. This is all part of the situation contextualizing what you can and cannot, should and should not do on behalf of your client.

Enter a disgruntled pub customer and a peeved pair of employees. The customer decides to tweet (via Twitter) his dissatisfaction with a bartender's performance at a site-specific pub, suggesting it was discriminatory toward him. Many of the customer's followers retweet the message. Followers of the customer's followers get involved and suddenly your client's name appears in about 11,000 tweets and retweets. The server's friend, also a pub employee, tweets a response in frustration, defending his friend. Suddenly, a rash of posts is made to your client's Facebook page, demanding an answer to the tweeted claims. A reporter calls you about the story. You know nothing. You shouldn't know anything because you are not contracted for social media purposes. You don't feel it is right to share that fact with the reporter. You speak to the reporter trying to let him down gently without seeming to be rude. You decide to monitor the pub chain's social media sites just in case the company decides to respond to the social media fervor that has developed. You watch and wait. On day 2 you find that an official Facebook status update is available denying any wrong doing. You also notice that some of the angrier posts from the day before seem to have disappeared. You wonder who or what devised the update. You also wonder who ordered the deletion of the posts. You say nothing. It is not your job to say anything. You wait some more. Customer fury over the parent company's seeming insensitivity to the discrimination claim gains steam. It is augmented by the fact that the customers whose Facebook posts disappeared become even angrier. They make additional posts to the company's Facebook fan page charging that only guilty companies delete posts. The same reporter calls you again about the story. You still know nothing. You try one more time to let the reporter down easily without being rude. You carefully craft your message because you want to maintain your positive relationship with the reporter and her employer. You are careful to control your voice so that you appear genuine and friendly. You share nothing off the record with her, not even the fact that your agency has nothing to do with the social media efforts of the restaurant because it is not contracted to do so. You can't because if you do it will appear as if you are trying to shift the blame or denigrate the agency in charge. If that story is made public to the restaurant, or even to your other clients, you would appear a bit shady in their eyes. It is just not the political think to do. You find yourself in a touchy situation facing a touchy problem. You continue to wait, watch, and self-reflect, searching for the right strategy. You don't have the legal right to "fix" the situation. You don't want to lose your restaurant client. You don't want to make an enemy of the reporter. You feel bad for your client and a bit frustrated with the agency contracted for social media purposes; you know social media and public relations efforts need to be strategically planned together. You are very careful in what you say about this because you realize that speaking up at the wrong time to the wrong people can damage your own business.

We hope that Heath's nine rhetorical factors are easily identified. If you have trouble identifying any of them in the above scenario, you probably forgot to start by pinpointing the rhetor from whose perspective you wanted to conduct your analysis. The most likely rhetor would be you. The following is our analysis of the situation:

Rhetor

- you as a public relations professional

Situation or problem

- you on retainer with the global pub chain for investor and media relations purposes
- your pub client's social media rhetoric invited a social media crisis for itself, but you are not contracted to manage it even though a reporter-as-opinion-leader thinks you are under contract

Audiences or publics

- current and prospective pub customers, social media followers with a vested interest in the pub, media members (intervening public), those interested in social justice, decision-makers in charge of your contract

Messages

- to you in a public format from the reporter as a public, "What do you know?"

- from you in a public format to the reporter, "I don't know anything, but I do value your relationship. Can you trust me on this one?"
- from you to your client through an interpersonal phone chat with the client VP for corporate communications, "I feel your pain and know you want social media as part of your strategic plan."

Message sources

- you, the reporter-as-opinion-leader and your public
- your client through the legal contract
- your client through social media posts
- the retained social media agency as social media choice maker
- social media participants through tweets and Facebook response threads

Images or opinions participants have of the sources

- the social media participants hold no image or opinion of the retained social media agency (that is the nature of the agency-on-retainer-for client-relationship)
- the social media participants hold a largely negative image of your client
- you hold a non-publicized (unarticulated) sense of disrespect of the retained social media agency
- you question to yourself the wisdom of your client in retaining the social media agency
- the reporter views you as a reliable and credible source
- your own clients perceive you as a professional worthy of representing them

Channels

- voice and print through telephone and digital posts, respectively
- Twitter and Facebook, as well as telephone communications
- print through the legal contract
- interpersonal through your last face-to-face meeting with your client

Opinion event

- the need for professional courtesy
- the need to keep contractual (legal) obligations
- the need to maintain your own professional integrity and credibility as a public relations professional in spite of your client's social media crisis that reflected on you
- your perception of your relationships with the reporter-as-opinion-leader
- stereotypes surrounding the public relations professional and reporter relationship

- your perception of the retained social media agency
- your perception of your relationship with the client's VP for corporate communication
- your perceptions of your client's communication strategy and history
- your perception of the power social media has to impact business as usual
- your client's perception of your professionalism and your professional abilities
- the fact that it has been a slow news week so far[19]

The lists provided for each of the eight factors in the hypothetical Pub example are not exhaustive. Remember, too, that the situation can involve multiple rhetors (social media participants, restaurant, retained social media agency, reporter, and so on) participating in the situation and bringing to it multiple interpretations and intents. As discussed earlier, the situation and its context call for at least one of five rhetorical responses: encouraging enlightened choice; adjusting organizations to people and people to organizations; building a case based on good reason; inviting people to use rhetoric as courtship: invitation and identification; and building identifications by shared perspectives, social construction of meaning, and connecting zones of meaning. If you were the public relations professional retained by the pub what response would you recommend and why would you recommend it? Public relations is the center of much of it.

Conclusion

Understanding public relations from the perspective of rhetorical theory helps us understand how dynamic and ever-changing message and meaning making really are. It sensitizes us to the ever-present contest in the message and meaning business as we use and misuse language and symbols. Examining a case from the eight rhetorical factors (situation, problem, rhetor, audiences or publics, messages, message sources, images, opinions, channels, and the opinion environment surrounding each statement) that are part of any public relations exigency helps us choose, or understand how we chose, a rhetorical response (encouraging enlightened choice; adjusting organizations to people and people to organizations; building a case based on good reason; inviting people to use rhetoric as courtship: invitation and identification; and building identifications by shared perspectives, social construction of meaning, and connecting zones of meaning). Rhetorical theory sensitizes us to the reality of public relations as an industry involving multiple rhetors addressing dynamic and ever-changing stakes in the marketplace wrangle of contested terrain.

Chapter Exercises

Case Application Lens: Rhetorical Theory

Public relations definition

Public relations is the process through which professional rhetors participate in multiple-rhetor contests to adequately address rhetorical problems faced by their employers, clients, and others in society; it involves explaining how organizations strategically or non-strategically manage their relationships through words, interests, opinions, and actions.

Rhetorical theorist intent

To examine the dynamic symbolic and language using process through which meaning is made in addressing rhetorical problems of marketplace wrangle or contested terrain, etc.

Rhetorical theory questions

1. When the public relations professionals in each case are viewed as rhetors, and the interplay between the organization and its vested publics as market place wrangle, contested terrain, or instances of finding and using all available means of persuasion, how would you describe WIGO? What is at stake?

2. How does viewing public relations as a participant in marketplace (of meaning) persuasion (also known as wrangle in the marketplace, marketplace wrangle, or contested terrain) influence your understanding of the profession?

3. Pull a case study or news release from your favorite organization's website. What parts of each become highly important as you look for how symbol and language use and misuse took place? Describe how the public relations initiative or "voice" within it portrays it as a rhetor.

4. Heath identifies seven rhetorical situations inviting public relations engagement: natural disasters; concerns voiced by others; recognition of problems that need to be addressed; choices, such as products or services; a matter of sound character; a matter of sound policy; and crisis response. Peruse news articles or news releases posted to the World Wide Web. See if you can find an example of an organization making each kind of response. Highlight the clues in what you find and share them with a classmate.

5. Use the cases or news releases you found for questions three and four. See if you can identify the following rhetorical factors in each one: situation, problem, rhetor, audiences or publics, messages, message sources, images or opinions, channels, and the opinion environment surrounding each statement. Do extra research if you need to about the situation at hand.

6. Again using the cases or news releases you found for questions three and four, see if you can identify the kind of rhetorical response the primary organization involved was making: encouraging enlightened choice; adjusting organizations to people and people to organizations; building a case based on good reason; inviting people to use rhetoric as courtship: invitation and identification; and building identifications by shared perspectives, social construction of meaning, and connecting of zones of meaning.

Opportunity for Praxis

To apply this chapter's information to the cases in Appendix B, see Appendix A:
____ Rhetorical Theory Key
____ Case Rubric Master

Notes

1. Heath, R. (1992). The wrangle in the marketplace: A rhetorical perspective of public relations. In R. Heath & E. Toth (Eds.), *Rhetorical and critical approaches to public relations* (pp. 17–35). Hillsdale, NJ: Lawrence Erlbaum, p. 17.
2. Heath, R. (2009a). The rhetorical tradition: Wrangle in the marketplace. In R. Heath, E. Toth, & D. Waymer (Eds.), *Rhetorical and critical approaches to public relations II* (pp. 14–47). New York: Routledge, p. 20.
3. Heath, R. (2009b), Section one: Rhetorical heritage and critical tradition. In R. Heath, E. Toth, & D. Waymer (Eds.), *Rhetorical and critical approaches to public relations II* (pp. 15–16). New York: Routledge, p. 15.
4. Heath, R. (1980). Corporate advocacy: An application of speech communication perspectives and skills and more. *Communication Education, 129*, pp. 370–377.
5. Heath, 1992, p. 17.
6. Ibid., p. 21.
7. Kenneth Burke is famous for writing a number of important works about rhetoric, including *Grammar of Motives* (1945) and *Language as Symbolic Action* (1966).
8. Burke, K. (1966). *Language as symbolic action.* Berkeley: University of California Press, p. 16.
9. Ibid.

10. Heath, 2009a, p. 20.
11. Our reason for being. (n.d.). Retrieved February 11, 2013 from http://www.patagonia.com/us/patagonia.go?assetid=2047&ln=140.
12. Profile statement. (n.d.). Retrieved February 11, 2013 from http://investor.columbia.com.
13. Hansen-Horn, T. & Horn, A. (2014), *Strategic planning for public relations: Beginning the journey*, New York: Peter Lang, pp. 59–60.
14. Heath, 1992, p. 25.
15. Heath, 2009a, pp. 34–35.
16. Heath, 1992, p. 25.
17. Heath, 2009a, pp. 36–39.
18. Hansen-Horn & Horn, 2014, p. 62.
19. Ibid., pp. 62–65.

CHAPTER SEVEN

Value in Applied Theory

Social Capital Theory

The ability to practice one- or two-way communication, make decisions based on "it depends," or organize through marketplace wrangle and contested meaning is viewed by social capital theorists as a product of the social capital associated with an organization. Proponents of social capital theory understand an organization as a network of past, present, developing, and anticipated internal relationships (useful or not useful) that's very existence depends on its suspension, if you will, within, or overlapping with, broader similar networks of external relationships. An organization's ability to wield power, rely on relationships of trust in times of crisis, successfully accommodate environmental activist demands, satisfy employees, meet client expectations, adapt to social changes, etc., depends on the kinds of relational networks (social capital) it has inside and outside its own boundaries. Its access to and ability to use its social capital as it works toward its goals is a determinant of how successful it will be. As a result, public relations is generally understood as the engagement and use of, or reliance on, social capital in the pursuit of organizational goals.

Social Capital as a Relational Network Resource

Largely a human trait or capability, social capital is embedded in or the product of relational and networked resources. In short, it's composed of connections resulting from communicative interactions at a variety of levels and can be viewed as an organizational resource (an organization can have more or less of it, and create more or less of it) that can be used for good or bad purposes. Relational networks can be enduring but are also malleable, which means they are impacted by every communicative exchange, real or imagined. They exist in the minds and perceptions of people as individual and/or collective constructs with organizational meaning. They are mitigated by senses of trust, credibility, reputation, image, behavior, honor, value, flexibility, adaptability, sustainability, reliability, productivity, and so on. They are the power behind public relations or the exigencies demanding public relations intervention. Relational networks can help organizations get things done, and they can aid in organizational protection, sustainability or advancement. Relational networks are seen by social capital theorists as highly valuable to organizational functioning, but the networks themselves are a bit elusive to pin down and define through a succinct description.

While possible only through human capability, it's important to note that social capital is not the same thing as human capital, though one cannot really exist without the other. Unlike relational networks that define and suspend an organization within other networks, human capital is the knowledge, skills, habits, experiences, personalities, etc., generally associated with a group of people as those individuals have value relevant to organizational goals. Human capital is pretty easily quantifiable; you can count number of people or hours available, ability to complete tasks, widgets produced each hour, and so on. Social capital is more elusive as the product of relational exchanges through communicative processes. How do you measure willingness to identify with a culture, trust levels, expected relational value, and so on? So, while relevant to it, human capital is just part of what makes social capital unique; it is not interchangeable with it.

Public relations scholars Erich Sommerfeldt and Maureen Taylor shed further light on our social capital understanding. They suggest that the leading social capital authors conceive of it "as the norms, cultural values and trust intrinsic to groups, organizations or communities. [As a result, social capital proponents are] … concerned with questions of how groups or communities 'develop and maintain their social networks and enhance their collective interests and identity' (Hsung & Breiger, 2009, p. 5)."[1] In other words, social capital involves relationships of trust (based on past actions, current promises and perceptions of those), understandings of performance retained and passed among organizational personnel, access to additional social capital from the networks that belong to organizations with which we are associated, and so on. It's a very complex concept yet also a very powerful one in the efficacy and success of organizational functioning and sustainability. It provides a powerful lens through which to view public relations.

Obligations and Expectations

Before the social capital discussion is continued, it's probably a good idea to more closely address the "capital" in social capital. It comes from communication-induced "changes in the relationships between actors."[2] Let's examine it more closely through something with which you are likely somewhat comfortable.

You're likely familiar with the idea of financial or economic capital, such as how much money you have in the bank, how much your car is worth, what kinds of credit limits you have, and so on. These are examples of financial capital belonging to you. Fortunately, J. Coleman's[3] explanation of social capital helps us transfer our understandings of financial capital to understandings of social capital from the viewpoint of obligations and expectations defined by *deposits*, *credit*, and *expenditures*.

> If A does something for B and assumes that B will reciprocate in the future, an expectation is established in A and an obligation incurred on the part of B. This obligation can be conceived as a credit slip held by A for the fulfillment of an obligation by B. These credit slips constitute a relational deposit that has a value that A can spend to accomplish various goals and objectives—unless, of course, the actor who has the obligation defaults on the debt.

For instance, you may have received a 1 a.m. Saturday call from a desperate friend. You had to wake up from a deep sleep to answer it (you only answered it because your friend already had "friend" social capital with you). You took the call and your friend asked you to drive to her place of work to jump her car's dead battery. You dragged yourself out of your warm bed, got out your car, drove across town, and rescued your friend. She later thanked you and you both drove to your respective homes. Your friend relied on her sense of social capital with you and exploited it for her gain. In this sense, exploitation refers to "to use," "call on," or "invoke." At the same time, through that exploitation process via the relational exchange (a change in the relation impacted by a communicative exchange), you expected that you earned some relational credit from your friend that you can, if you want to, use at a later time because of your friend's changed sense of obligation (or enhanced credit with her you now have on deposit). In fact, should you have car trouble, need a ride somewhere, or need a place to couch surf for a weekend sometime in the future you'll likely assume your friend will come to your rescue without hesitation. Of course, only if she has the same expectations for her "jumped your car for you" obligation as you do, will this *expectation—obligation* relationship work out as you intend. However, the friend interpretation may not be correct at all. It may be that your friend called you for a jump, because you "owed" her a favor from something she had previously done for you. Or it could be that she is your girl ... friend and you expect to be called to come to her rescue when she has trouble. If this is the case, the larger relational exchanges and structure of the pre-existing relationship build a volunteer sense of expectation and obligation within it. As you might imagine at this point, our expectation—obligation scenarios with deposits, credits, and expenditures can go on and on, so we'll stop here.

It's pretty easy to imagine relationships built on networks of communicative exchanges as "money in the bank" in the "jump my car" scenario. However, the obligations and expectations inherent in social capital are "created through ... communicative exchanges and they both contain actor beliefs about past and future exchanges."[4] They differ from financial obligations and expectations in one substantial way; financial debt is easily quantified and, as such, repaid or exchanged. Social capital credit is not easily measured, exchanged, or repaid. The amount available; its character; its ability to be used, reinforced, or responded to are hard to describe, much less know with certainty. Social capital exists in the minds of people not in the form of coins, bills, or numbers. Additionally, while a financial "debt can be sold or passed on to another individual or organizations ... social capital is rooted in and constrained by the particular relationship in which it emerges,"[5] making it difficult if not impossible to pass on. It gets more complex at the organizational level. Organizations are not people, yet they are created by and comprised of people. Hence, the necessary condition of social capital, human capability, is inherent in organization. In fact, some social capitalist theorists argue that an organization only exists because of social capital, of some sense of shared and recognized relational networks and obligations—expectations exchanges. In this sense, public relations is often called upon to assist in facilitating shared senses of relational networks or because of them. And, sometimes, overlapping and/or environmental networks of social capital demand public relations intervention for organizational purposes. At any rate, a public relations professional's ability to rely on social capital to accomplish organizational goals demands that he understand it, have access to it, and be able to leverage it for his public relations purposes.

Ideally, and drawing on the works of Harvard University political scientist and renowned social capital theorist Robert D. Putnam, public relations professional R. Cawley casts social capital as a great public relations opportunity.[6] Cawley argues that public relations is uniquely positioned to create and exploit two types of social capital, bonding and bridging. *Bonding social capital* is the ability to build a sense of "shared identity that provides a cultural bond among members of an organization" that leads to great level of demonstrated organizational success. *Bridging social capital*, however, is much more challenging to create. As the real public relations challenge, Cawley argues, it is the relational networks and all that comes with them that can "reach across divisions and distances [not only geographical divisions and distances] to build ongoing relationships between disparate organizations." In fact, Cawley argues that public relations might be well served with a redefinition. It could be, he says, "understood as the practice of creating organizational social capital." At first glance, Cawley's definition seems an obvious departure from understanding public relations as planned and strategic results-driven communicative effort with the publics in mind. However, if we substitute "creating organizational capital" for "planned and strategic results-driven communicative effort" we have a definition worth spending some time exploring. We have, public relations is creating organizational capital with the publics in mind.

Levels of Social Capital

Generally speaking all social capital, including bonding and bridging, can be understood at one of three levels: micro, macro, and meso. At the *micro-level* it's understood as the connections one individual has with other people and group memberships. The term micro refers to individual and individuals. From this view of social capital, two important factors influence an individual's ability to successfully use her connections in the pursuit of her goals. The first factor is the size of her network, and the second is "the size and depth of the capital the other parts of [her] network have and to which [she] gains access."[7] A case in point is your own LinkedIn account. If you don't have one, you have no LinkedIn social capital that you can use as you pursue your goals. If you do have an account, and let's say that you do, the number of first-, second- and even third-level LinkedIn connections that you have indicates something about your LinkedIn social capital to help you reach a goal. For our purposes here, let's say you want to find your first full-time public relations position. If you have 15 first-level LinkedIn connections, your network likely has very little social capital that you can use to land the desired job. However, if you are after a position at FleishmanHillard and the account director filling the position is networked to you through LinkedIn as a second-level connection, you may be able to use the social capital possible through that relationship to land the job, especially if the connection you both have in common is your former internship supervisor who has since moved on to join FleishmanHillard. In this case, you may be able to contact your former supervisor and ask him to put a good word in on your behalf with the account director. Indeed, if the position is advertised through LinkedIn, it may be that the hiring account director will view your LinkedIn profile and find (on his own because prospective employers do peruse your social media accounts) your first-level connection to your former internship supervisor and, thus, conclude your application is worth further review. The possibilities for differing LinkedIn scenarios are many.

Social capital can also be understood at the community or national levels. This is the *macro-level*. The focus is on how social capital is impacted by and impacts community, national and cultural trends, as well as their outcomes. For instance, the social capital the US has with the government and populace of Mexico (two different relationships) hugely impacts its ability to regulate illegal drugs coming across the border. For instance, the network of relationships that US law enforcement groups have with Mexican law enforcement groups come into play here. So do networks or relationships of trust among US border patrol groups and Mexican border patrol groups. In another vein, when the US provides humanitarian aid to drought-stricken African countries, we might argue that social capital is again hugely impactful. The US ability to actually get aid where it needs to go, and to the people in desperate need, depends on its social capital with relevant African governments, aid groups on the ground in Africa, relationships with respective guerilla leaders, and pre-existing forms of social capital with the groups of receiving people.

Between the micro- and macro-levels of relational networks is the meso-level, also known as the level of organizational functioning. Public relations scholars V. Hazleton & W. Kennan[8] view social capital at this level, especially as it impacts the ability of the public relations profession to accomplish its mission. The idea is that successful organizational relational networks can help the organization owning them accomplish its public-relevant goals. Social capital impacts an organization's ability to influence and/or adapt to other organizations.

Some public relations scholars take the discussion a step further and try to understand it from all three levels while examining the interplay among micro-, meso-, and macro-level social capital as it impacts public relations efficacy. "Social capital is thus a process and an outcome, and is relevant to the success of an individual actor at the micro-level, an organization at the meso- level, and to an entire community or society at a macro-level."[9] If we return to the US efforts to regulate illegal drugs coming across the US-Mexican border, and look at WIGO from all three levels we can anticipate the following: At the macro-level (national and/or community) the degree to which the US government has social capital (positively perceived relationships of trust) established with national leaders in the Mexican government will impact whether or not "friendly" illegal drug control courses of action can be negotiated between the two governments. In addition, the degree to which the US and Mexican governments, respectively, have the same kinds of social capital with border communities, will profoundly influence the two governments' ability to enact the planned actions. At the meso-level (organizational), the degree to which border patrol agencies from both countries have desirable social capital relationships with each other and border town leadership, will determine what can be accomplished. Finally, at the micro-level (individual) the social capital that US and Mexican government officials have with border patrol and border community officials will, again, profoundly impact what goes one.

The application of social capital theory to public relations lets us examine the power relational networks can and do have in organizational action and sense-making. In short, "social capital is the ability that organizations have of creating, maintaining, and using relationships to achieve desirable goals."[10] Of course, it also makes sense to argue that to be successful, a public relations department or practitioner must have access to or reserves of social capital, and it must be used in a strategic ways.

Social Capital Management Outcomes

Interestingly, Hazleton and Kennan identify three kinds of outcomes that social capital management can net: "increased and/or more complex forms of social capital, reduced transaction costs and organizational advantage," making sure to note that the outcomes can be positive or negative and "can be characterized along a continuum that ranges from the highly concrete to highly abstract."[11] This means that when social capital is exploited (used) by the organization to which it belongs we can expect organizational effect. When managing its social capital in pursuit of organizational goals, there's almost always one or many effects on the organization's current levels of social capital, hence *increased and/or more complex forms of social capital*. It may come in the form of additional connections to or within the existing networks, more intellectual capital (business-related knowledge), or new relationships and networks. It might also come in the form, when management is not a success, of more complicated and hard-to-use social capital such as tenuous employee relations or distant media relations. For example, when successfully exploited and relationally managed in the area of pre-existing media relations relationships, it can lead to enhanced meso-level social capital with relevant media. If poorly managed, it can lead to resistant or hostile relationships with relevant media and, hence, more complex social capital or reduced amounts of it. A second outcome is *reduced transaction costs*, though not in the traditional sense of buying and selling. This outcome relates to levels of trust and impacts on trust levels in doing business; they are "grounded in the available stock of social capital"[12] and come in the form of lawsuits against the organization (such as sexual harassment, racial discrimination, etc.), intentional subpar production levels (sabotaged production levels), labor union issues, employee theft, etc. In understanding costs from the lens of social capital, the intent of its theorists is to highlight costs related to the absence of "associational capital that directly breeds mistrust, hostility, suspicion, and hate and encourages costly and prolonged conflict. Employee theft, for example, reflects the absence of a relational context in which a norm resides producing a set of expectations and obligations regarding theft."[13] A third outcome, *increases in organizational advantage,* involves any result that helps the organization to conduct business as usual while successfully managing the complex networks of relationships within it and within which it exists. Increases in "productivity, efficiency, customer satisfaction, net asset value, stock value, etc."[14] are possibilities. Of course, the reverse is also true and unsuccessful relational management can lead to less productivity, efficiency, customer satisfaction, net asset value, stock value, etc.

Maintaining and/or working to develop new networks, and relationships within current networks valued as organizational capital, can be engaged in more strategically if we keep in mind the social capital management outcomes. We may end up with increased and/or more complex forms of social capital, reduced transactions costs, and/or organizational advantage. Knowing what we want or need, with a view to what the outcomes can be, can help organizational leadership practice public relations more selectively and powerfully.

Conclusion

Social capital theorists bring to us the idea of relational networks as valuable organizational resources. Based on systems of obligations and expectations; debt, credit, and expenditures; an organization's social capital (it can have more or less of it); be it bonding, bridging, or something more; exists at and across three levels: micro (individual), meso (organizational), and macro (community and national). The outcomes generally associated with successful social capital management are increased and/or more complex forms of social capital, reduced transaction costs, and organizational advantage.

Chapter Exercises

Case Application Lens: Social Capital Theory

Public relations definition

Public relations is the engagement and use of, or reliance on, an organization's social capital (relational networks) in the pursuit of organizational goals; public relations is used to develop and maintain social networks and enhance their collective interests and identity in a series of relational credit, debt, and expenditure through communicative exchanges of obligations and expectations

Social capital theorist intent

To understand the public relations professional's ability to rely on social capital to accomplish organizational goals; how it can be understood, accessed, and leveraged for public relations purposes is of utmost importance

Social capital theory questions

1. Find two case studies. How would you describe the social capital belonging to each organization involved in each case?
   a. How much social capital does each organization have and why do you say that?
   b. Discuss each organization in terms of evident bonding social capital, bridging social capital, or something more that has or has not been exploited. What were the cues you used to reach your conclusions?
   c. Describe how the involved organizations did or did not appropriately access needed social capital to achieve their goals or objectives?
   d. Describe how the involved organizations did or did not appropriately leverage needed social capital to achieve their goals or objectives?
2. Using the same two cases you found for question one, do your best to identify and describe the social capital that exists for the vested organization at the micro-, meso-, and macro-level.
   a. Which, if any, does it appear that the public relations professional helped the organization access and exploit?
3. Imagine that you were asked to explain the five social capital characteristics of a public relations opportunity to your mom. Develop a hypothetical example from which she can understand expectations, obligations, credits, deposits, and expenditures from a social capital perspective of public relations.
4. Silpada fine jewelry (www.silpada.com) recently announced that it was closing the business. While its media message cited "changes in buying behaviors," read at least three articles (not written by a Silpada representative) about the announcement, and develop an explanation of what happened from a social capital perspective.
5. You might want to develop an explanation of what happened as undesirable social capital outcomes in the form of decreased and/or more complex forms of social capital, increased transaction costs, and organizational disadvantage.

Opportunity for Praxis

To apply this chapter's information to the cases in Appendix B, see Appendix A:
_____ Social Capital Theory Key
_____ Case Rubric Master

Notes

1. Sommerfeldt, E. & Taylor, M. (2011). A social capital approach to improving public relations' efficacy: Diagnosing internal constraints on external communication. *Public Relations Review, 37*, p. 198.
2. Hazleton, V. & Kennan, W. (2000). Social capital: Reconceptualizing the bottom line. *Corporate Communications, 5*(2), p. 82.
3. Coleman, J. (1988). Social capital in the creation of human capital. *The American Journal of Sociology, 94*(1), p. S102.
4. Kennan, W. & Hazleton, V. (2006). Internal public relations, social capital, and the role of effective organizational communication. In C. Botan & V. Hazleton (Eds.), *Public Relations Theory II* (p. 323). Mahwah, NJ: Lawrence Erlbaum.
5. Ibid., p. 323.
6. Cawley, R. (2010, Winter). Creating social capital: The great opportunity for public relations. *Public Relations Strategist, 6K*-011008.
7. Ihlen, O. (2009). *Public relations and social theory.* New York: Routledge, p. 74
8. Hazleton & Kennan, 2000 and Kennan & Hazleton, 2006, pp. 311–338.
9. Sommerfeldt & Taylor, 2011, p. 197.
10. Kennan & Hazleton, 2006, p. 322.
11. Hazleton & Kennan, 2000, p. 84.
12. Ibid., p. 86.
13. Ibid.
14. Ibid.

Preface and Instructions for Use

In our quest to help you more fully understand the complexity and interconnectedness of public relations in a practical way (and be more comfortable with its nature), we developed a "key" representing the essential factors of each chapter. The keys we developed for your use correspond with the chapters and the development of content in them.

Chapter One: Case Kind
Chapter Two: Strategy
Chapter Three: Economic Area, Organization Type, PR Situations & Contexts, and PR Specializations
Chapter Four: Value in Applied Theory: Excellence Theory
Chapter Five: Value in Applied Theory: Contingency Theory
Chapter Six: Value in Applied Theory: Rhetorical Theory
Chapter Seven: Value in Applied Theory: Social Capital Theory

Appendix A concludes with a Case Rubric Master designed to accommodate the analyses you arrive at when you apply any or all of the keys to one of the cases found in Appendix B. The process is really quite systematic and we are convinced that you will find it easy to use. You can work from the conclusions you record on the Case Rubric Master, while referencing any notes you may have made on individual keys, in discussions with others. Your conversations won't be very interesting if you don't read the corresponding chapters before trying to apply the keys.

A-1. Case Kind

Case Title

Case Kind: Use this key to examine a case and determine, using the descriptions provided here (as well as those in your textbook), what kind of case classification most closely represents it. You can later transfer your choices to the **Case Rubric** Master. Write Y for yes and N for no in the boxes provided below.

	Y/N	Case Kind Key	Description
H		Historical	What is being studied has already occurred; the study looks back in an attempt to explain what and why something occurred and how the outcome was managed; it provides detail only found in hindsight
HL		• Linear approach	A historical study that begins with an analysis of the case background and moves systematically to an evaluation of the impact made or not made; the situation is presented as static from beginning to end; provides hindsight certainty
HP		• Process approach	A historical study that frames public relations as an ongoing process; introduces the elements of feedback and accommodation to the case account; introduces readers to in process or in progress evaluation and the idea of response/adjustment; the points at which adjustments were are made are highlighted; provides processural possibilities
GB		Grounded-business	Offers case background in the form of some history, financial data, and communication data and asks reader to make decisions or recommendations based on his analysis of the narrative; hypothetical for heuristic purposes

A-2. Strategy

Case Title

Strategy: Use this key to examine a case and determine, using the descriptions provided here (as well as those in your textbook), what kinds of strategies (assumed or obviously employed) characterize it. You can later transfer your choices to the **Case Rubric** Master. Write Y for yes and N for no in the boxes provided below.

	Y/N	Strategy Key	Description
S1		Prescriptive	Importance placed on how strategy, itself, should be defined; assumption is the professional knows what the strategy is, she just needs to find the best way to go about formulating it
S2		Descriptive	Professionals not as interested in prescribing best practices of strategy as they are in being able to identify and describe how it unfolds as it is imagined and communicated; what transpires is described as strategy
S3		Transfor-mative	Professional operates with the assumption that change is inevitable apart from her interventions so she imagines strategy as something that will reconfigure itself, or be reconfigured, to accommodate change
S4		Emergent	Professional recognizes strategy as it happens or emerges across time; assumes that what's intended meets a changing reality and is modified; plan based only in so far as the strategist plans to plan and re-plan
S5		Linear	Similar to prescriptive, plan based, professionals view themselves as agents of power and change so it is their job to plan, implement, and change strategy relevant to WIGO across time
S6		Adaptive	Professionals prioritize organizational objectives but without assuming they are free to act on them at will; assume that adjustments will have to be made relevant to the environment or WIGO on a continual basis

S7		Interpretive	Professional does not hold to linear or adaptive ideas, instead believes all action is only possible in cooperation with others than her client; believes an organization exists only at the permission of those it impacts
S8		Deliberate	Professionals assume planned strategy is best and presuppose organizational profitability and sustainability; all about organizational position and goal achievement
S9		Plan	Professionals assume the use of a consciously intended course of action or set of guidelines
S10		Ploy	Still plan-based, but simply a strategy maneuver to outclass, outperform, get the jump on something, capitalize on an unanticipated endorsement, or counteract undesirable publicity; often embedded within a planned strategy
S11		Pattern	Gives credence to plan and ploy, but focuses on how strategy is defined by patterns in a stream of actions, does not assume prescription but recognizes patterns that limit and facilitate strategy
S12		Position	Professionals focus on WIGO external to the organization as more important that WIGO internal to the organization with the intent of positioning the organization within its environment for success; may do this through plan, ploy, and position while making modifications to patterns
S13		Perspective	Professionals focus largely on internal WIGO and their ability to interpret it as most important contributors to strategy; try to understand WIGO from a position collective perspective taking

What evidence do you find of the codification-elaboration-conversion process? Refer to chapter two.

A-3. Economic Area

Case Title

	Y/N	Economic Area Key	Description
Economic Area: Use this key to examine a case and determine, using the descriptions provided here (as well as those in your textbook), what kinds of economic areas characterize it. You can later transfer your choices to the **Case Rubric Master**. Write Y for yes and N for no in the boxes provided below.			
B2B		Business-to-business	Serves the needs of businesses and not individuals; involves contractual obligations between organized corporate groups
B2C		Business-to-consumer	Involves meeting the needs and wants of individuals, who consume something, with products, services, or ideas
B2G		Business-to-government	Involves non-government organizations doing business directly with government offices and enterprises at local, state, national, and international levels; governed by government rules

A-4. Organization Type

Case Title

	Y/N	Organization Type Key	Description
Organization Type: Use this key to examine a case and determine, using the descriptions provided here (as well as in your textbook), what kinds of organization type or types characterize it. You can later transfer your choices to the **Case Rubric Master**. Write Y for yes and N for no in the boxes provided below.			
FP		For-profit	Exists solely for the purposes of making money; required to pay taxes on its profit
NP		Non-profit (philanthropically funded)	Business is not conducted solely for the purpose of making money but, instead, is undertaken for a cause or special interest; characterized by different tax laws; philanthropically funded

NGO		Non-government organization	A non-profit that operates at the international level and is not part of the US government (though it can receive grants from the US government)
SE		Social enterprise non-profit (self-funded)	A non-profit that exists for the purpose of making money and to address a cause or special interest; all profits are directed back into the organization and its efforts; its own for-profit business efforts fund it
GVT		Government	Highly regulated activity with rules coming from the government; operate totally under the purview of national, state, or local governments; sole purpose is public service and they answer to the public because their existence is made possible from public funds

A-5. PR Situations and Contexts

Case Title

PR Situations & Contexts: Use this key to examine a case and determine, using the descriptions provided here (as well as those in your text book, what kinds of PR situations and contexts characterize it. You can later transfer your choices to the **Case Rubric** Master. Write Y for yes and N for no in the boxes provided below.

	Y/N	PR Situations & Contexts Key	Description
1A		Advancement	Fundraising and political representation for academic organizations; sometimes used interchangeably with "development"
1B		Campaigning and debating	Relating to local, state and federal level activity for the purposes of elections, voting, and/or legislation
1C		Cause marketing and branding	Matching a for-profit organization's marketing efforts with a charitable organization's cause/goals for the purpose of favorable perception building

1D		Community relations	Usually geographically designated, but can also occur in digital communities; for the purpose of relationship building and/or maintenance between operating organizations and the people of the communities in which they exist
1E		Corporate communications	Generally referring to internal public relations activities at large for-profit organizations, although some government offices are similarly named
1F		Corporate social responsibility	Referring to organizational vision and activity designed to act ethically and make a positive impact in areas from which it benefits or serves
1G		Crisis communication and/or management	Predates actual organizational crises; can preempt crises, purpose during crises is to provide factual, timely, and situation-relevant information to all vested parties while working for a timely return to "regular" operations
1H		Development	Referring to fundraising and resourcing efforts for all non-profit organizations; sometimes used interchangeably with "advancement"
1I		Image and reputation management	Referring to efforts to build and/or maintain an organization's multifaceted collection of public perceptions into a desirable end result; reputation refers more than image to perceptions of past actions and intents
1J		Integrated marketing communications	Referring to initiatives undertaken with the understanding that every possible vehicle of organizational communication is perceived by recipients as coming from one indistinguishable source, therefore, all communicative efforts should be complementary in some way.
1K		Issues management	The address of emerging issues for the sake or organizational pursuits or before they can negatively impact doing business as usual

1L		Lobbying	Involves formal and informal efforts; paid lobbyists represent the interests of employers and advocate at local, state, and federal levels; grassroots activism takes place from the efforts of non-paid advocates in attempts to drive public activism
1M		Marketing communications	Referring to communication initiatives supporting consumer and/or trade promotions; Not to be confused with IMC
1N		Media relations	Referring to long- and short-term relationship development with, as well as strategic communication efforts directed at, media members relevant to your organization's goals
1O		Public affairs	Referring to efforts to interpret and impact political and/or social issue regulation as they have potential to impact business as usual
1P		Risk communication	Involves strategic messaging designed to reduce perceptions of and/or the reality of conditions that can bring harm to publics; often able to preempt crisis
1Q		Special event planning	Referring to the planning and execution of meetings, conventions, tradeshows, ceremonies, team building activities, and the like; designed for public relations purposes
1R		Strategic communication	Sometimes used interchangeably with public relations, referring to coordinated communication efforts to net desirable organizational impact
1S		Sustainability	Referring to efforts to insure long-term organizational livelihood; sometimes used interchangeably with corporate social responsibility

A-6. PR Specializations

Case Title

PR Specializations: Use this key to examine a case and determine, using the descriptions provided here (as well as those in your text book, what kinds of PR specializations characterize it. You can later transfer your choices to the **Case Rubric** Master. Write Y for yes and N for no in the boxes provided below.

	Y/N	PR Specializations Key	Description
2A		Agency Public Relations	Services provided for a fee at client request; can consist of any of the other specializations.
2B		Aviation Relations	Initiatives to represent the interests of all level of airports, travelers and cargo systems, aircraft manufacturers, and service providers
2C		Conference and convention relations	Special event services, relationship building among businesses, and professional services representation
2D		Consumer relations	Services to build iconic brands and brand reputation for loyal consumption
2E		Digital communications	Social media strategies and tactics, among others, as used to provide relevant messages and representation to consumers of electronic media
2F		Education relations	Efforts on behalf of elementary, middle, high school, and post-high-school organizations in cooperation with the Department of Education
2G		Employee relations	Often neglected, this includes treating employees as a valued public, recognizing them as brand ambassadors and word-of-mouth sources; sometimes called corporate communications
2H		Entertainment public relations	A catchall for strategic work with television, movie, music, fashion, radio, athletic, and event-related celebrities
2I		Environmental or conservation relations	Involving efforts to preserve the environment, natural resources, animal life and/or gain permission to do business in protected areas; generally an area of robust activism

2J		Fashion relations	Truly a global industry, it involves efforts to define latest trends, follow celebrities, and communicate beauty
2K		Fundraising	Services to elicit voluntary financial contributions from relevant publics, largely a responsibility of the non-profit arena
2L		Government relations	Efforts to work within laws and regulations enforced by the US government (or any government), influence legislation and leaders, or change policy
2M		Healthcare communications	A growing area in light of the US-push for preventative measures and a rapidly aging public, it involves work on behalf of hospitals, insurance companies, special interest groups, and the like
2N		International relations	Involves building and negotiating relationships with nondomestic governments, etc., and working with groups such as the IMF; it often involves questions of policy
2O		Investor and financial relations	Highly regulated by the federal agencies, this involves initiatives to communicate financial statuses in ways beneficial to all vested parties
2P		Maturing publics relations	A rapidly growing public, it involves issues of health care, geriatric care, palliative care, and long-term support, as well as vested interests in retirement, travel, and the like
2Q		Member relations	Like employee relations, this involves working with an external public. However, the voluntary nature of members is a significant differentiator. Services include making sure members retain their membership through satisfaction brought about by communication to them and of their interests
2R		Relations with special publics	Identified as specific groups clustered around special interests determined by demographics and psychographics
2S		Sports public relations	As a valuable source of entertainment and international unity, efforts to represent the interests of sports-related publics is key

2T		Travel and tour-ism relations	Image and reputation are the foundation of the health of this industry, as are vital sources of state and national income; generally relates to hospitality as well
2U		University relations	Services to tell a university's story and its prom-ise to those holding a real or potential vested interest in it
2V		Volunteer relations	Directed at members and non-members, these are a defining part of allegiance to causes, activist activities, and so on; also a source of employee relations activities

A-7. Excellence Theory

Case Title

> Excellence Theory: Use this key to examine a case and determine, using the questions an descriptions provided here (as well as those in your textbook): what is most obvious, least obvious, most important, least important, etc. from an excellence theory lens. You can later transfer your choices to the Case Rubric Master. Write Y for yes and N for no in the boxes provided below.

PR Defined

The management of communication between an organization and its public

Theorist Intent

To determine best practices for accomplishing organizational goals; best practices are differentiated by purpose, organizational goal, public relations contribution to goal, nature of communication, communication model, and nature of research for success

Theory Lens

- Which of the four models was used? What was the result?
- Which of the four models could have been used? Why?
- Which of the four models should have been used? Why?

Y/N	Excellence Theory Lens	Questions, frames for analyses, descriptions
Purpose		
	Propaganda	To create buzz, hype, or advocacy; truth not essential
	Dissemination of information	To provide fact-backed information; assumption is public needs it as a service
	Scientific persuasion	To use formative research to develop initiatives to meet organizational goals
	Mutual understanding	To use research and dialogue to reach mutual understanding and benefits
Organizational goal		
	Environmental control/ domination	To get public to do what the organization wants
	Environmental adaptation/ cooperation	To serve the public by providing it what it needs
	Environmental control/ domination	To get the public to do what the organization wants
	Environmental adaptation/ cooperation	To adjust the organization to the public and the public to the organization
PR contribution to goal		
	Advocacy	Persuasion regardless of truth; not necessarily unethical
	Dissemination of information	Provision of information judged relevant and needed by public
	Advocacy	Persuasion based on public research; goals incorporate public feedback
	Mediation	Dialogue facilitation between organization and relevant publics; research important
Nature of communication		
	One-way, complete truth not essential	One-way, no feedback loop, public perception not part of one-way process

	One-way, truth important	One-way, fact-finding important to goals, strategy, and tactic development; feedback not important in goal development
	Two-way, imbalanced effects based on research intent	Two-way with a feedback loop through research (focus groups, Internet surveys, response options, etc.); feedback used in goal, strategy, and tactic development
	Two-way, cooperative balanced effects	Two-way with ongoing dialogue for goal-setting and strategy and tactic development; feedback is very important to all understandings and initiatives; mutuality is key
Communication model		
	Source to receiver	Sender encodes, sends across channels, receiver decodes
	Source to receiver	Sender encodes, sends across channels, receiver decodes
	Source to receiver accounting for feedback	Sender encodes based on formative research with public, sends across channels, receiver decodes but can provide responses through feedback loop
	Group to group	All relevant parties play a part in the sending, encoding, responding, research in a continual process
Nature of research or success of efforts		
	Very little, counting house	Almost no research done except, perhaps, to find best ways to persuade public; efforts evaluated by counting tickets, attendance, etc.
	Little but readability and readership	If public is aware of, pays attention to, understands, and retains information sent
	Formative, evaluative of attitudes	Research done to help form goals, strategies, and tactics to be public-specific; impact on attitudes or behavior determines success

Formative, evaluative of under-standing and common goals	Research done to help form goals, strategies, and tactics to be public-specific; accomplishment of dialogue among relevant parties, and establishment and attainment of mutually beneficial goals determines success
Excellence PR model found in case:	
Press agentry/publicity	Most efforts mass media focused with the goal of creating buzz, hype, or advocacy with little regard for truth; little research required; not necessarily unethical
Public information	Distribution of information, not necessarily with persuasive intent; fact-finding for content assumed to be needed by public
Two-way asymmetrical	Research conducted for purpose of persuasion/advocacy; feedback loop for the purposes of more sophisticated persuasion initiatives; purpose of accomplishment of organization's goals
Two-way symmetrical	Intent is mutual understanding and benefits; research conducted for the purposes of understanding and balanced purposes; relationship building is a key focus

A-8. Contingency Theory

Case Title

Contingency Theory: Use this key to examine a case and determine, using the questions an descriptions provided here (as well as those in your textbook): what is most obvious, least obvious, most important, least important, etc. from a contingency theory lens. You can later transfer your choices to the **Case Rubric Master.** Write Y for yes and N for no in the boxes provided below.

PR Defined

The strategic management of conflict and competition in the best interests of an organization and, when possible, also in the interests of key publics

Theorist Intent

To understand how public relations leads the way in the recognition of threats, and adopting stances to conflict and competition, in an "it depends" advocacy to accommodation manner that helps accomplish organizational goals

Theory Lens

- Is there competition? If so, describe it as you perceive it.
- Is there conflict? If so, describe it as you perceive it. How relevant is the conflict to the organization's stated objectives? How relevant should it be?
- Was a threat (or threats) perceived? If so, describe the process by which you think the public relations professional appraised it via the primary and secondary appraisal processes. If a threat was appraised, where would you place the process on the "dimensionality of threats" model? Why?
- What stance (or stances) on the contingency continuum appears to have been adopted? Why do you think the organization seems to have taken the stance it did? Does the stance seem to change over time? How is the stance different relevant to each key public, or is it?
- What factors (of the more than 80 identified) seem to have contributed the most to the stance/s the organization took? What led to the "factors" conclusions you made?

Y/N	Contingency Theory Lens	Description
Competition		Organizations and publics compete for resources such as marketshare, contracts, shipping rights, etc.
	Was there any? If so, what was it about or at stake?	
	If there was competition, how relevant was it to organizational goals?	

Conflict		Occurs when organizations attack ideas, perceptions, interpretations, character, etc., through communication; can involve competition or appraised threats
	Was there any? If so, what was at stake or being contested?	
	If there was conflict, how relevant was it to organizational goals?	
Threat		Consists of the interplay between demand and resource appraisals [ability to overcome or thwart threat], and perception or assessment of danger, uncertainty, and required effort inherent in the situation; occurs in three dimensions
	Was there a threat appraised? If so, where would you place it on the Dimensionality of Threats model?	
—	—Dimension one —external	litigation, government regulation, potentially damaging publicity, scarring of organization's reputation, legitimating activists claims
—	—internal	economic loss or gain from implementing various stances, marring of employees or stockholders' perception of the company, marring of the personal reputations of the company decision makers

—	—Dimension two: threat level	
—	—low	not very relevant to organizational goals or sustainability
—	—medium	pretty relevant to organizational goals or sustainability
—	—high	very relevant to organizational goals or sustainability
—	—Dimension three: duration	
—	—short-term	won't last very long
—	—long-term	will likely last a long time and remain relevant
Stance		**Accommodation-Advocacy continuum; an organization can adopt one or more per public or for a singular public; ranges from pure accommodation to please public or adapt to external factors at all costs, to pure advocacy to resist and/or control**
	Apology and restitution	Accept blame, apologize to vested parties, and make wrongs right
	Capitulation	Give in to all accusations and demands, blame acceptance and apology not automatic
	Compromise	Give something to get something in what is not a win-win situation
	Negotiation	Work together to define situation and relevant accommodations
	Collaborating	Work together to redefine WIGO and courses of action
	Cooperation	Appearing to collaborate while working for the organization's best interests
	Avoiding	Ignoring
	Compromising	Work together to define give and take in what is not a win-win situation

Contending	Publicly debating	
Competition	Work against each other to win	
Arguing	Debate to win	
Public relations	Advocate through strategic communicative initiatives in the organization's interests	
Competing litigation	Appeal to the law or courts to determine all	
Factors contributing to stance/s		
Organizational characteristics *(internal)—check the ones you believe are impactful factors in the situation*	__ Open or closed culture __ Dispersed widely geographically or centralized __ Level of technology the organization uses to produces its product or service __ Homogeneity or heterogeneity of officials involved __ Age of the organization/value placed on tradition __ Speed of growth in the knowledge level of organization uses __ Economic stability of organization __ Existence or nonexistence of issues management official or programs __ Organization's past experiences with the public __ Distribution of decision-making power __ Formalization: number of roles or codes defining and limiting the job __ Stratification/hierarchy of positions __ Existence of influence of legal department __ Business exposure __ Corporate culture	
PR department characteristics *(internal)*	__ Total number of practitioners and number of college degrees __ Type of past training: trained in PR or ex-journalists, marketing, etc.	

	___ Location of PR department in hierarchy: independent or under marketing umbrella/experience encroachment of marketing/persuasive mentality ___ Representation in the dominant coalition ___ Experience level of PR practitioners in dealing with crisis ___ General communication competency of department ___ Autonomy of department ___ Physical placement of department in building (near CEO and other decision makers or not) ___ Staff trained in research methods ___ Amount of funding available for dealing with external publics ___ Amount of time allowed to use dealing with external publics ___ Gender: percentage of female upper-level staff/managers ___ Potential of department to practice various models of public relations
Characteristics of dominant coalition (top management) *(internal)*	___ Political values: conservative or liberal/open or closed to change ___ Management style: domineering or laid back ___ General altruism level ___ Support and understanding of PR ___ Frequency of external contact with publics ___ Departmental perception of the organization's external environment ___ Calculation of potential rewards or losses using different strategies with external publics ___ Degree of line manager involvement in external affairs

Internal threats (how much is at stake in the situation) *(internal)*	__ Economic loss or gain from implementing various stances __ Marring of employees' or stockholders' perceptions of the company __ Marring of the personal reputations of the company's decision makers
Individual characteristics (PR practitioners, dominant coalition, line manager) *(internal)*	__ Training in diplomacy, marketing, journalism, engineering, etc. __ Personal ethics __ Tolerance or ability to deal with uncertainty __ Comfort level with conflict or dissonance __ Comfort level with change __ Ability to recognize potential and existing problems __ Extent of openness to innovation __ Personality: dogmatic, authoritarian __ Communication competency __ Cognitive complexity: ability to handle complex problems __ Predisposition toward negotiations __ Predisposition to altruism __ How individuals receive, process, and use information and influence __ Familiarity with external public or its representative __ Like external public or its representative __ Gender: female versus male
Relationship characteristics *(internal)*	__ Level of trust between organizations and external public __ Dependency of parties involved __ Ideological barriers between organizations and public
Threats *(external)—check the ones you believe are impactful factors in the situation*	__ Litigation __ Government regulation __ Potentially damaging publicity

		__ Scarring of company's reputation in business community and in the general public __ Legitimizing activists' claims
Industry environment *(external)*		__ Changing (dynamic) or static __ Number of competitors/level of competition __ Richness or leanness of resources in the environment
General political/social environment/external culture *(external)*		__ Degree of political support of business __ Degree of social support of business
The external public (group, individual, etc.) *(internal)*		__ Size and/or number of members __ Degree of source credibility/powerful members or connections __ Past successes or failures of groups to evoke change __ Amount of advocacy practiced by the organization __ Level of commitment/involvement of members __ Whether the group has public relations counselors or not __ Public's perception of the group: reasonable or radical __ Level of media coverage the public has received in the past __ Whether representatives of the public know or like representatives of the organization __ Whether representatives of the organization know or like representatives from the public __ Public's willingness to dilute its cause/request/claim __ Relative power of the organization __ Relative power of the public
Issue under question *(external)*		__ Size __ Stake __ Complexity

A-9. Rhetorical Theory

Case Title

> **Rhetorical Theory**: Use this key to examine a case and determine, using the questions an descriptions provided here (as well as those in your textbook): what is most obvious, least obvious, most important, least important, etc. from a rhetorical theory lens. You can later transfer your choices to the **Case Rubric Master**. Write Y for yes and N for no in the boxes provided below.

PR Defined

The process through which professional rhetors participate in multiple-rhetor contests to adequately address rhetorical problems faced by their employers, clients, and others in society; it involves explaining how organizations strategically or non-strategically manage their relationships through words, interests, opinions, and actions.

Theorist Intent

To examine the dynamic symbolic and language-using processes through which meaning is made in addressing rhetorical problems of contested terrain, etc.

Theory Lens

- When the public relations professionals in a case are viewed as rhetors, and the interplay between the organization and its vested publics as marketplace wrangle, contested terrain, or instances and finding and using all available means of persuasion, how would you describe WIGO? What is at stake?
- How does viewing public relations, in each case, as a participant in marketplace (of meaning) persuasion influence your understanding of the profession?
- What parts of each case become highly important as we look for how symbol and language use and misuses took place?

Y/N	Rhetorical Theory Lens	Questions, frames for analyses, descriptions
Rhetorical situation		**Inviting rhetorical response via public relations**
	Natural disasters	Such as hurricanes, earthquakes, tsunamis, and tornados that do massive damage and significantly impact the organization
	Concerns voiced by others	Largely questions of safety, best practices, ethical behaviors, future plans, etc.

Recognition of problems that need to be addressed	Responses to public demand or desires (such as simple cell phones), emerging physical trends (such as diabetes-related wounds and treatment needs), etc.
Choices, such as products or services	Best solutions to perceived problems, product, or service choice that fill ethical desires, etc. Is the problem (not necessarily pejorative) recognized? Is it met? Should it be? How well?
A matter of sound character	Conversations about questions of ethical intent or behavior, best practices for environmental sustainability or corporate citizenry, etc.
A matter of sound policy	Often hotly contested terrain about human or animal rights, use or preservation of natural resources, etc. Questions if the organization's past, current, or proposed behavior is in its and the public's best interests. Policies such as the legalization of marijuana and workplace productivity, or mandating that all freshmen or sophomores live in college-approved housing are questions of policy
Crisis response	Response to tragedy or significant interruption to business as normal in a way that meets federal guidelines, but also indicates the organization's sympathy (not necessarily accepting blame) for those impacted and its willingness to do what it can to reduce impact; goal to resume normalcy as soon as possible
Rhetorical factors or dynamics (can you figure them out?)	**These characterize and invite WIGO and a rhetorical response**
Situation	Communicative context that requires or allows a strategic, or non-strategic, response
Problem	Arises from the situation as a perceived exigency needing addressed as it affects organizational functioning or goals
Rhetor	The one facing or engaging a situation calling for a response to a problem

Audiences or publics	Changing with the issues or across time, they hold a vested interest in the situation and organization and are perceived, by the organization, as relevant to it
Messages	Symbolic (including language and imagery) representations that elicit meaning
Message sources	Those from whom, what, or where the messages come
Images or opinions	Remembrances from language, symbols, conversations, experiences, and perceptions
Channels	Mode/Mediums through which messages are sent, represented, received, or exchanged
The opinion environment, or call for statement, surrounding each statement	Social, political, economic, and cultural rhetorical messages perceived by any or all participants as relevant to WIGO
Rhetorical responses to a problem	**What the organizations may engage via public relations**
Encouraging enlightened choice	Appeal to agree with one point of view, make one choice in preference to another—the rationale for rhetoric
Adjusting organizations to people and people to organizations	Appealing to those outside the organization to adjust their views of it or use their own appeal to get organizational leaders to adjust to their ways of thinking
Building a case on good reason	Using public relations initiatives to appeal to virtue, fact, and sound reasoning that offers positive solutions to personal and collective problems
Inviting people to use rhetoric as courtship: invitation and identification	Using communicative appeals to help get a public to identify with, or more closely with, an organization; branded merchandise, stories, tag lines, etc., are examples

Building iden-	Developing and executing an appeal to share one
tifications by	point of view or perspective as opposed to another;
shared per-	promotes a shared sense of the world
spectives, social	
construction	
of meaning,	
and connect-	
ing zones of	
meaning	

A-10. Social Capital Theory

Case Title

Social Capital Theory: Use this key to examine a case and determine, using the questions an descriptions provided here (as well as those in your textbook): what is most obvious, least obvious, most important, least important, etc. from a social capital theory lens. You can later transfer your choices to the **Case Rubric Master**. Write Y for yes and N for no in the boxes provided below.

PR Defined

The engagement and use of, or reliance on, an organization's social capital (relational networks) in the pursuit of organizational goals; public relations is used to develop and maintain social networks and enhance their collective interests and identity in a series of relational credit, debt, and expenditure processes through communicative exchanges of obligations and expectations.

Theorist Intent

To understand the public relations professional's ability to rely on social capital to accomplish organizational goals; how it can be understood, accessed, and leveraged for public relations purposes is of utmost importance.

Theory Lens

- How would you describe the social capital belonging to each organization involved in the case?
- How much social capital does each organization have and why do you say that?

- Describe how the involved organizations did nor did not appropriately access needed social capital to achieve their goals or objectives?
- Describe how the involved organizations did or did not appropriately exploit (leverage) needed social capital to achieve their goals or objectives?

Y/N	Social Capital Theory Lens	Questions, frames for analyses, descriptions
Kinds of social capital		
	Bonding	A sense of shared organizational identity (at any level and of any kind of organization) providing a cultural bond among members and leading to levels of organizational success
	Bridging	A sense of ability to develop relational networks across organizational divisions and distances (not just geographical) to build new or ongoing relationships between disparate organizations
	Other	Not necessarily bonding and bridging, seems different in essence but worthy of note
Levels of social capital		**Can occur at one level or among multiple levels**
	Micro-level	Connections one individual has with other people and group memberships; important is the size of the individual's own network, as well as the number of connections the individual has access to (and can exploit) through his/her own network; LinkedIn first, second, etc., levels of connections is one example
	Meso-level	Relational networks existing at the organizational, or group to group level; examples are relationships between an organization's PR department and a media outlet group, the PR department and the Security and Exchange Commission, etc.
	Macro-level	Relational networks existing at the community or national levels; focus is on how social capital is impacted by and impacts community, national, and cultural trends, as well as their outcomes; the social capital present between the countries, and mitigating resolutions between them, relevant to the US-Mexican border is an example

Five characteristics of each public relations opportunity	Can occur at the micro-, meso-, or macro-level (call also occur among and between in the same situation)
Expectations	A does something for B with the assumption that B will reciprocate in the future so an expectation is established in A
Obligation	A does something for B with the assumption that B will reciprocate in the future so an obligation is incurred on the part of B
Credit	The result of B's obligation to A, represented and held by A like a credit slip to be redeemed at another time until B fulfills his obligation to A
Deposit	A relational thing; can be imagined as the value represented by the credit slip help by A that represents the relational value between A and B that A can spend to meet his goals ... unless B defaults on the obligation
Expenditure	The exploitation (use) of the relational deposit created by B's obligation to A, and represented when A acted with an expectation of B; removes or changes (even enhances) the original notion of credit and deposit from the relationship
Possible outcomes of social capital management	**Can be positive or negative in light of organizational goals, and characterized from highly concrete to highly abstract**
Increased and/ or more complex forms of social capital	Additional connections to or within the existing networks, more intellectual capital, or new relationships and networks
Reduced transaction costs	Related to levels of trust and impacts on trust levels; grounded in the available stock of social capital; related to presence or absence of associational capital
Organizational advantages	Outcomes that help an organization do business as usual while maintaining complex networks of relationships; come in the form of increased productivity, efficiency, customer satisfaction, nets asset value, stock value, etc.

A-11. Case Rubric Master

Case Title

> **Case Rubric Master:** Transfer the case assessments you recorded on the other keys to this sheet. You can use this sheet to facilitate discussion and refer to individual keys as needed.

	Y/N	Case Kind
H	___	Historical
HL	___	• Linear
HP	___	• Process
G	___	Grounded–business

	Y/N	Strategy
S1	___	Prescriptive
S2	___	Descriptive
S3	___	Transformative
S4	___	Emergent
S5	___	Linear
S6	___	Adaptive
S7	___	Interpretive
S8	___	Deliberate
S9	___	Plan
S10	___	Play
S11	___	Pattern
S12	___	Position
S13	___	Perspective

	Y/N	Economic Area
B1	___	B2B usiness-to-business
B2	___	B2C Business-to-consumer
B3	___	B2G Business-to-government

	Y/N	Organization Type
FP	___	For-profit
NP	___	Non-profit
NGO	___	• Non-governmental organization
SE	___	Social enterprise non-profit
GVT	___	Government

	Y/N	PR Situations & Contexts
1A	___	Advancement
1B	___	Campaigning & debating
1C	___	Cause marketing & branding
1D	___	Community relations
1E	___	Corporate communications
1F	___	Corporate social responsibility
1G	___	Crisis communication and/or management
1H	___	Development
1I	___	Image & reputation management
1J	___	Integrated marketing communications
1K	___	Issues management
1L	___	Lobbying
1M	___	Marketing communications
1N	___	Media relations
1O	___	Public affairs
1P	___	Risk communication
1Q	___	Special event planning
1R	___	Strategic communication
1S	___	Sustainability

	Y/N	PR Specializations
2A	___	Agency public relations
2B	___	Aviation relations
2C	___	Conference & convention relations
2D	___	Consumer relations

2E	___	Digital communications
2F	___	Education relations
2G	___	Employee relations
2H	___	Entertainment public relations
2I	___	Environmental or conservation public relations
2J	___	Fashion relations
2K	___	Fundraising
2L	___	Government relations
2M	___	Healthcare communications
2N	___	International relations
2O	___	Investor & financial relations
2P	___	Maturing publics relations
2Q	___	Member relations
2R	___	Relations with special publics
2S	___	Sports public relations
2T	___	Travel & tourism relations
2U	___	University relations
2V	___	Volunteer relations
	___	

Y/N	Excellence Theory
	Purpose
___	Propaganda
___	Dissemination of information
___	Scientific persuasion
___	Mutual understanding
	Organizational goal
___	Environmental control/domination
___	Environmental adaptation/cooperation
	PR contribution to goal
___	Advocacy
___	Dissemination of information
___	Mediation

	Nature of communication
____	One-way, complete truth not essential
____	One-way, truth important
____	Two-way, imbalanced effects based on research intent
____	Two-way, cooperative balanced Effects
	Communication model
____	Source to receiver
____	Source to receiver accounting for feedback
____	Group to group
	Nature of research or success of efforts
____	Very little, counting house
____	Little but readability & readership
____	Formative, evaluative of attitudes
____	Formative, evaluative of understanding & common goals
	Excellence PR model found in case
____	Press agentry/publicity
____	Public information
____	Two-way asymmetric
____	Two-way symmetrical

Y/N	**Contingency Theory**
	Competition
____	Was there any? What's at stake?
____	How relevant was it to organizational goals?
	Conflict
____	Was there any? What's being contested?

——	How relevant was it to organizational goals?	
	Threat	
——	Any appraised? Where would you place it on the Dimensionality of Threats model?	
—— ——		Dimension one external internal
—— —— ——		Dimension two: threat level low medium high
—— ——		Dimension three: duration short-term long-term
	Stance	
——	Apology & restitution	
——	Capitulation	
——	Compromise	
——	Negotiation	
——	Collaborating	
——	Cooperation	
——	Avoiding	
——	Compromising	
——	Contending.	
——	Competition	
——	Arguing	

____	Public relations
____	Competing litigation

	Factors contributing to stance
	Organizational characteristics (list the top 5)
1	
2	
3	
4	
5	
	PR department characteristics (list the top 5)
1	
2	
3	
4	
5	
	Characteristics of dominant coalition (list top 3)
1	
2	
3	

1	Internal threats (list one)

	Individual characteristics (list to 5)
1	
2	
3	
4	
5	

1	Relationship characteristics (list one)

1	External threats (list one)

1	Industry environment (list one)

	General political/social environment/external culture (describe)

	The external public (list the top 3)
1	
2	
3	
	Issue under question (describe)

	Rhetorical Theory
	Name the rhetor or rhetors
Y/N	The rhetorical situation was?
___	Natural disaster
___	Concerns voiced by others
___	Recognition of problems that need to be addressed
___	Choices, such as products or services
___	A matter of sound character
___	A matter of sound policy
	Rhetorical factors of dynamics
___	Situation
___	Problem
___	Rhetor
___	Audiences or publics
___	Messages

____	Message sources
____	Images or opinions
____	Channels
____	The opinion environment, or call for statement, surrounding each statement
	Rhetorical response to problem
____	Encouraging enlightened choice
____	Adjusting organizations to people and people to organizations
____	Building a case on good reason
____	Inviting people to use rhetoric as courtship: invitation and identification
____	Building identifications by shared perspectives, social construction of meaning, and connecting zones of meaning

Y/N	Social Capital Theory
	3 levels of social capital
____	**Micro-level:** Describe what exists (relevant to the objectives):
____	**Meso-level:** Describe what exists (relevant to the objectives):
____	**Macro-level:** Describe what exists (relevant to the objectives):
	Characteristics of the opportunity (describe them)
____	Expectations

____	Obligations
____	Credit
____	Deposit
____	Expenditure
	Social capital management outcomes
____	Increased and/or more complex forms of social capital
____	Reduced transaction costs
____	Organizational advantages
	Does the organization have more or less social capital by the case end? At which levels?

Public Relations Cases for Praxis

Preface and Instructions for Use

Appendix B consists of 11 case studies of significant recent and ongoing public relations activity in the US and, to some degree, internationally. They were included as a way to introduce you to a wide array of public relations situations and contexts calling for all variety of specializations. They also illustrate the dynamic and ever-changing nature of the industry. They expand across all kinds of case, strategy, economic, and organization types. You can use the keys found in Appendix A to help you analyze each case by case kind, strategy used, economic area involved, organization type, PR situations and contexts involved, and PR specializations called for in it. Additionally, as you use the chapter and theory-relevant keys (excellence theory, contingency theory, rhetorical theory, and social capital theory) to analyze WIGO in each case, you will gain new insights into possibilities and experience the value of praxis.

Cases included:

1. Update: March of Dimes Rebrand
2. Inside Pediatrics Children's Mercy Kansas City
3. Vanity Fair Women Who Do LiftTOUR
4. TouchNet + Heartland

5. WeatherTech Super Bowl Ad Buy
6. ZF Race Reporter: Europe, Japan and the US
7. Pinnacle Not So Silent Night
8. Lee Jeans—Influencer Relations
9. Fight CRC One Million Strong Collection
10. Tips for Kids—Seventeen Years Later
11. Dairy Queen's Fan Food Not Fast Food Campaign: Retrospective Cases Analysis from the Outside

B-1. Update: March of Dimes Rebrand

The initial March of Dimes Rebrand campaign undertaken by March of Dimes in partnership with Crossroads was first reported in Strategic Planning for Public Relations: Beginning the Journey (see chapter 9). It's brought up to date here to illustrate to readers that a rebrand is a continuous event; it does not end with a calendar year or at the end of the printed page. The MOD rebrand continues, moving from re-establishing relevance to being able to focus on its core mission of fighting premature births. It's branded its relevance with its annual Premature Birth Report Card for each state.—Submitted by Crossroads President Mike Swenson

Background Since 2014 and Current Evaluation

- In 2006 the March of Dimes realized its image needed to be more relevant, relatable, and positive.
- Though targeting all moms with its messages, the majority of moms did not know what it stood for and its corporate partners wanted a brand that resonated more easily with consumers.
- The March of Dimes successfully worked with the Kansas City–based public relations agency Crossroads to bring its brand into the twenty-first century and stand for a solution, not a problem.
- The March of Dimes successfully flipped its message of prematurity prevention (something most people did not view as relevant to them) to "stronger, healthier babies," something just about everyone can relate to.
- It launched its ongoing "Strong Start" campaign.
- Unaided awareness among moms increased substantially and its corporate partners felt an energizing and inspiring reconnect with the March of Dimes brand.

- The historic Walk America, the organization's primary fund raising event, was successfully renamed and branded as Walk for Babies, something everyone can easily understand.
- At the close of 2015, the March of Dimes had re-established its connection to its major publics and been able to turn its reconnect-rebrand efforts from there to its primary aim, leading the way in fighting prematurity.
  - It now has the credibility and resonance allowing it to lead the fight against a current leading cause of premature birth defects, elective inductions.
- At the close of 2015, the March of Dimes is widely known for its annual production of the Premature Birth Report Card for each state and the US as a whole. (See http://www.marchofdimes.org/mission/prematurity-reportcard.aspx for the latest report.)
  - The Premature Birth Report Card is produced by March of Dimes and made available in November, which is National Prematurity Month.
- The local and national media are highly vested in the annual Prematurity Report Card, appreciating the data, graphics, and comparisons made possible by it.
- Following pitches to and news release distributions to top tier media outlets, March of Dimes spokespersons appeared regularly in 2013, 2014, and 2015 interviews with local and national media outlets wanting to know the latest about prematurity trends and prevention. Additional non-interview generated relevant stories were also featured by a multiplicity of media.
  - 2013: 237 news hits; 18,103,123 impressions for an estimated $150,329 in ad value.
  - 2014: 2,384 news hits; 309,767,046 impressions for an estimated $901,986 in ad value.
  - 2015: 4,139 news hits; 204,836,666 impressions for an estimated $6,089,571 in ad value.
- March of Dimes corporate sponsorships remain strong, with sponsors indicating that the brand is relevant, relatable, and positive-focused.
- The March of Dimes partnerships with the Association of State and Territorial Health Officers and many hospitals across the country continue to flourish.
- Department of Health and Human Services continues to work closely with the March of Dimes, in 2016 citing the March of Dimes Birth Defects Foundation as the first option in under its "Find an Expert" in prenatal care web section.

Background for Initial Rebrand Efforts (Reprinted with Permission)

- President Franklin D. Roosevelt founded the March of Dimes as a not-for-profit organization in 1938 in response to the US polio epidemic.
- Its primary goal was polio prevention.
- Its teamwork with scientists and volunteers led to the introduction of the polio vaccine and the almost complete eradication of the disease in the US in 1955.
- Following the successful introduction and use of the polio vaccination, the March of Dimes focused its efforts on the prevention of birth defects and infant mortality.
- As of 2003, more than 500,000 babies were born prematurely, and a record 31% increase in premature births between 1981 and 2003, the prevention of birth defects and infant mortality remain the March of Dimes focus.
- In 2005, the March of Dimes found that its brand did not seem to resonate with moms, corporate partners, and others.
- In 2006, the March of Dimes approached Crossroads for help because of the agency's cause-marketing expertise and not-for-profit organization success.
- Crossroads conducted qualitative research with internal audiences, corporate sponsors, medical professionals, donors, and moms as a way to explore startling statistics regarding premature birth and brand awareness from the *Gallup Consulting's National Brand Study for March of Dimes.*
- Crossroads' research found the following:
  - Most people did not know what the March of Dimes was.
  - The March of Dimes messaging and imagery focused on prematurity, a message that did not resonate with 55% of moms because they did not believe that it was a problem in 2006.
    - Moms were influenced by medical personnel, other moms and grandmothers, and online opinion leaders.
  - The March of Dimes Walk America signature event was not used to communicate the organization's mission and connect emotionally with its audiences and, in fact, most people did not know the event's purpose.
  - Unaided brand awareness had fallen to an all-time low of 9%, down even from its 1993 level of 22%.
  - Major corporate sponsors were considering ending March of Dimes support.
- Crossroads' research also found that the brand was perceived as outdated, irrelevant, difficult to relate to, and problem- instead of solution-focused.

- ○ An audit of March of Dimes messaging and collaterals confirmed the felt disconnect. Prior to 2006, messaging and collaterals had highlighted sick babies instead of healthy babies, problems instead of solutions.
- ○ Corporate partners had designed and produced their own March of Dimes marketing materials in attempts to reimage them as more positive; the March of Dimes identity program was not perceived as clear, simple, and consumer relevant.
- Increasing rates of premature births and related defects had made it imperative that the March of Dimes remain committed to its cause of ensuring healthy babies. However, the March of Dimes messaging strategies and tactics had led to a critical disconnect with its major publics. The March of Dimes faced an immediate need that would take several years to redress.

Statement of the Opportunity

- In 2006, the March of Dimes had the opportunity to refresh the March of Dimes brand and connect with all consumers—especially moms and established corporate partners—by aligning its messaging with mom-driven values and interests.

Goal

- To modernize the image of the March of Dimes by making it stakeholder relevant through a focus on the March of Dimes solutions for healthy babies.

Objectives

- To stand for a solution, not a problem.
- To associate the brand with a personal and passionate tone.
- To position the March of Dimes as a relevant and relatable resource for all moms.
- To recast the March of Dimes as a champion for all babies.

Publics

- The *primary public* was "all moms."
- *Secondary publics* included corporate sponsors, March of Dimes employees, March of Dimes volunteers, relevant medical personnel, and interested nonspecified March of Dimes benefactors.

Messages

Primary

Moms: (1) The March of Dimes celebrates the wonder of babies. (2) The March of Dimes is a champion for all babies. (3) We understand. (4) The March of Dimes has been behind Nobel Prize–winning research and solutions for healthy babies. (5) We want to inspire you and the health of your baby. (6) Working together for stronger, healthier babies.

March of Dimes corporate sponsors: (1) The March of Dimes celebrates the wonder of babies. (2) What we do speaks to your consumers. (3) Your help is still needed to help celebrate the wonder of babies. (4) Working together for stronger, healthier babies.

March of Dimes employees: (1) The March of Dimes celebrates the wonder of babies. (2) Your help is needed to celebrate the wonder of babies. (3) We are all working together for stronger, healthier babies.

March of Dimes volunteers: (1) The March of Dimes celebrates the wonder of babies. (2) Your help is needed to celebrate the wonder of babies. (3) We are all working together for stronger, healthier babies.

Relevant medical personnel: (1) The March of Dimes celebrates the wonder of babies. (2) We understand. (3) We need your help to help us keep helping. (4) We are all working together for stronger, healthier babies.

Nonspecified benefactors: (1) The March of Dimes celebrates the wonder of babies. (2) You can join in the wonder.

Secondary

Moms: (1) We march for all babies. (2) Premature birth is still a problem and it continues to increase even in the US (3) You can stop much of the problem. (4) We are here to help you. (5) Full-term gestation and safety from the risk of prematurity occur only at 39 weeks and later.

March of Dimes corporate sponsors: (1) The March of Dimes celebrates the wonder of babies. (2) Our message does "speak" to your consumers. (3) Your help is still needed to celebrate the wonder of babies.

March of Dimes employees: (1) Thank you for your commitment to wonder. (2) Help the March of Dimes clarify its stand for all babies. (3) The March of Dimes needs you to help it clarify its message of wonder. (4) The March of Dimes values you and your commitments.

March of Dimes volunteers: (1) Thank you for your commitment to wonder.

Relevant medical personnel: (1) The March of Dimes celebrates your commitment to the wonder of healthy choices and healthy babies. (2) We need your help to change the fact that only 25% of women are accurate in their knowledge that full-term gestation occurs at 39 weeks and later.

Nonspecified benefactors: (1) Here is how you can celebrate the wonder.

Strategies

- To invoke a new contemporary brand that reflects all babies in terms of the new organizational identity program and its personality as energizing, celebratory, fresh, inspired, and confident.
- To use consistent positive messaging that makes the March of Dimes commitments relevant to all babies, based on the reengineered mission of "We help moms have full-term pregnancies and research the problems that threaten the health of babies."
- To incorporate contemporary and relevant messengers and messenger sources as part of the message.
- To use shared celebratory moments and humor, when appropriate, to deliver the March of Dimes messages.
- Evolved strategy: Beginning in 2010, capitalize on initial campaign success to augment the seriousness of the messaging to increase awareness of prematurity as the leading cause of newborn death worldwide and promote intervention willingness.

Tactics

All Strategies

- Rewrote organizational mission to "We help moms have full-term pregnancies and research the problems that threaten the health of babies."
- Developed and implemented a new March of Dimes Branding Guide including new logo, color palette, and new approach to photography.
  - The central color of purple was chosen for its biological sex neutrality and its graphic value and intensity characteristics.
- Changed name of Walk America to March for Babies to emphasize the organization's mission and not just the event.
- Redesigned and used website as host to campaign launch and showcase for new brand tone and personality.

  o Central launch message focus was solutions for "questions all mothers ask."
- Developed long-term partnerships with established mommy bloggers who write about their experiences in ways that resonate with other moms and, in so doing, reinforce the March of Dimes message.
- Designed and delivered integrated messages through established channels for communication such as print advertising, the March of Dimes website, Facebook fan page and posts, Twitter, and corporate communications.
- Shared anticipated or remembered celebratory moments for all babies through specific multimedia delivered PSA message campaigns.
  o Stronger, Healthier Baby campaign
  o Coming Home campaign
  o A Healthy Baby is Worth the Wait campaign

Timeline

- Spring and summer 2006: Brand image, identity, and messaging research
- Summer 2006: Recommendations for rebrand
- Fall 2006–2010: Rebrand; messaging for resonation, relevancy, and consistency
- 2010: Increase seriousness of messaging to include prematurity seriousness and intervention choices
- 2012: Continue with the long-term rebrand efforts and consistency of messaging

Budget

- Nearly $150,000
  o Redressed as needed

Evaluation

In process for all objectives (all evaluation is in process as the campaign continues)
- As of January 2013:
  o Unaided awareness of the March of Dimes was up from 9% in 2006 to 25%.
  o The March of Dime mission awareness was up 23% among moms.
  o The March of Dime image measure among mothers was up 32%.
  o The March of Dimes was second only to the American Cancer Society in unaided awareness among moms.

o All 2006 corporate sponsors stayed with the March of Dimes and new partnerships have been established.

o The March of Dimes has seen since the launch of the "Coming Home" PSA and supporting communication a 10% improvement among mothers and a 17% improvement among the general population in the seriousness with which they view premature birth.

o In 2010, the campaign success established the foundation for increasing the seriousness of messaging as it related to premature birth and volunteerism in redressing risk and death rates.

o The rebrand and consistent messaging have attracted the attention of the Department of Health and Human Services, with a request for advance viewings of the PSAs and incorporation of the messaging in the Strong Start campaign.

o The rebrand and consistent messaging have led to partnerships with the Association of State and Territorial Health Officers and many hospitals across the country.

B-2. Inside Pediatrics Children's Mercy Kansas City

Inside Pediatrics is an Emmy Award-winning series following the medical journeys of families and the life-changing experiences that unfold inside Children's Mercy Hospital in Kansas City, Missouri. It just completed season two in 2015, with a third season planned for 2017. The Inside Pediatrics efforts have won many prestigious industry awards including an Emmy, a 2016 PRSA Silver Anvil, a KC PRSA Gold PRISM, 10 Non-Profit Connect Philly awards, and two gold SMCKC awards.—Shared by Children's Mercy Communications and Marketing.

Background

• Children's Mercy is the only free-standing children's hospital between St. Louis and Denver.

• Its mission is to "improve the health and well being of children by providing comprehensive, family-centered health care and committing to the highest level of clinical and psychosocial care, and to research, academic, and service excellence."

• Its vision is to "be a national and international leader recognized for advancing pediatric health and delivering optimal health outcomes through innovation and high-value, integrated systems of care."

• Children's Mercy provides comprehensive care for patients from birth to 21.

- Children's Mercy was the first hospital in Missouri or Kansas to receive Magnet designation in 2003 from the American Nurses Credentialing Center for superior nursing quality, an honor it now has received four consecutive times.
- Children's Mercy is consistently ranked among the leading children's hospitals in the nation. In 2016, Children's Mercy was once again ranked by *US News and World Report* as one of America's best pediatric hospitals in all ten pediatric specialties rated.
- Children's Mercy is home to the region's only Level IV Neonatal Intensive Care Unit (NICU).
- It employs more than 700 pediatric specialists in more than 40 specialties; many of its specialties are certified or recognized as national leaders by leading organizations.
- More than 100 physician scientists, and others, are involved each year in leading research projects.
- An academic medical center, Children's Mercy trains more than 450 medical students, 100 residents, and 99 fellows each year.
- As a leader in pediatric research, Children's Mercy is engaged in more than 140 clinical trials at any one time.
- In 2015, it admitted 14,538 patients, recorded 185,295 emergency/urgent care visits, performed 18,982 in- and outpatient surgeries, and made 6,264 medical transports.
- In 2015, its service depended on 6,294 full time staff, 753 medical staff, and 785 volunteers.
- As a well-loved Kansas City organization by families and staff, Children's Mercy continually looks for innovative ways to celebrate families and showcase staff.
- Already trusted to treat common conditions such as asthma, flu, bumps, and bruises, Children's Mercy wanted to bring wide exposure to the expertise in and promise of its specialty care units, the emergency room, and the operating room.
- Children's Mercy was aware of a docu-series successfully produced and premiered by another children's hospital.
  - Coolfire Studios of St. Louis had served as the production company.
  - The success of the other docu-series suggested the possibility that a similar approach would work for Children's Mercy Kansas City as a venue through which to provide viewers with an unprecedented look behind the walls of the hospital into the world of doctors, nurses, patients, and families while sharing the inspiring stories that happen every day at the hospital.

Background to Implementation

- The series title *Inside Pediatrics* was aptly chosen.
- Coolfire Studios indicated interest in filming and producing a docu-series for Children's Mercy of Kansas City and was contracted.
- KMBC-TV 9 committed to airing the docu-series as the hospital's broadcast partner.
- Six 22-minute episodes were planned with filming to take place in the summer months of 2014 with the first episode airing that fall.
- Episode time slots were likely to vary because of KMBC's lineup commitment, and the docu-series would be up against heavily marketed, long-established programs as well as other less-established programs that would compete for holiday season and turn of the year time.
- Patient privacy and comfort had to remain top priorities.
- Consent agreements had to be carefully articulated to assure the production and sustainability of the docu-series.

Situation Analysis

While a beloved KC organization, Children's Mercy knows that unparalleled affection within the community does not always represent a complete understanding of its full scope or breadth of services. In addition, Children's Mercy is committed to recruiting and retaining the best staff possible while working hard to make them feel appreciated. Finally, in keeping with the continually changing communications landscape, as well as the power of moving video and the public's love of reality-type shows, Children's Mercy was in a position to bring innovation to its story-telling goals. The recent docu-series success associated with another children's hospital suggested a similar opportunity for Children's Mercy Kansas City.

Statement of the Opportunity

Children's Mercy Kansas City had the opportunity to use a docu-series format to tell inspiring and encouraging stories that would connect and engage staff, patient families, and friends.

Goal

- To bring stories of hope and inspiration to its friends and family through a reality-like docu-series providing an unprecedented look at the extraordinary things that go on behind the walls of the hospital as a means of celebrating its families and showcasing its staff.

Objectives

- To receive solid ratings, and to not finish last any one night.
- To foster a sense of total employee engagement even though it was impossible to feature all 6,000+ strong staff on air.
- To surpass the social media benchmarks set by the other children's hospital at the end of its docu-series, especially its 1,980 Facebook fans.
- To generate Children's Mercy Kansas City editorial coverage in spite of *Inside Pediatrics'* close alignment with its broadcast partner KMBC.
- To generate any perceptible higher level of job applications sent through Human Resources as a result of increased awareness and interest.

Publics

Service lines and corresponding staff: To tell its story, and to tell it well, it needed the support of staff in the key service lines that would be featured. The docu-series would provide a transparent look into the work they do daily to help children and families facing difficult medical situations. The cameras would be there to capture their medical expertise, but also the raw emotions and stresses they deal with on a day-to-day basis.

Physicians: Without their full support and vision for the docu-series, it could not take place. Their willingness to lend their expertise and be filmed while they worked was also of upmost importance. They understood the demands of the docu-series, but their concern was for their patients' care. At all times, they were mindful of each family's right to privacy. They were cautiously excited about the opportunity to show the greater community the great work that happens at Children's Mercy. They take great pride in the mission of the hospital and work they do. They understood the filming would show their great successes, but also expose some of the difficult choices and vulnerable moments they face in dealing with critically ill children.

All Children's Mercy staff: The buy-in of all staff was essential to the success of the filming and the associated publicity that would surround the series' debut. Their willingness to be filmed while they worked was also of utmost importance, if the opportunity should present itself. Having the docu-series filmed at Children's Mercy brought a great source of pride, even for those not directly involved in filming. It would also expose the highs and lows of their daily work lives to those viewers outside the hospital walls. It was important to gain the support of this audience who would be critical to success and had the potential to be its best ambassadors.

Families and patients: Without the support of families and child patients the series could not be produced. The raw emotion of their experiences, the inconveniences and uncertainty of film production, as well as the uncertain nature of the illnesses and treatments with which they were dealing all had to be considered when they were approached for inclusion in an episode. It's been the experience of Children's Mercy that most of its families and patients are more than willing to share their stories of struggle and inspiration. In addition, if they were pleased with the episodes they would be natural ambassadors. Their privacy, security, and health had to remain a priority.

KMBC viewers: KMBC loyalists would be those most likely to hear about Inside Pediatrics from the series media host. In addition, their enthusiasm for the episodes would need to trump their remorse at any programming that was moved because of the showings. This group could be great series ambassadors.

Social media enthusiasts: Children's Mercy's general Facebook page already had a significant number of followers, many active with it throughout the year. The Children's Mercy Twitter account also had a robust number of followers. In addition, many of the hospital's families and patients were avid consumers of social media, as were its employees. Social media messaging, when done well, was likely to elicit a lot of excitement for Inside Pediatrics. The intent was to develop a fan base for Inside Pediatrics from the hospital's current social media fans, as well as new fans.

Potential staff: The docu-series would show a glimpse of why Children's Mercy is rated among the best places to work in Kansas City to new graduates, and those looking for new employment options from custodial, to nursing, to administrative, to specialty services, to physicians. If they heard about Children's Mercy through Inside Pediatrics, and could view what went on "from an inside perspective", they may develop a high awareness and interest in career possibilities with the hospital.

Local and national media: As a highly important intervening public (and KMBC as a primary public) their interest in, reviews of, and coverage of the publicity efforts leading up to the docu-series debut, as well as the episodes themselves, was paramount to generating viewership and desired positive responses.

Children's Mercy fan base: These were current and past families, employees, donors, volunteers, referring physicians, etc. Their previous and current support of the hospital merited that its fans be kept up-to-date about docu-series intent and progress, as well as receive celebration invitations when appropriate.

Messages

Primary and Secondary

Service lines and corresponding staff: (1) Be our partners. (2) Participate in showcasing what makes Children's Mercy great. (3) Celebrate your patients and families. (4) Help us give the world an inside look at the expertise and research that brings hope to your patients and families. (5) Celebrate your colleagues. (6) Excuse the temporary filming inconvenience.

Physicians: (1) Be our partners. (2) Participate in showcasing what makes Children's Mercy great. (3) Celebrate your patients and families. (4) Help us give the world an inside look at the expertise and research that brings hope to your patients and families. (5) Celebrate your colleagues. (6) Excuse the temporary filming inconvenience.

All Children's Mercy staff: (1) Be our partners. (2) Participate in showcasing what makes Children's Mercy great. (3) Celebrate your patients and families. (4) Help us give the world an inside look at the expertise and research that brings hope to your patients and families. (5) Celebrate your colleagues. (6) Excuse the temporary filming inconvenience.

Families and patients: (1) Be our partners. (2) Help us give the world an inside look at the expertise and research that brings support and hope to your family. (3) Help us celebrate your victories. (4) Excuse the temporary filming inconvenience. (5) You can choose not to participate at any time; just say the word. (6) We'll guard your privacy, safety, and health.

KMBC viewers: (1) Inside Pediatrics is brought to you by KMBC to let you see inside your beloved KC Children's Hospital. (2) It's the kind of programming you expect.

Social media enthusiasts: (1) Inside Pediatrics gives you an unprecedented look into the expertise and stories of hope and inspiration behind the walls of Children's Mercy Kansas City. (2) Watch your feeds for important news and updates; be an Inside Pediatrics Facebook fan; share on our behalf; let us know what you think using #InsidePediatrics. (3) We'll make everything mobile optimized just for you.

Potential staff: (1) Inside Pediatrics gives you an unprecedented look into the expertise and stories of hope and inspiration behind the walls of Children's Mercy Kansas City. (2) It's a great place to work. (3) Imagine your potential as part of our staff.

Local and national media: (1) We've done something you'll want to talk about. (2) Inside Pediatrics gives you an unprecedented look into the expertise and stories of hope and inspiration behind the walls of Children's Mercy Kansas City. (3) It's a series of stories your viewers/readers/listeners can love. (4) Be part of sharing something great.

Children's Mercy fan base: (1) We've done something you'll want to know about. (2) Inside Pediatrics gives you an unprecedented look into the expertise and stories of hope and inspiration behind the walls of Children's Mercy Kansas City. (3) It's a series of stories you can love. (4) Share in something great.

Strategies

1. Invite special services staff, top doctors, and select families and patients to be partners with Children's Mercy.
2. Keep it real, all the time.
3. Invite annual celebrity participants in the Big Slick fundraising event benefitting the hospital to lend their support to Inside Pediatrics.
4. Keep feedback opportunities open and responsive at all times.
5. Celebrate the series debut in big ways.
6. Be social with interaction opportunity as a key driver.

Tactics

Strategy one tactics: *Invite special services staff, top doctors, and select families and patients to be partners with Children's Mercy.*

- Personal invitations in face-to-face conversations and meetings featuring an outline of the project and potential benefits, with an invitation to be a partner.
  - A number of physicians consented to be partners.
  - The opportunity to film 28 families from 22 different cities across five states was secured.
  - Participating patients ranged in age from 34 weeks gestation to 17 years old.
- Maintained close contact with all volunteer participants, emphasizing that participation could be discontinued at any time without penalty.
- Interpersonal communication was the key.

Strategy two tactics: *Keep it real, all the time.*

- No staged scenes.

- Filming access to operating room, treatments, and family reactions were secured with "good taste" and "a sensitive touch for raw emotion" kept in place.
- A public relations team staff member was always on hand as a liaison.
- Filming took place in the hospital and in homes.
- Months of reviews followed the filming for the purposes of editorial adjustments and promotion appropriateness.

Strategy three tactics: Invite annual celebrity participants in the Big Slick fundraising event benefitting the hospital to lend their support to Inside Pediatrics.

- Celebrities Paul Rudd, Jason Sudeikis, Rob Riggle, David Koechner, and Eric Stonestreet agreed to participate in film scenes.
- Celebrity Paul Rudd agreed to serve as the Inside Pediatrics narrator, and attend the red-carpet premiere party event.

Strategy four tactics: Keep feedback opportunities open and responsive at all times.
- A Communications and Marketing team staff member was always on hand as a liaison.
- Production meetings were scheduled regularly as a means of message and schedule management.
- Each episode was carefully reviewed by strategic staff with the objective of "letting it be authentic while remaining sensitive to the significance of what went on and the visual enormity of some of the images."
  o Occasional adjustments of graphic images, etc., were made.
- Any participant, especially families and patients, could discontinue their engagement at any time.
- Months of reviews followed the filming for the purposes of editorial adjustments and promotion appropriateness.
- Coolfire Studios' expertise was highly valued.
- KMBC insights were invited throughout the process.

Strategy five tactics: Celebrate the series debut in big ways.

- Augment celebration through branded marketing materials.
- Throw a red-carpet style premiere party inviting doctors, top donors, hundreds of guests, and Inside Pediatrics stars (the families).
- Throw employee premiere parties.
- Provide Inside Pediatrics coverage at every available internal contact point.
- Invite, through news releases, advisories, event invitations, back-scenes access, etc., local and national media to celebrate the series with us.

Strategy six tactics: Be social with interaction opportunity as a key driver.

- Developed Inside Pediatrics website.
- Founded an Inside Pediatrics Facebook fan page encouraging followership as well as story-telling and episode review.
- Created and urged the use of #InsidePediatrics via Children's Mercy's established Twitter account, and others, as well as in web content and media pitches.
- Posted series stories to the intranet with opportunities for response.

Timeline

- 13 weeks of filming in early 2014.
- Post-film months of review were conducted.
- Premier parties hosted during the fall holiday season leading up to the series debut in December 15, 2015.
- Introduced all episodes between December 15 and 22, 2014 via KMBC.

Evaluation

To receive solid ratings, and not to finish last any one night.

- Episodes 1 and 2 aired back to back and beat everything on TV except Survivor's season finale (nearly 70,000 households). These numbers did not include DVR views (anecdotal evidence suggests several households recorded the episodes for later viewing).
- Episode 3 performed better than Entertainment Tonight (ET), the show it bumped, reaching nearly 60,000 households. These numbers did not include DVR views (anecdotal evidence suggests several households recorded the episodes for later viewing).
- Episodes 4, 5, and 6 ratings were lower as we neared the holidays, but still performed well against the competition.

To foster a sense of total employee engagement even though it was impossible to feature all 6,000+ strong staff on air.

- More than 450 employees were filmed, directly or indirectly, in the episodes allowing almost 8% direct employee involvement.
- Hundreds of employees attended the "employee premier parties" and 70% of them indicated that they were "proud," "grateful," hopeful," and "blessed" to be part of Children's Mercy.

- Intranet stories about Inside Pediatrics brought an 86% increase in story views.
- Anecdotal evidence from involved doctors demonstrated highly positive results. In the words of one doctor, "I cannot thank you enough for giving me this to remain grounded in the work I do, and educate so many on why our work at CMH is so important."

To surpass the social media benchmarks set by the other children's hospital at the end of its docu-series, especially its 1,980 Facebook fans.

- The Inside Pediatrics Facebook page had 5,200 fans after the first season of the series compared to the total of 1,980 set as the benchmark to surpass.
- In the first season, #InsidePediatrics was mentioned 2,400 times the week of the episodes.
- The episodes, web extras, and series trailer were viewed 51,000 times on YouTube.
- InsidePediatrics.com was visited by 16,900 users.

To generate Children's Mercy Kansas City editorial coverage in spite of Inside Pediatrics' close alignment with its broadcast partner KMBC.

- Inside Pediatrics in association with Children's Mercy Kansas City was featured in 79 local, regional, and national online, print, radio, and TV stories.
  - KMBC mentioned the series 25 times in newscasts on KMBC and KCWE between December 15 and 21, 2015.
  - Mentions and coverage still continue.

To generate any perceptible higher level of job applications sent monthly through Human Resources as a result of increased awareness and interest.

- Job applications increased by approximately 50 per week when compared to number of applicants per week one year ago during the same time period.

Continuing Evaluation.

- The original six 22-minute Inside Pediatrics episode debut was so successful that Coolfire Studios was retained again and a second season (four episodes plus one special episode) was filmed and produced. Episode 1: "A Brighter Future" aired December 16, 2015 at 7:00 p.m.; Episode 2: "Medical Mysteries" aired December 16, 2015 at 7:30 p.m.; Episode 3: "Hurry Up and Wait" aired December 23, 2015 at 7:00 p.m.; and Episode 4: "Hopes and Dreams" aired December 23, 2015 at 7:30 p.m. on KMBC. In support of

American Heart Month, a fifth and special episode, "The Heart of Children's Mercy" was aired February 16, 2016 with a premier party in support of it attended by movie star and Inside Pediatrics narrator Paul Rudd.

- ○ The Inside Pediatrics Facebook page fan levels reached the number of 7,254 by May 31, 2016 (an increase of 2,054 over the first season's tally).
- ○ A third season is planned for 2017.

B-3. Vanity Fair Women Who Do LiftTOUR

Vanity Fair was in search of a unique messaging strategy that would help it resonate more closely with its target market. With the help of Crossroads, Vanity Fair launched the nationwide bus tour, Women Who Do LiftTOUR benefitting Dress for Success. The results exceeded expectations. The campaign was a 2015 KC PRSA gold PRISM winner, and the 2015 Best in Show winner.—Submitted by Crossroads President Mike Swenson

Background

- Vanity Fair Lingerie was a nearly 100-year-old lingerie brand with an awareness problem in a category that was missing the mark with its number one customer—women.
- Other "sexy" lingerie brands seemed to believe that women care only about attracting fleeting and impersonal male attention while "boring" lingerie brands subjected women to a sea of same, frumpy undergarments.
- It's known that not every woman wants to be an "angel" and no woman wants to be plain.
- A competitor audit revealed that no other lingerie brand was speaking to women in a real, authentic way.
- Vanity Fair lingerie products are sold in Kohl's, Macy's, JCPenney, and Sears among others.
- Vanity Fair lingerie is worn for its undeniable support, lift, and a little bit of luxury.
- Market research characterized Vanity Fair's target market individual as someone who
  - ○ is classic and confident.
  - ○ leads a very sensible and well-balanced life focused around her family, friends, faith, and fitness.
  - ○ seeks out timeless styles that are comfortable to wear.
  - ○ exudes grace and sophistication in the way she dresses and presents herself every day.

- o values confidence and being "put together."
- o is busy running businesses, families, government, etc., (is part of Women Who Do).
- o yearns for support and inspiration that comes from connecting with other women and celebrating their collective power.
- o is found in communities across the US.
- o is influenced by traditional media.
- o is a follower of blogs she judges relevant to her interests and lifestyle.
- It's recommended that women receive a proper bra fitting at least once a year, but most do not.
- It's estimated that eight of 10 women wear the incorrect bra size.
- Women indicated that they do not get fitted because they don't have time or they want to avoid the intimate nature of a bra fitting.
- The data clearly show that women like helping other women; this is especially true of Vanity Fair customers.
- Cause marketing is known as a valuable option for companies wanting to reach their targets in unique ways.
- A careful audit of Vanity Fair Lingerie's product lines, the Vanity Fair target market, and possible cause organizations revealed that Dress for Success was an excellent cause partner.
  - o Dress for Success is a global non-profit organization dedicated to promoting the economic independence of disadvantaged women by providing professional attire, a network of support, and career development tools. (www.dressforsuccess.org)
  - o Dress for Success provides professional and appropriate attire, including undergarments. It can only accept brand new undergarments, which means its inventory is always low. Vanity Fair lingerie and the company's commitment to helping others was a perfect complement to the Dress for Success need for undergarments.
  - o The Dress for Success dedication to promoting the economic independence of disadvantaged women was closely aligned with Vanity Fair's Women Who Do position.
- Vanity Fair embarked on the Women Who Do LiftTOUR—a nationwide bus tour with a focus on fit and philanthropy.

Situation Analysis

The Vanity Fair brand was not resonating well with its target market—women. The women it needed to reach were very busy, valued confidence, prized authenticity, busy "doing," liked helping other women, did not get an annual bra fitting, and the majority (80%) were likely wearing ill-fitting bras. Vanity Fair faced a unique challenge and opportunity in its goal to build lingerie brand awareness and resonation among its target market. In consultation with Crossroads, it was anticipated that a Vanity Fair-sponsored LiftTOUR fitting and philanthropy mobile event, benefitting a cause, was optimal for reaching the Vanity Fair market in a unique and welcome way.

Statement of the Opportunity

- To build brand awareness by coming to women where they shop in a unique, sophisticated, private, and authentic way that allowed them to feel good while doing good.

Goal

- To spread awareness of the Vanity Fair brand while helping women across the country feel good while doing good in their own communities.

Objectives

- To secure 120 local and national media and blog placements covering the LiftTOUR and Women Who Do message.
- To fit 5,000 women on the LiftTOUR—and subsequently, donate 5,000 bras to Dress for Success.
- To garner 200 million impressions for the Vanity Fair brand annually (not just from Women Who Do LiftTOUR).

Publics

Women in Vanity Fair's target market: These women were very busy, valued confidence, prized authenticity, busy "doing," liked helping other women, did not get an annual bra fitting, and the majority (80%) were likely wearing ill-fitting bras. They tended to shop at Kohl's, Macy's, JCPenney, and Sears stores. As busy doers, they needed convenience. As confident yet faith and family focused, they needed sophisticated privacy. And, they needed the opportunity to feel vested in their do good opportunities.

Local and national media: A primary and intervening public, local and national media were still highly important in creating buzz about the LiftTOUR bus as it made its scheduled stops, as well as about the double-benefits to participating women—personalized bra fitting and donation of new bras through Dress for Success in her own community.

Influential bloggers: These were fashion, lifestyle, and mom bloggers who best aligned with Vanity Fair's product and brand story. Their cumulative reach and impact through opinion leading were highly important to supporting the authenticity of the LiftTOUR event. The credibility of the Women Who Do message could be credited or discredited by influential bloggers, especially by those who were part of Vanity Fair's target market.

Messages

Primary

Women in Vanity Fair's target market: (1) Visit the local LiftTOUR and help a woman in need. (2) We want you to feel good while doing good. (3) We fit with your desires to feel good and do good. (3) We make it easy to feel good and do good.

Local and national media: (1) The LiftTOUR models Vanity Fair's commitment to helping women feel good and do good all across the country. (2) Vanity Fair's LiftTOUR partnership with Dress for Success demonstrates its commitment to helping women everywhere.

Influential bloggers: (1) We'll give you something that will benefit you, let you feel good and do good, and to blog about that your followers will love. (2) Lead the way in helping women feel good and do good.

Secondary

Women in Vanity Fair's target market: (1) We are part of your confidence, style, and "do good" lifestyle. (2) We're bringing sophisticated fit to you. (3) You can help other women in your community through your LiftTOUR participation and our partnership with Dress for Success.

Local and national media: (1) Great visual opportunity of helping Women Who Do feel good and do good. (2) Cover local authenticity as Vanity Fair's LiftTOUR partners with local Dress for Success groups; we're coming to you.

Influential bloggers: (1) Get your own LiftTOUR experience. (2) First-hand experience makes for best blogging content.

Strategies

- Emphasize significance and credibility behind LiftTOUR launch and reintroduction of the brand as fresh and relevant.

- Highlight authenticity of feel good while doing good opportunity and appeal to sense of philanthropy.
- Offer high profile visual message.

Tactics

Strategy 1 tactics: Emphasize significance and credibility behind LiftTOUR launch and reintroduction of the brand as fresh and relevant.

- Earned, paid, and owned media coverage correlating with the tour.
- Hosted pre-LiftTOUR launch event at Gramercy Park Hotel in NYC for influential retailers, traditional media representatives, and select bloggers to introduce the tour.
  - Included Dress for Success and Vanity Fair leadership.
  - Invited guests offered personal bra fitting
  - Allowed fitted guests to donate one new bra to Dress for Success through the Vanity Fair partnership.
- Hosted eight exclusive blogger events targeting fashion, lifestyle, and mom bloggers, as an introduction to the Women Who Do LiftTOUR, opportunity for personal fittings, receipt of a Vanity Fair product of their choice, opportunity to donate through Dress for Success on a personal "handwritten" note.
- LiftTOUR bus fitting room design and tour schedule plan was fresh and relevant.

Strategy 2 tactics: Highlight authenticity of feel good while doing good opportunity and appeal to sense of philanthropy.

- Offered a mobile, yet beautiful, sophisticated, and private fit lounge to Women Who Do across the United States, in 12 major markets, that let local women feel and do good, and let others know.
  - Arranged 71 different location stops through Dallas, Phoenix, San Diego, Los Angeles, Chicago, Detroit, NYC, Philadelphia, Cleveland, Atlanta, and Miami at local Kohl's, Macy's, JCPenney, and Sears locations.
  - Offered one-on-one personal and private fittings from Vanity Fair.
  - Allowed participants to write a personal note to a Dress for Success recipient of a donated bra.
  - Encouraged participants to take photos and videos with the Vanity Fair "I Support …" signs, ranging from "I support … Strong Women," to "I Support … Paying it Forward," to "I Support … Everybody" and share these stories on their own personal social media channels.

- Earned, paid, and owned media coverage before, during, and after each local stop including radio remotes, geo-targeted social posts, and local influencer and media outreach.
- Hosted eight exclusive blogger events targeting fashion, lifestyle, and mom bloggers, as an introduction to the Women Who Do LiftTOUR, opportunity for personal fittings, receipt of a Vanity Fair product of their choice, opportunity to donate through Dress for Success on a personal "handwritten" note.

Strategy 3 tactics: *Offer high profile visual message.*

- LiftTOUR bus wrap time-lapsed video for public consumption.
- LiftTOUR bus wrap as a moving billboard.
- LiftTOUR bus as a standing advertisement when in local parking lots associated with tour stops and Vanity Fair retailers.
- Earned, paid, and owned media coverage before, during, and after each local stop including radio remotes, geo-targeted social posts, and local influencer and media outreach.

Timeline (15 weeks)

- Pre-July 14, 2014 Women Who Do LiftTOUR Vanity Fair and Dress for Success partnership launch event at the Gramercy Park Hotel in NYC.
- July 14, 2014 Women Who Do LiftTOUR kickoff at Vanity Fair's headquarters in Bowling Green, Kentucky.
- 71 stops, in 12 major markets, between July 14 and October 31, 2014.
  - July 17—Bowling Green, Kentucky at Vanity Fair's headquarters
  - July 22—Dallas
  - July 29—Phoenix
  - August 5—San Diego
  - August 11—Los Angeles
  - September 2—Milwaukee
  - September 15—Detroit
  - September 23—NYC
  - October 6—Philadelphia
  - October 14—Cleveland
  - October 21—Atlanta
  - October 28—Miami

Budget

$900,000 including cost of bus and bus wrap.

Evaluation

Summative

Secure 120 local and national media and blog placements covering the LiftTOUR and Women Who Do message.

- 333 earned media and blog stories netting 141.5 million earned media impressions.
  - Specifically, 33 blog posts totaling 500,000 impressions.
- 141.5 million earned media impressions accounted for 4.532 media mentions.
- 4,532 social media mentions netted 7.2 social media impressions.

Fit 5,000 women on the LiftTOUR—and subsequently, donate 5,000 bras to Dress for Success.

- 5,681 bra fittings.
- 5,402 Dress for Success donations.

Garner 200 million impressions for the Vanity Fair brand annually (not just from Women Who Do LiftTOUR).

- The Women Who Do LiftTOUR accounted for 150 million impressions, more than 75% of the annual Vanity Fair goal of 200 million.
- Total of 242 million impressions for the Vanity Fair brand.

B-4. TouchNet + Heartland

TouchNet retained Trozzolo Communications Group to communicate a company merger to clients and other vested publics. The client retained Trozzolo with a 12-hour deadline to produce a comprehensive 120 day reputation and brand management proposal. The results exceeded expectations. The campaign was a 2015 KC PRSA Gold PRISM Winner, Best of Show finalist and 2016 PRSA Silver Anvil award winner.—Submitted by Trozzolo Communications Group Brand Strategist Jeff Madden

Background

- TouchNet Information Systems, Inc., a small, privately held company, serves the higher education marketplace with commerce management software that assists colleges and universities in streamlining financial transactions.
- TouchNet helps meet the challenge of running campus business more efficiently.
- University clients can use TouchNet's software and services to automate campus commerce and integrate commerce transactions.
- The TouchNet use promise is transformation from costly, paper-intensive business processes to a unified, secure digital environment with real-time data.
- With approximately 700 existing clients, TouchNet was acquired by Heartland Payment Systems.
- Heartland is a Fortune 1000 company (50 times larger than TouchNet) specializing in secure payment processing.
- With only 12 hours' notice (due to Heartland's publicly traded status), Trozzolo was called upon and retained to help manage the brand merger.
- Trozzolo had 12 hours to draft and present a 120-day plan to the client before the decision-makers boarded a plane back to the corporate office.
- In-depth discussions were held with TouchNet and Heartland leadership and 20 employees.
- Existing research and sentiment regarding TouchNet and Heartland brands was analyzed for satisfaction rates, brand salience and value, and the like.
- Similar acquisitions by Heartland, and other technology companies serving the higher education market, were analyzed with the objective of reviewing strategies and tactics used compared to results.
- Research demonstrated that TouchNet had a solid brand image.
- The only negative TouchNet finding was client concern that a large company takeover would net change and more work for the colleges (bureaucracy).
- TouchNet clients voiced appreciation for their ability to talk to top Touch-Net leaders.
- TouchNet clients were clear that they enjoyed their relationships with their existing product and service teams.
- Heartland had an equally solid brand image despite a major security breach in 2009. Since the breach, the company had worked hard to re-establish its brand as a leading payment processor.
- Many of Heartland's core philosophies mirrored TouchNet's.

- The combined resources of both companies could further help the higher education market reach its goals.
- The biannual COMTEC tradeshow was a primary face-to-face opportunity to communicate brand and position.
- It was important, at the next COMTEC tradeshow, that a comprehensive and coordinated enhanced brand message be delivered at all contact points.
- It was possible that struggling competitors would use the acquisition against TouchNet in competitive selling scenarios.
- Industry data indicated that mergers and acquisitions can net significant employee attrition.
- TouchNet retained 190 employees at the date of the announced merger.
- Industry data indicated that mergers and acquisitions can net significant client loss.
- TouchNet had 700 active clients at the date of the announced merger.
- Industry data indicated that mergers and acquisitions can significantly impact the value of publicly traded companies and their portfolios.
- Trade publications were and are clearly known as a key intervening public venue for all specialized industry restructuring.
- Timing was a primary challenge because trade publications work one month out.
- As the public relations representative, Trozzolo had to work under a tight deadline with new contacts from a Fortune 1000 company; contacts who had other priorities, including other acquisitions.

Situation Analysis

Publicly-traded Heartland's acquisition of the much smaller private company, TouchNet, and the subsequent brand initiatives, was necessarily time sensitive given SEC regulations, stock values, and relevant media editorial timelines. Both companies had solid brands and positive positions with their clients and within their respective industries. TouchNet's continued ability to service its clients was significantly enhanced with the addition of Heartland's payment solutions to its lineup. While adding a highly valuable brand to its portfolio, Heartland knew, as did TouchNet, that it needed to clearly and positively represent TouchNet's new structure and enhanced services while preventing significant client or employee loss.

Statement of the Opportunity

To announce the acquisition of TouchNet by Heartland, and communicate the added service benefits from the merger while retaining clients and employees.

Goals

- To do no harm.
- To build on and enhance the TouchNet and Heartland brands.

Objectives

- To retain the existing 700 TouchNet clients and ensure that 90% of the top 50 clients remained 120 days following the announcement.
- To retain the 190 existing TouchNet staff members and ensure that 90% remained 120 days after the announcement.
- To ensure that attendance at the biannual COMTEC event did not decline.
- To ensure that branding was cohesive, specifically in the messaging made available to COMTEC attendees.
- To attract 10 new prospects, within a year, as a result of the announcement and merger communication initiatives.

Publics

TouchNet employees: The 190 TouchNet employees were part of the organization's salient and well-received pre-merger brand. The service they provided to 700 clients was positively reviewed and valued by those clients. As with any merger, the affected employees needed clarity in a situation bound to bring uncertainty.

TouchNet clients: All 700 clients were impacted by the merger and announcement. They needed clarity in a situation bound to bring uncertainty. Reassurance of continued quality of service and leadership access was key.

Heartland employees: A strategic group of Heartland employees was key to the merger and announcement, as well as a seamless transition to a new organizational structure that welcomed TouchNet as a member of the corporate portfolio and enhanced both brands.

TouchNet Prospects: Current and enhanced service prospects needed retained and developed to provide future business growth. They clearly needed to know Touch-Net advantages in light of their needs.

Messages

Primary

TouchNet employees: (1) We value you. (2) We value your service.

TouchNet clients: (1) TouchNet quality and service will continue. (2) The future TouchNet service portfolio can give you even more. (3) It's a plus.

Heartland employees: (1) Help us accept, assimilate, and enhance the TouchNet brand and its + value.

TouchNet prospects: (1) TouchNet + brings even more.

Secondary

TouchNet employees: (1) We want to keep you.

TouchNet clients: (1) We want to keep your business. (2) We won't make more work for you. (3) TouchNet can do even more for you through Heartland technology. (4) You'll still have friendly access.

Heartland employees: (1) We'll help you support the merger.

TouchNet prospects: (1) TouchNet + has even more to offer you with the merger.

Strategies

- Utilize existing communication channels to reassure all priority publics that the acquisition meant only better things moving forward.
- Position the merger as an opportunity for both companies to "move forward."
- Communicate that TouchNet's knowledge and technology, combined with Heartland's payment solutions, was sure to help ensure edge-to-edge commerce possibility and sustainability.
- Position the acquisition as an addition (a plus) to TouchNet's existing positioning instead of an entire rebrand.

Tactics

Strategy 1 tactics: Utilize existing communication channels to reassure all priority publics that the acquisition meant only better things moving forward.
- Use of brand + enhancement and not rebrand.
- Key message development for use in employee training.
- Employee training to facilitate brand enhancement and seamless transition.
- Talking points developed and distributed to leadership.
- Sales presentation and proposal content rewritten and implemented.
- Trade public ads devised as a 2-step tactic, theme "moving forward."

Strategy 2 tactics: Position the merger as an opportunity for both companies to "move forward."

- Media message strategy, emphasizing enhancement and moving forward, sent to corporate (Heartland as a Fortune 1000 company controlled media relations).
- Trade publication moving forward ads designed and first one contracted, enhancement from design and paid placement of second ad.
- Rebranded newsletter produced and distributed to clients and prospects.

Strategy 3 tactics: *Communicate that TouchNet's knowledge and technology, combined with Heartland's payment solutions, was sure to help ensure edge-to-edge commerce possibility and sustainability.*

- COMTEC key talking points developed and implemented as graphics, launch video, traditional collaterals, etc.
- COMTEC open mic forum planned and implemented.
- Rebranded newsletter developed and distributed to clients and prospects.

Strategy 4 tactics: *Position the acquisition as an addition (a plus) to TouchNet's existing positioning instead of an entire rebrand.*

- Enhanced logo, refined brand standards, business card redesign, letterhead redesigned, envelopes and other relevant contact points redesigned and produced.
- Sales presentation and proposal content rewritten and implemented.
- Rewritten sales presentation proposal content reviewed, compared to feedback, and refined.
- First and second trade publication moving forward ads.

Timeline

- 12 hours from initial contact: produced a 120 day first step acquisition announcement and merger message
- 30 days from acquisition: research-driven brand recommendations, key message development, employee training, staff rally, enhanced website messaging, advice relayed to Heartland's corporate communication department, fresh ads for two key trade publications, enhanced and refined collaterals.
- 60 days from acquisition: new sales presentations and proposals content developed, new ads launched in two key trade publications, distribution of rebranded newsletter, planning for COMTEC in process.
- 90 days from acquisition: messaging produced and approved for use at November COMTEC event.

- 120 days from acquisition: evaluation of phase one and plan for phase two, launch second ad in trade publications to enhance moving forward message, launch of refined sales and marketing materials.

Budget

More than $20,000

Evaluation

In Process

- Revision of sales presentation and proposal content
- Employee conversations.
- 120 day review and evaluation in anticipation of phase two

Summative

To retain existing 700 TouchNet clients and ensure that 90% of the top 50 clients remained 120 days following the announcement.

- All existing 700 clients were fully retained. Many expressed excitement about the new opportunities and engaged TouchNet for additional software products and services.

To retain 190 of existing TouchNet staff members and ensure that 90% remained 120 days after the announcement.

- TouchNet lost only one employee out of 190 during the transition.

To ensure that attendance at the biannual COMTEC event did not decline.

- Attendance at the biannual event increased by more than 10%.

To ensure that branding was cohesive, specifically in the messaging made available to COMTEC attendees.

- The client claimed it was among the best work Trozzolo had ever done for it.
- Executives and the CEO from Heartland invited the Trozzolo team to present at a companywide retreat.
- TouchNet staff stated they felt a real vision for the company. They were energized and ready for the next chapter.

- The TouchNet brand is now the most admired brand in the corporate portfolio.

To attract 10 new prospects, within a year, as a result of the announcement and merger communication initiatives.

- Since the acquisition, TouchNet added more than 26 new clients, which was double the amount added in the pre-acquisition year.

Unanticipated impact: Sister companies within the Heartland Campus Solutions umbrella adopted the idea of adding value with the + and used some of the messaging to position what their company + TouchNet would provide to the higher education market.

B-5. WeatherTech Public Relations Super Bowl Ad Buy

A rather small company compared to the traditional Super Bowl advertisers, WeatherTech leaders knew, in 2013, that it was ready to take the opportunity as a means of building brand awareness and giving the American people something to talk about. It did just that and has become, as what is anecdotally known, the "darling" of the Super Bowl advertisers.—Submitted by Kyle Chura Associates

Background

- WeatherTech, headquartered in Bolingbrook, Illinois, has long been recognized by the discerning automotive enthusiast as a supplier of accessories of unparalleled quality.
- Best known for its WeatherTech DigitalFit® FloorLiners™ and commitment to all-American manufacturing, the company supplies products to many automobile manufacturers as an original equipment supplier.
  - All-American manufacturing began in 2007.
  - Its products are not just for car enthusiasts.
- Mission: "Our mission is quite simple at WeatherTech Direct, LLC. We strive to continually exceed our customers' expectations, and it shows not only in every product that wears the WeatherTech brand, but in our culture as well."
- WeatherTech is very public about its commitment "to favor the American economy."
- It is also public about its commitment to "work hard to stay adamantly aware of sustainability and environmental best practices."

- It supplies products as an Original Equipment Supplier (OEM) to many auto manufacturers.
- It supplies accessories to all four German luxury automobile manufacturers.
- WeatherTech recently earned ISO/TS 16949 Quality Standard certification from the International Automotive Task Force (IATF) and International Organization for Standardization (ISO) technical committee.
- WeatherTech employs 1,100 employees.
- Its product development engineers utilize the most sophisticated tools available for data capture and reverse engineering of complex vehicle geometry such as floor surfaces, cargo areas, window openings, or fenders. As a result, the customer is assured the highest standards are met in terms of product fit and finish.
- American promise: "We at WeatherTech Direct, LLC are proud of our investment in the American manufacturing infrastructure and truly understand the marketplace we serve. Through creativity, productivity and innovation—with an eye toward conservation, we will continue to develop the finest automotive accessories you can purchase to protect or enhance your vehicle ownership experience—simply-put, doing things right."
- WeatherTech's marketing focus is to sell its automotive accessories through its website, www.weathertech.com, or over the phone at 1-800-car-mats.
  o Its floor mat sales are predicated on how consumers can protect their second largest investment (to their home), their automobile.
  o 75% of WeatherTech's sales are direct to consumer.
- By the close of the 2013–2014 fiscal year, WeatherTech surpassed $400 million in annual sales.
- WeatherTech retained Pinnacle Advertising and Marketing four years prior to 2014 with the goal of growing the business to the point at which advertising in the Super Bowl made sense.
- The auto industry, especially auto makers, had a long Super Bowl advertising tradition.
- According to CEO and Found David MacNeil, improvements in the economy, WeatherTech's own sales trends, and the Super Bowl reach of nearly 112 million viewers (most who were car owners), WeatherTech knew the time was right to advertise during the Super Bowl.
- WeatherTech bought a 30-second spot during the second quarter of the 2014 Super Bowl.

- WeatherTech knew it would be the smallest company advertising in the Super Bowl, but that could be a publicity and word-of-mouth "something to talk about" advantage.
- In 2013, Chrysler had unwittingly set the stage for WeatherTech when it debuted its Clint Eastwood narrated "Half Time in America" ad, which focused on the automaker's commitment to rebuilding America, and Detroit, one step at a time.
  o WeatherTech's commitment to Made in America, by Americans, with American resources would resonate perfectly with the rebuild idea.
- WeatherTech was clearly aware that Super Bowl ads were valuable marketing and public relations awareness tools.
- First and second quarter spots were sold at significantly higher prices than were third and fourth quarter spots because of the greater likelihood that all viewers would be exposed to them or avoid the risk of the game being a "blow-out" and losing viewership.
  o The average cost for a 2014 30-second spot was $4 million, or $133,000 a second.
- WeatherTech wanted exposure to the diverse cross section of Super Bowl viewers and, it wanted to give them something to talk about.
  o National media coverage and word-of-mouth buzz were key desirables as it started to showcase its digitally imaged floor liners, among other products, as the quality American choice.

Situation Analysis

WeatherTech's product, sales, and distribution numbers had reached the point where its decision-makers knew it could take its spot as a Super Bowl advertiser. A successful advertising debut would position the company for further growth; the Super Bowl was judged as a best venue for the kind of large-scale exposure that the company wanted. Its proposed ad and complementary public relations initiatives were designed to position WeatherTech as "something to talk about" and, as an American manufacturer committed to country and quality auto products that owners wanted in their vehicles (to protect their second largest investments).

Statement of the Opportunity

Small yet mighty, WeatherTech had the opportunity to showcase its brand, and its commitment to quality domestic manufacturing, in a large way through strategically placed and public relations supported Super Bowl advertising as part of its managed path of growing its brand image by leveraging Super Bowl viewership.

Goal

- To present WeatherTech and its quality auto accessory products to Americans in a high profile and enduring way, while clearly emphasizing WeatherTech's commitment to made in America, by Americans, with American resources with products meant for everyone.
- Not everyone who purchases WeatherTech products reads Car & Driver, Road and Track, etc. Anyone who drives a car is the market for WeatherTech products. The Super Bowl spot allowed the company to gets its message to the public utilizing the most watched television program of the year.

Objectives

- To extend the WeatherTech brand to the Super Bowl's nearly 112 million viewers.
- To communicate WeatherTech's commitment to Made in America, by Americans, with American resources.
- To give Super Bowl XLVIII viewers something to talk about.
- To reaffirm WeatherTech's position as the market leader.

Publics

Super Bowl viewers: Anticipated to total nearly 112 million, 2014 Super Bowl viewers would consume media leading up to the Super Bowl, were avid consumers of the ads and halftime show, and would pay close attention to the game until a winner clearly emerged. The vast majority owned autos or were influencers of someone who owned one. A large majority were in a position to buy WeatherTech products. According to Experian Simmons, part of Experian Research Services, the following was also true of Americans who called themselves NFL fans at Super Bowl time:

- The average percentages of household income are as follows: $75,000–$99,999—16%, $100,000–$149,999—15%, Less than $25,000—13%, $60,000–$74,999—12%, $150,000–$249,999—9%, $50,000–$59,999—9%, $30,000–$34,999—5%, $45,000–$49,999—5%, $25,000–29,000—5%, $35,000–$39,999—4%, $40,000–$44,999—4%, and $250,000 or more = 4%.

- Americans who earn more than $250,000 in annual household income are 29% more likely to call themselves an NFL fan compared to the average American.
- Americans who earn between $150,000 and $249,999 in annual household income are 27% more likely to call themselves an NFL fan compared to the average American.
- Americans who earn between $100,000 and $149,999 in annual household income are 24% more likely to call themselves an NFL fan compared to the average American.
- Americans who earn between $75,000 and $99,999 in annual household income are 17% more likely to call themselves an NFL fan compared to the average American.
- Americans who earn less than $25,000 in annual household income are 44% less likely to call themselves an NFL fan compared to the average American.
- In addition, and also according to Experian Simmons, the average NFL fan's anticipated next vehicle purchase (new or used) is: new—50%, used—42%, no response—8%.

Finally, because of its avid consumption of media messaging prior to and after the Super Bowl, this public would anticipate the ad, know when it was slated to appear, and engage in word-of-mouth buzz about it before, during, and after the Super Bowl. This would set the stage for increased brand awareness as a precursor to additional sales opportunities within a large cross-section of Americans.

Media pre-, during, and post–Super Bowl: Media members were and are huge primary and intervening audiences for the Super Bowl. While auto- and sports-related media, especially members of the network slated to air the Super Bowl itself, were of high priority, other media members were also important. Because the Super Bowl is one of the most widely anticipated and viewed events of the year, viewing/listening reading audiences anticipate Super Bowl, including Super Bowl ad, coverage of the event in a pre-event, event, and post-event format. In addition, all media members were generally interested in the Super Bowl and in what advertisers would advertise. Without pre-event coverage of the WeatherTech ad, many viewers would likely miss it. With successful pre-event coverage, viewers would anticipate the ad, know when it was slated to appear, and engage in word-of-mouth buzz about it before, during, and after the Super Bowl. National media were prioritized because of the scope of the Super Bowl. Local media, it was assumed, would take their lead from the national media. To set the stage for the desired WeatherTech conversation, national media had to start talking about it before the ad's actual February 2, 2014 debut.

Messages

Primary

Media pre-, during, and post–Super Bowl: (1) Be in the know about a small company spending big Super Bowl ad money. (2) WeatherTech can do the "you can't do that" American manufacturing. (3) Our 2014 Super Bowl ad is worth talking about.

Super Bowl viewers: (1) WeatherTech is something to talk about. (2) We're all about American and American made. (3) WeatherTech products are for you and your second largest investment, your automobile.

Secondary

Media pre-, during, and post–Super Bowl: (1) Check into and talk about our American made commitment. (2) We're not going away. (3) Our commitment and quality are not going away; we belong in the Super Bowl ad lineup.

Super Bowl viewers: (1) Check us out. (2) Our digitally designed floor mats are for you. (3) Visit www.weathertech.com or call 1-800-Car-Mats to get what you want.

Strategies

- Be memorable.
- Be real.
- Think multi-year conversation with the Super Bowl as a driver.

Tactics

Strategy 1 tactics: Be memorable.

- The 2014 Super Bowl "You Can't Do That" ad featured WeatherTech's commitment to domestic manufacturing, labor, and resources instead of its products, as a direct in-your-face humorous approach to the assumption that true domestic manufacturing can't be done on a sustainable scale.
  o From a 2014 Forbes article, "But in MacNeil's response, as in the Super Bowl Commercial, was: 'We didn't listen to the experts.'"

- The ad used humor to showcase the challenges faced when trying to manufacture products in the US, with a focus on WeatherTech's commitment to doing just that.
- WeatherTech's status as the smallest advertiser in the Super Bowl was a position. As such, it was a memorable position.
- The second quarter buy that guaranteed viewership was needed to make the ad memorable to a large scale public.

Strategy 2 tactics: Be real.

- The ad, and all pre- and post-ad public relations messaging clearly supported WeatherTech's commitment to American made, by Americans, with American resources.
- All ad actors in the 2015 and 2016 ads were volunteer WeatherTech employees; the 2015 and 2016 ads were produced by local production companies.
- Ad quality and "story" were judged as "real" in copy meetings and by viewers at air time.
- Socratic Technologies' two-phase Super Bowl testing found: "All three proprietary Socratic tools used to test the 53 Super Bowl commercials measured high scores for WeatherTech in the crucial areas of engagement, persuasion, positive messaging, brand recognition, and increased purchase intent. The biggest surprise was, the commercial for WeatherTech, the Illinois-based "accessories company."
- The 'You Can't Do That' challenge resonated with subjects who recognized the commercial itself, and interest in the brand amplified as the commercial progressed. WeatherTech's 'Made In America' spot scored some of the highest points we've seen from a Super Bowl commercial. It seems America does aspire to a 'can do' attitude. This commercial performed well on all metrics and scored significantly above average in major indices. WeatherTech's commercial ranked #1 out of the 53 commercials we tested."

Strategy 3 tactics: Think multi-year conversation with the Super Bowl as a driver.

- Included only minimal product emphasis as a purposeful strategy to leave media something to talk about, viewers wanting more, and to lay the groundwork for a continued 2015 Super Bowl ad opportunity.
- Posted "Automotive Floor Mat Maker WeatherTech Will Run Ad During the Super Bowl" news release to PR Newswire, January 23 to create pre-event buzz.
  o Also sent news release and pitch to targeted media.
  o Included an at demand hyperlink for downloadable ad teaser.

- ○ Included offer for a downloadable copy of the ad by directly contacting Kyle Chura Associates.
- Hosted "You Can't Do That" at www.weathertech.com post-Super Bowl ad debut for continued viewing and as the first driver in an anticipated multi-year conversation (www.weathertech.com/youcantdothat).
- Founder and CEO made available for media interviews with national and other relevant media, among them Forbes, USA Today, The Wall Street Journal, AP, New York Times, Chicago Tribune, etc.
- Clearly assumed a significant Super Bowl lineup position as a second quarter advertiser.

Timeline

- 2000: Retained Pinnacle to drive sales and set stage for Super Bowl ad buy.
- 2000–2014 Implemented system of WeatherTech talking points and media training completed with WeatherTech leadership team.
- 2013: Committed to 2014 Super Bowl ad development and spot buy process.
- 2014: Released pre-Super Bowl to strategic media to generate media and consumer anticipation.
  - ○ Embargoed ad to strategic date.
- January 23, 2014: News release posted to PR Newswire and distributed to national media list.
- February 2, 2014: "You Can't Do That" debuted during the second half of the Super Bowl.
- February 2, 2014: "You Can't Do That" available to the public immediately following the Super Bowl at www.weathertech.com/youcantdothat.
- February 3, 2014: News release featuring ad success distributed to target media.
- Pre and post February 2, 2014: MacNeil interviews granted, and additional media resources produced and distributed.

Budget

- 30-second spot purchase price averaged $4 million with additional funds needed for second quarter spot buy.
- Ad production costs.
- Associated public relations fees.
- Total: More than $4.5 million.

Evaluation

In process

- Prior to its February 2, 2014 Super Bowl debut, WeatherTech received specific pre-ad coverage from national media such as the New York Times in its "NY Times Showcase," and its "NY Times High Stakes section," and the Chicago Tribune, USA Today, and more.
  - As an example, the 2014 NY Times circulation rate on all days but Sunday was more than 2 million. Sunday circulation was more than 2.5 million. USA Today averaged a daily circulation of more than 4 million, and the Chicago Tribune more than 300,000.

Summative

To extend the WeatherTech brand to the Super Bowl's nearly 112 million viewers.

- Successfully secured a 30-second spot in the second quarter of the February 2, 2014 Super Bowl.
  - Pre-ad coverage was substantive (see above).
- Successful national reviews.
  - Topped Socrates Technologies' list (see above).
  - Ranked 28/53 on USA Today Ad Meter, with a 5.8 score.
  - CommuniScore gave the ad a "better than average" score.
  - Buzzone Model gave the ad a "better than average" score.

To clearly communicate WeatherTech's commitment to made in America, by Americans, with American resources.

- Ad content clearly communicated messages through copy and visual imagery.
- A February 17, 2014 USA Today feature clearly covered the WeatherTech story, commitment, and products through words and photos/digital slide show.
- Nearly every piece of garnered coverage highlighted WeatherTech's intended messages of Made in America commitment, among them Forbes, Wall Street Journal, NY Times, and multiple others through AP distribution.

To give Super Bowl XLVIII viewers something to talk about.

- Pre-event discussions of the WeatherTech Super Bowl ad occurred in almost all national media and continued for several weeks.
- Nearly 112 million viewers tuned into the Super Bowl during the second quarter.

- USA Today's Ad Meter final rankings placed "Made in America" as 28th of 53 in its ad lineup with a score of 5.58.
- Posted "WeatherTech Super Bowl Ad Scored Big with Fans and Ad Watchers" news release to PR Newswire, and pitched to targeted media February 3, 2014.
  - WeatherTech's own social media interactions from followers indicated high support for the made in America message and the quality of its products.
- As anticipated, while viewers responded positively to "You Can't Do That," they also indicated that were ready for more process and product coverage than was found in "Made in America," something the company planned to supply in its 2015 Super Bowl ad.
  - WeatherTech had clearly positioned itself for a 2015 Super Bowl ad "America at Work" showcasing major WeatherTech product lines, manufacturing processes, and Americans doing the work.
- WeatherTech evidenced significant increases in phone and internet traffic, up nearly 50% over 2013.
- WeatherTech brand recognition increased among the general US public driving double-digit sales growth from 2013 to 2014.
- A 2015 "America at Work" 30-second spot was produced and contracted for the first half of the game.
  - Positioned WeatherTech for a 2016 ad featuring WeatherTech's pride in its American workforce that produces products in America for international distribution.
  - Posted "WeatherTech Returns as Advertiser to Super Bowl Telecast" news release to prweb.com and distributed to targeted national media January 20, 2015.
    - Also sent news release and pitch to targeted media.
    - Included an at demand hyperlink for downloadable ad teaser.
    - Included offer for a downloadable copy of the ad by directly contacting Kyle Chura & Associates.
- Excellent media coverage, fan buzz, and web/phone traffic, as well as sales (double digit again).
  - Web traffic, consumer calls to 1-800-Car-Mats increased significantly over 2014.
  - WeatherTech sales increased by double digits over 2014.
  - Web data, using the metric "sessions" indicated the following: February 1–March 1, 2014 with 1,641,275 sessions and February 1–March 2, 2015 with 2,401,125 sessions.
  - A 2015 media highlight was being featured on ABC World News Tonight with David Muir.

- ○ Set the stage for a 3rd Super Bowl ad in 2016, "Resources" which aired February 7 amidst the publicity generated from the strategic release of the "WeatherTech Back for Third Year as Super Bowl Advertiser" release on January 28 featuring a downloadable teaser, and an embargoed downloadable copy of the ad by contacting Kyle Chura & Associates.
- ○ A 2016 media highlight was being featured on ABC World News Tonight with David Muir, the second year for this high-level coverage.

To reaffirm WeatherTech's position as the market leader.

- WeatherTech remains the clearly most talked about auto accessories manufacturer.
- Anecdotal evidence suggests that WeatherTech has become the "darling" of Super Bowl advertisers; it remains the smallest advertiser in the lineup that generates a lot of buzz.
- WeatherTech has evolved to global exporting of its products.

B-6. ZF Race Reporter/Fan Reporter Program: Europe, Japan, and the US

German technology company ZF Friedrichshafen AG (ZF) used public relations and marketing strategy to build brand awareness and enhance corporate reputation in the US. It did this through a strategic corporate partnership with a newly formed racing series and the introduction of its ZF Race Reporter/Fan Reporter program.— Submitted by Head of Sponsoring and Motorsports Communication at ZF Friedrichshafen Moritz Nöding

Background

- ZF is a global leader in driveline and chassis technology as well as active and passive safety technology in segments such as passenger cars, commercial vehicles, marine, wind power, industrial applications, and motorsports.
- ZF is a business-to-business brand and, with that, has to accommodate the challenges associated with extending its brand beyond its business partners to create external brand awareness and demand.
- ZF is headquartered in Friedrichshafen, Germany with its North American headquarters in Northville, Michigan.
- ZF has multiple US manufacturing plants including those in Kentucky and Michigan.

- Mission/Corporate Statement: "Our enthusiasm for innovative products and processes and our uncompromising pursuit of quality have made us a global leader in driveline and chassis as well as active and passive safety technology. We are contributing towards a sustainable future by producing advanced technology solutions with the goal of improving mobility, increasing the efficiency of our products and systems, and conserving resources."
- ZF has a 100-year tradition of motorsports racing as an avenue for product performance testing, and public relations and marketing opportunities.
- It has a dedicated ZF Motorsports website at http://www.zf.com/motorsports.
- In 2012, ZF successfully introduced its ZF Race Reporter/Fan Reporter program to Europe at the Deutsche Tourenwagen Masters (DTM), the German Touring Car Masters.
  o The Race Reporter/Fan Reporter Program provided behind-the-scenes glimpses into the technology used in race cars; it also allowed fans to participate in behind-the-scenes reporting.
  o From ZF's website: "The ZF Race Reporter Program brings fans behind the scenes to learn interesting facts, race history and technical aspects of race engineering. Fans can get even closer to the action by submitting a motorsports-related question for the chance to become a winning ZF Fan Reporter!"
- In 2013, ZF successfully introduced its ZF Reporter/Fan Reporter program to Japan at the Super GT (Grand Touring Series).
- At the same time as it was bringing its ZF Race Reporter/Fan Reporter program to Europe and Japan, ZF wanted a way to penetrate the US auto market in a significant way through sustainable multi-year messaging.
  o According to Strategy Analytics, the US spent $181 billion in advertising, or $546 per capita in 2014, followed by a 2015 increase to $187 billion total.
  o The US is one of the most difficult and expensive markets in the world to penetrate with new messaging.
- While not as popular as oval track racing in the US, road racing continues to increase in popularity; its popularity in Western Europe, ZF's home base, was already well established.
- Auto racing is a primary automobile, automobile parts, and automobile accessories testing environment. It also provides the opportunity for sponsorships, advertising, and public relations initiatives targeted to racing enthusiasts, auto businesses, and relevant media.
- Pre-2013 found ZF Motorsports in the US auto market, but largely restricted to auto racing teams already familiar with its products and ZF

Motorsports. ZF had some established B2B awareness, but its larger US brand awareness level was limited.

- The US auto market is clearly distinguished from other markets by a public expectation for big power and unparalleled endurance.
- In 2014, the American Le Mans Series merged with the Rolex Sports Car Series to form the United SportsCar Championship under the International Motorsports of America (IMSA) sanctioning body. It marked the formation one of the largest road racing race series in the US.
    ○ TUDOR was the title sponsor until 2016, making it the TUDOR United SportsCar Championship.
    ○ WeatherTech assumed title sponsorship in 2016, which served to change the series name to the IMSA WeatherTech SportsCar Championship.
- Because it was just newly formed, the TUDOR United SportsCar Championship brand had an awareness rating in 2014 of next to nothing, according to IMSA President & COO Scott Atherton.
    ○ This placed the series at or below ZF brand awareness and corporate reputation levels.
    ○ It is known as an environment which promotes technological transfer from race car to road car.

Situation Analysis

In 2013, ZF was ready to demonstrate to the US market that its engineering excellence guaranteed that it provided better products than its competitors. ZF brand awareness and corporate reputation levels were limited in the already over-saturated US promotional market. Its recent success with motorsports partnerships and its ZF Race Reporter/Fan Reporter program in Germany's DTM and Japan's SuperGT series, suggested that it could do something similar to successfully penetrate the US market for the purpose of sustained messaging. The well-known US appetite for big power and unparalleled endurance resonated with the quality of ZF's products and engineering technology. The 2014 debut of the TUDOR United SportsCar Championship series appealed to ZF on many levels, especially the opportunity to build ZF brand awareness and corporate reputation along with helping do the same for the race series.

Statement of the Opportunity

ZF had the opportunity to leverage advantages presented by the newly introduced TUDOR SportsCar Championship series, as an avenue through which it could increase its own brand awareness and build ZF's corporate reputation in the US market.

Goal

- To enhance its corporate reputation in the already over-saturated US promotional market, while leveraging the company's series involvement to help drive awareness of its products and engineering excellence.

Objectives

- To increase ZF brand awareness in the US market through unique entry points for large-scale and targeted messaging.
- To increase ZF brand awareness in the US market, specifically among US auto manufacturers, owners future talent, and motorsports enthusiasts through the successful introduction of its Race Reporter/Fan Reporter program.
- To position the company to transfer technology that was developed on the race track straight to the production line.
- To set the stage for original equipment manufacturer (OEM) conversations.

Publics

Traditional media (paid and non-paid): Both a primary and intervening audience, this included national media such as newspapers (USA Today), television (Fox Sport 1), magazines (Racer, National Speed Sport News, and AutoWeek), and radio (IMSA Radio). Members of this public were interested in what the ZF partnership meant for the Championship series, real-time race performance facts and quotes, as well as the interest value the Race Reporter/Fan Reporter videos might hold for their audiences. Text, audio, video, and still images were valued. Paid and unpaid opportunities were anticipated.

Social media (owned and not owned): This included the IMSA TUDOR/Weather Tech SportsCar Championship website, ZF, and motorsports bloggers; e-newsletter recipients; ZF YouTube channel; ZF Motorsport Facebook and other motorsports fan pages administrators; and ZF Twitter influencers. Social media interests are similar to those of traditional media. Text, audio, video, and still images are valued.

Race fans: Most US road racing fans are also car owners and car enthusiasts. The vast majority like road racing because they are fans of high horse power performance cars. They are avid consumers of all racing series media, whether traditional or non-traditional. The large majority own smart phones and have "on demand" information, interaction, etc., at their disposal. They enjoy the excitement of being at the track and use racing apps (like the IMSA app) to follow the on-track action in real time, making it their own individual experience. The typical IMSA fan has a passion for brands, high level of education, high level of income, and high net worth. Fans tend to be affluent, married, male, and 52 years of age. Seventy-five percent are likely to try a sponsor's product or service, while 83% state that sponsorship of a race series makes them feel good about a product; they are likely to recommend it to someone else.

Race teams/drivers/owners: Race teams, drivers, and owners are always on the lookout for product partnerships that help underwrite their efforts, as well as chances to experience the benefits of the best race performance products and engineering available. They are car owners and enthusiasts.

Auto manufacturers: Auto, auto parts, and auto accessories manufacturers are always on the lookout for opportunities to pursue OEMs, parts, and accessories that complement their manufacturing and marketing plans.

Messages

Primary

Traditional media (paid and unpaid): (1) Our partnership is one of excellence and commitment that benefits your publics. (2) Listeners, viewers, readers, followers will want to get behind-the-scenes insights. (3) A different race fan will get to be our fan reporter at each of the race tracks ZF has announced on its race schedule. *Secondary*: (1) We have the content and collaterals to help you do your job and engage your audience.

Social media (owned and not owned): (1) Our partnership is one of excellence and commitment that benefits your followers/fans. (2) Followers will want to get behind-the-scenes insights. (3) A different race fan will get to be our fan reporter at each of the race tracks ZF has announced on its race schedule. *Secondary*: (1) We have the content to help you do your job and engage your audience.

Race fans: (1) ZF is a committed series and fan partner. (2) You get behind-the-scenes insights from us. (3) You can be our fan reporter. *Secondary*: (1) We have the auto technology and expertise you want. (2) Make it your own experience.

Race teams/drivers/owners: (1) ZF is a committed series and fan partner. (2) Join us in providing behind-the-scenes insights, data collection included. *Secondary*: (1) We have the auto parts and expertise you need.

Auto manufacturers: (1) We have the technology and expertise you need.

Strategies

- Use innovative approaches to spotlight ZF performance and engineering.
- Be relevant to auto manufacturers, retailers, and enthusiasts in the US.
- Bring fans closer to the action and provide racing insights from experts who understand the many complex facets of the motorsports industry.

Tactics

Strategy 1 tactics: Utilize innovative approaches to spotlight ZF performance and engineering. (2014–2016)

- In 2014, ZF entered into and announced one of the first corporate partnerships with the newly formed TUDOR United SportsCar Championship.
  - Announced via Championship series-sponsored press conference, releases, etc.
  - Received promised partnership publicity efforts, signage, etc., for partnership duration.
- In 2014, ZF announced its Race Reporter/Fan Reporter program as part of its involvement in the newly formed TUDOR United SportsCar Championship series.
- In 2015–2016 ZF continued the TUDOR United SportsCar Championship (becoming the IMSA WeatherTech Sports Car Championship in 2016) partnership.
- In 2014–2016 ZF continued the Race Reporter/Fan Reporter program.

Strategy 2 tactics: Be relevant to auto manufacturers, retailers, and enthusiasts in the US. (2014–2016)

- The extended Championship series partnership communicated ZF's commitment to the US auto racing industry, and general auto market.
- ZF product performance on track demonstrated ZF quality.
- ZF product and service support teams on site demonstrated ZF commitment.

Strategy 3 tactics: Bring fans closer to the action and provide racing insights from experts who understand the many complex facets of the motorsports industry. (2014–2016)

- The ZF Motorsports Race Reporter/Fan Reporter program was carefully planned, with US preferences in mind, to provide behind-the-scenes insight about product and track performance, engineering excellence and, when strategic, ZF products and expertise.

- The ZF Motorsports Race Reporter/Fan Reporter program was open to all interested fans with the invitation to apply found at www.zf.com and widely communicated through owned, paid, earned, and shared media.
- ZF retained talent to script, shoot, edit, and produce three videos (one featuring the on-site track, one featuring technology, and a third featuring a pre-qualified fan in interview action) prior to six or seven selected IMSA WeatherTech SportsCar Championship races. 2014: Daytona International Speedway, Sebring International Raceway, Detroit Belle Isle Park, Watkins Glen International, Indianapolis Motor Speedway, Circuit of the Americas (COTA), and Road Atlanta. 2015: Daytona, Sebring, Detroit, Lime Rock Park, Road America, COTA, and Road Atlanta. 2016: Daytona, Sebring, Detroit, Canadian Tire Motorsport Park (CTMP), COTA, and Road Atlanta.
- Promoted all three videos from each race through traditional media as near to race time as possible.
- Promoted all three videos from each race through owned social media channels (Facebook, Twitter, YouTube, Instagram) associated with ZF Motorsport, earned motorsports media outlets, and others as near to race time as possible. Social promotion was critical.
- Published high res photos from the race track prior to each race and posted them (with appropriate messaging) to Facebook, Twitter, and Instagram as near to race time as possible.
- Timeliness is an important factor. All three videos were to be shot, edited and posted before the main event race started or shortly thereafter. This gave, the targeted audience an immediate connection to the race weekends as well as allowed ZF to take advantage of race weekend "media talk," social media buzz, and all other race related internet traffic in a timely manner.

Timeline

- 2013: ZF ready for the US market with 2014 brand awareness and corporate reputation preparations underway.
- January 2014: ZF TUDOR United SportsCar Championship partnership announced at a press conference at Daytona International Speedway leading into the Rolex 24 At DAYTONA race.
- January 2014: Race Reporter/Fan Reporter program announced at the same press conference the series partnership was announced.

- 2014–2016: TUDOR United SportsCar Championship (became WeatherTech SportsCar Championship in 2016) partnership retained.
- 2014–2016: ZF Race Reporter/Fan Reporter program maintained.

Budget

Nearly $1 million in total from 2014 to 2016 for all cumulated ZF motorsports communication activities in the US (activation projects, social media, press relations, etc.)

Evaluation

Summative

To increase ZF brand awareness in the US market through unique entry points for large-scale and targeted messaging.

- Secured a successful three-year (and counting) partnership with the newly formed TUDOR United SportsCar Championship (became WeatherTech SportsCar Championship in 2016) series.
- The WeatherTech SportsCar Championships series is broadcast via Fox Sports 1 to more than 85 million homes, as well as being streamed live to international fans.
- The three-year visual representation of ZF kept the company top-of-mind with those involved in or covering the series.
- The quality of the Championship series positively impacted the ZF brand in the US through association and earned media coverage.

To increase ZF brand awareness in the US market, specifically among US auto manufacturers, owners future tanent, and motorsports enthusiasts through the successful introduction of its Race Reporter/Fan Reporter program.

- The Championship partnership, and accompanying IMSA promotion of ZF, kept ZF top-of-mind for three years in 37 races throughout the US.
  - ZF signage was present at all of the races, specifically in the paddock as well as in prominent track positions where available.
- Public views of the Race Reporter/Fan Reporter videos demonstrated increasing brand awareness, as well as the value associated with ZF's corporate reputation and its ability to deliver what its target publics wanted in its series videos. It's important to note that 2014 viewers had to "pull" the

videos to them, so the act of video watching indicated a willing engaged individual. Post-2014, saw a Facebook change when videos auto-played; this increases plays but deceases seconds viewed.

- o 2014: All three videos delivered for fan consumption through ZF's You-Tube channel, with Facebook video posts and Twitter tweets also drivers. Total YouTube views among all 21 videos totaled 9,092. Total views via Facebook (controlling for a 4-race delay for Facebook content) totaled 18,830. Total ZF brand and corporate exposure was nearly 28,000, though Facebook did not make analytics for viewed videos available until race six.
- o 2015: All three videos delivered for fan consumption through ZF's You-Tube channel, with Facebook video posts and Twitter tweets also drivers. Total YouTube views among all 21 videos totaled 8,751. Total impressions via Facebook totaled more than 6.5 million. Total Twitter impressions totaled more than 600K. Total ZF brand and corporate exposure was more than 7.1 million.
- o 2016: All three videos delivered for fan consumption through ZF's You-Tube channel, with Facebook video posts and Twitter tweets also drivers. Total YouTube views among 18 videos totaled more than 13,6480. Total impressions via Facebook were more than 6.3 million, and via Twitter more than 1.7 million.
  - The 2016 video views attested to the growing video popularity which, in turn, illustrated the ZF's growing brand awareness and enhanced corporate reputation in the US.

To position the company to transfer technology that was developed on the race track straight to the production line.

- ZF's standing partnership access to Championship series participants allowed it to track and record the performance data of select products. The race and fan reporter videos were able to highlight some of these partnerships and provided data.
- The technical videos served as collaborative on-track ventures and testimonies to what ZF was all about.

To set the stage for original equipment manufacturer (OEM) conversations.

- The success of ZF's three-year Championship series partnership, as well as the more than 3 million views of its Race Reporter/Fan Reporter videos to date, did much to set the stage for ensuing OEM conversations.

B-7. Pinnacle Not So Silent Night

Not So Silent Night was the result of the combined efforts of Pinnacle Entertainment, Ameristar St. Charles, River City, and sponsor partner KLOU. In 2014, the 2-year tradition of offering a life-sized gingerbread house dining experience and showcasing the culinary arts team talent while providing philanthropic support to the Center for Hearing & Speech was successfully expanded to two properties.—Submitted by Director of Public Relations at Pinnacle Entertainment Roxann Kinkade

Background

- Pinnacle Entertainment, Inc. is a dynamic and growing casino entertainment company with nearly 15,000 team members.
- Pinnacle Entertainment owns and operates 15 gaming properties located in Colorado, Indiana, Iowa, Louisiana, Mississippi, Missouri, Nevada, and Ohio.
- Pinnacle's culture is guided by its values—integrity, care, excellence, innovation, and ownership.
- At the core of Pinnacle Entertainment's corporate philosophy is a commitment to the communities in which it operates—not only as a major employer, but as a significant contributor to local schools, infrastructures, and charities.
- The last few months of the year are known commonly as the "Giving Season" for the non-profit community. As the holidays near, it may be that people feel encouraged to give more generously.
  - In 2007, The Center on Philanthropy (COP) at Indiana University found that respondents reported giving about 24% of their annual total between Thanksgiving and New Year's Day.
    - A more recent COP study focused on high-net worth donors (defined as households with income greater than $200,000 and net worth over $1,000,000) found that 42.7% of those surveyed gave more during the holidays than the rest of the year; 44.4% reported giving "about the same."
- Ninety percent of Americans celebrated Christmas, Kwanza, or Hanukah in 2013, according to the National Retail Federation.
- Ninety percent of Americans will donate to charity during the holiday season. According to a 2013 Charity Navigator poll, 90% of poll participants donated in 2012 with more than 91% intending to give in the 2014 season.
- A Pew Research Center survey conducted in December of 2013, among a representative sample of 2,001 adults nationwide, explored Christmas

plans, childhood traditions, and likes and dislikes about the holiday season. It found that most Americans say gathering with family and friends is what they most look forward to about Christmas and the holidays, one-third say they dislike the materialism of the holidays, one-fifth dislike the expenses associated with the season, and one-tenth dislike holiday shopping and the crowded malls and stores.

- Ameristar St. Charles and River City both have traditions of supporting the community through donations and volunteerism.
  - o Philanthropic funds had been directed by River City to the Center for Hearing and Speech in previous years.
    - The Center for Hearing and Speech is a local organization that works to improve the quality of life for individuals with hearing and speech disorders by providing high-quality services regardless of ability to pay.
- Ameristar St. Charles and River City employees were known to give back to others during the holiday season.
- Ameristar St. Charles and River City culinary arts teams were known as creative, fun, and the best in the market. Chef Stephan was the reigning American Culinary Federation National Pastry Chef of the 2014 Year.
- The life-sized gingerbread house building opportunity was already part of River City holiday tradition.
  - o In 2013 its efforts raised $2,000 for the Center for Hearing and Speech.
  - o 2014 was the third year for the gingerbread project at River City, thus making it less of a news story.
- The local Christmas station KLOU had an established history of supporting the Center for Hearing and Speech.
  - o KLOU's weekly reach was more than 800,000 St. Louis residents.
- Ameristar St. Charles and River City each had solid Twitter followers and a significant number of Facebook likes. Both social media platforms were promising low-cost avenues for strategic messaging.

Situation Analysis

Ameristar St. Charles and River City approached the 2014 holiday season recognizing the popularity of the 2012 & 2013 gingerbread dining experience at River City, anticipating space at both properties for 2014 life-size gingerbread houses, celebrating their award-winning national chefs, and anticipating continued support from Pinnacle for the properties' community commitments. The situation was optimal for increasing efforts in 2014 to provide guests with exclusive gingerbread house holiday dining experiences at both properties while supporting the local Center for Hearing and Speech.

Statement of the Opportunity

Pinnacle Entertainment had the opportunity to expand the 2012 and 2013 gingerbread house exclusive dining success to both of its St. Louis properties, showcase its talented and award-winning culinary arts team in the building of two life-size gingerbread houses for guests' exclusive holiday dining experiences, while also benefitting the Center for Hearing and Speech.

Goal

- To position Ameristar St. Charles and River City Casino as the top attractions in St. Louis at which to make memories during the holiday season, showcase the talent of the culinary arts team, and raise philanthropic dollars for the local Center for Hearing and Speech.

Objectives

- To offer the public an exclusive opportunity to create holiday memories by dining inside life-size gingerbread houses during the Thanksgiving to Christmas holiday season.
- To help more team members engage in the community by providing the opportunity to create the house at their property, take care of it, and serve guests dining in that house.
- To showcase the talent of the culinary arts team through the creation of the gingerbread houses and the special holiday menus served to the exclusive house guests.
- To generate $5,000 from the $25 non-refundable gingerbread dining experience donation reservation fees as philanthropic support for the Center for Hearing and Speech, ideally generating 100 reservations for each property's gingerbread house dining experience.
  - o 246 dining slots could be accommodated at each site, controlling for 45 minute dining experiences.

Publics

Team members: The excitement for and talent from the culinary arts team was essential to the success of the house building. In addition, their enthusiasm would translate to enthusiasm from other team members. Word-of-mouth among all team members would transfer to word-of-mouth local buzz.

Holiday celebrants wanting a unique dining experience, especially guests in the St. Louis market: Largely assumed to be locals in the St. Louis area, these people were part of the 90% of Americans who celebrate the holiday seasons, indicating that spending time with family and friends was their favorite part of the celebrations. These people also likely fall into the majority of Americans who give philanthropically between Thanksgiving and Christmas. As locals, they were likely familiar with KLOU The Christmas Station. Many were also voluntarily connected to the properties as Twitter and Facebook followers.

Local media: An intervening public, its help was needed to let as many people as possible know of the gingerbread house exclusive dining experience. Included in the list of targeted media were KLOU and its companion stations at iHeartMedia, local television stations (the visual opportunities were superb), local print media (the opportunity to interview and photograph locals was welcomed), and food writers (these persons are always interested in what celebrity chefs are doing).

Messages

Primary

Team members: (1) Let's celebrate the holidays with the life-size gingerbread building tradition. (2) Let's see who can be the most creative in building a dream life-size gingerbread house. (3) Let's give our guests a memory-making holiday experience.

Holiday celebrants wanting a unique dining experience, especially guests in the St. Louis market: (1) Make Ameristar St. Charles and River City part of your holiday tradition. (2) 100% of your reservation donation benefits the Center for Hearing and Speech. (3) You can help others while enjoying a holiday tradition with your friends. (4) The executive pastry chefs at Ameristar St. Louis and at River City have been named American Culinary Federation Pastry Chefs.

Local media: (1) Ameristar and River City are proud of their community partnerships and they donate hundreds of thousands of dollars to support their communities each year. (2) The executive pastry chefs at Ameristar St. Louis and at River City have been named American Culinary Federation Pastry Chefs. (3) 100% of reservation donations benefit the Center for Hearing and Speech. (4) We'll share details about the creative elements of the houses as we receive them.

Strategies

- Partner with iHeartMedia, specifically KLOU 103.3 The Christmas Station, for promotion purposes.

- Develop key messages supporting Ameristar St. Charles and River City as the top attractions at which to make holiday memories.
- Leverage uniqueness and scope in house building.

Tactics

Strategy 1 tactics: Partner with iHeartMedia, specifically KLOU 103.3 The Christmas Stations, for promotion and endorsement purposes.

- New releases to local target media.
- Media advisory inviting media to watch and chronicle home-building.
- KLOU-produced and broadcast public service announcements.
- Depend on KLOU to utilize its digital followings to bring awareness to the event.

Strategy 2 tactics: Key messages supporting Ameristar St. Charles and River City as the top attractions at which to make holiday memories.

- News releases to local target media.
- Media advisory inviting media to watch and chronicle home-building.
- Facebook and Twitter messaging.
- Pre-event opening property signage.
- Event weeks property signage.
- Website content: Ameristar St. Charles, River City, KLOU, Center for Hearing and Speech.
- Printed special gingerbread dining menus.
- Selfie-station for guest use, selfie-contest offered exclusively through KLOU.
- Staff training using key messages.
- Question and answer talking points.
- Back of house signage and information emails (for internal use).
- Provide $100 gift certificates with one-night hotel stay to direct KLOU selfie contestants to property sites.

Leverage uniqueness and scope in house building.

- Each house could accommodate six guests.
- The exclusive dining experience was available for breakfast, lunch, and dinner.

- 1,300 pounds of gingerbread, 395 pounds of powdered sugar, 70 pounds of Rice Krispy treats, 51 pounds of modeling chocolate, 20 pounds of Isomalt, and additional miscellaneous products were used in the house structures.

Timeline

- Media pitches made and releases sent November 11.
- Reservations taken November 11 to December 24.
- Property pre-event signage and web content in place November 15 to 24.
- Donation (nonrefundable reservation) seating available November 24 to December 24 from 7 a.m. to 11 p.m.

Budget

- $400 in collateral materials for each property.
- Nearly $8,000 donated by Paric Corporation—Costs associated with 1,300 pounds of gingerbread, 395 pounds of powdered sugar, 70 pounds of Rice Krispy treats, 51 pounds of modeling chocolate, 20 pounds of Isomalt, and additional miscellaneous products used in the house structures.
- The wages and salaries associated with the 70 team members it took to build the houses—Ameristar Facilities and Bakery TMs donated labor.

Evaluation

In Process

- A new Union Station holiday family experience competed for guests' attention.

Summative

To offer the public an exclusive opportunity to create holiday memories by dining inside giant gingerbread houses during the Thanksgiving to Christmas holiday season.

- KLOU, as the sponsor partner, provided 15 live promotions per week for a total of 90 spots, 15 recorded promotions per week for a total of 90 spots, website event listings on all six iHeartMedia radio stations, and Not So Silent Night promotion on its homepage for four weeks.
- Chef John Johnson was interviewed on the Michelle Esswein talk radio show on NewsTalk 97.1.
- One unique television story aired on KDSK's Show Me St. Louis was broadcast four times.

- 10 unique print stories were secured, nearly all of them mentioning such words as family, tradition, and holiday and thereby positioning Ameristar St. Charles and River City as places at which to create holiday family traditions.
  - Every press article mentioned the 100% tax deductible donation reservation to the Center for Hearing and Speech.
  - Every press article mentioned the culinary skill of the chefs.
  - Three of the 10 articles mentioned Chef Stephan as the reigning AFC National Pastry Chef of the Year.
- 15 positive guest tweets were received via Twitter, with 115 tweets total including those generated by Pinnacle, KLOU, and the Center for Hearing and Speech.
- A total of 2,000 organic Facebook likes, comments, and shares were generated.

To help more team members engage in the community by providing the opportunity to create the house at their property, take care of it, and serve guests dining in that house.

- More than 70 team members were involved in building the houses.
- Many team members helped care for the houses and served guests in the houses.

To showcase the talent of the culinary arts team through the creation of the gingerbread houses and the special holiday menus served to the special house guests.

- Chef Jon Johnson was interviewed on the Michelle Esswein talk radio show on NewsTalk 97.1
- Three of the ten media articles generated mentioned that Chef Stephan was the reigning AFC National Pastry Chef of the Year.
- All chefs voice enthusiasm and excitement as they drew up their house-building plans and moved to execution.
- Participating guests voiced enthusiasm for the special menus and dining experience.

To generate $5,000 from the $25 non-refundable gingerbread dining experience reservation fees as philanthropic support for the Center for Hearing and Speech, ideally generating 100 reservations for each property's gingerbread house dining experience.

- 260 reservations total (131 at St. Charles and 129 at River City) surpassing the targeted 100 reservations per property, and 200 total reservations by 60.
- $6,500 raised, surpassing $1,500 more than the $5,000 objective.

B-8. Lee Jeans—Influencer Relations

Lee Jeans works regularly to counter the lingering stereotype that its jeans are not "style right" or "socially acceptable" for out-of-home situations. It partnered with Crossroads to positively impact the perception of Lee Jeans among key influencers. The results exceeded the objectives. The campaign was a 2015 KC silver PRISM winner.—Submitted by Crossroads President Mike Swenson

Background

- Lee Jeans is a 125-year-old American denim manufacturer.
- Its product line includes affordable, great fitting, and fashionable jeans for men, women, and children.
- Despite its commitment to fashion-forward style and excellent fit for all shapes and sizes, the Lee Jeans brand still nets unfavorable impressions that include: 1980s light blue jeans, loose and durable construction worker, or "mom and dad" jeans.
- Despite the company's efforts, many consumers do not believe Lee Jeans are "style right" nor are they acceptable for "socially exposed" out-of-home situations such as the office, date night, or dinner or drinks with friends.
- Lee Jeans is still one of the top denim brands in the US, competing with Levi's, Wrangler, American Eagle Outfitter, and Old Navy.
- Lee's segmentation research coins its target customer as a confident daily enthusiast who is characterized as being a father or mother, having an independent income, and enjoying fashion and style with a focus on comfort.
- Lee's consumer research shows that people who try Lee buy Lee.
- Crossroads had a pre-established relationship with Lee's in-house product designers and trend experts that let it glean product and trend expertise and stay abreast of enticing information that can be shared with magazine editors.
- Editors look to Lee as a fashion resource, frequently approaching Crossroads (as its PR representative) with questions such as, "What are the up-and-coming back pocket denim trends?" and "What do men look for when making denim purchases?"
- Key influencer endorsements and praise are especially impactful when trying to refine and redefine senses of style and brand image in the fashion and style industries, the jeans market was no exception.
- Lee had just introduced its new Curvy Fit, Easy Fit, and Modern Series collections.

- Favorable online content and national fashion and lifestyle magazine content were known to drive product purchase.

Situation Analysis

In its commitment to making its brand image more relevant as style right and socially acceptable for out-of-home situations, Lee knew it needed to convince key influencers first. Key influencers, including all kinds and levels of traditional media and their digital counterparts, as well as the growing sphere of bloggers, are powerful trend and style setters in the fashion industry. Lee's own insight from consumer research showing that people who try Lee buy Lee, was an excellent platform from which to approach and convince key influencers.

Statement of the Opportunity

To invite key influencers, or representatives of key influencer media, to try Lee so they could "buy" Lee as style right and socially acceptable out-of-home wear, or even start wearing Lee Jeans themselves.

Goal

- To positively impact the perception of Lee Jeans among key influencers, as well as promote the launch of the new Curvy Fit, Easy Fit, and Modern Series Collections.

Objectives

- To improve the perceptions of Lee Jeans in the online space, improvement demonstrated by amount and type of coverage, as well as source of coverage. Intent: host fun blogger events and outfit 20 influencers, attend Dad 2.0 Summit and outfit 200 attendees who Tweet their experiences.
- To improve the perceptions of Lee Jeans within national and lifestyle magazines where favorable endorsements drive product purchase, improvement demonstrated by amount and type of coverage, as well as source of coverage. Intent: Secure at least 20 fashion placements in targeted national magazines.

Publics

Market editors: Already following Lee Jeans product and brand developments, as well as participants in pre-established relationships with Crossroads as a conduit for Lee advice and insights into style and trends, they valued timely information and product samples that allowed them to do their jobs. They were open to new information, even information that would elevate the Lee Jeans brand. Heavily inundated with email and phone pitches, they welcome face time and personal communication.

Bloggers: Those most relevant to the Lee Jeans brand are always on the lookout for new and relevant blog material. They are characterized by a sense of independence and entrepreneurialism. Heavily inundated with email and phone pitches, they welcome face time and personal communication. Their days are characterized by hit and miss pitch relationships from companies that simply "want something" from them. Most female bloggers find trying on jeans to be very intimidating. Male bloggers don't feel they have time to shop or try a new style. Many bloggers were known to view Lee jeans as a "mom or dad" jean brand from the 1980s. Lee Jeans viewed top bloggers in Minneapolis and Dallas as key targets. The Dad 2.0 Summit is host to many of the country's most influential male bloggers.

National Media: Always interested in soft stories such as hot looks for the next season, Lee Jeans could provide them with content. The best way to do this, and one of the most efficient, was through a co-operative satellite media tour bringing with it its own personality endorsement.

Men and women who qualify as confident daily enthusiasts: Some of these people were current brand loyalists, but many were not. They are interested in style, comfort, fashion, and affordability, though not in cheap products. Many have an outdated and false impression of Lee Jeans. They are highly mobile, likely to be moms and dads, and are consumers of and influenced by traditional and social media.

Messages

Primary

Market editors: (1) We'll keep you abreast of jeans style and trends. (2) Our Curvy Fit, Easy Fit, and Modern Series collections are just what your consumers want in style and fit.

Bloggers: (1) What about Lee? (2) Try Lee and you will like Lee. (3) Your Lee experience is something your readers will want to read about.

National media: (1) We can give you the hot looks for fall. (2) We give you Gracie Gold.

Men and women who qualify as confident daily enthusiasts: (1) Lee Jeans IS for you. (2) Our new stylish Curvy Fit, Easy Fit, and Modern Series collections are just what you want in style and fit.

Secondary

Market editors: (1) Lee Jeans set the trends. (2) We are just as stylish and socially acceptable as our competitors, maybe even more so. (3) We have something for everyone.

Bloggers: (1) Try Lee Jeans and you will wear Lee Jeans. (2) Gracie Gold endorses Lee Jeans. Now that is something to blog about. (3) Lee Jeans is style right and socially acceptable.

National media: (1) Lee Jeans can provide you with leading opinions and video about fall trends, what's in, and what's out. (2) Lee Jeans comes to you endorsed by a recognized industry opinion leader.

Men and women who qualify as confident daily enthusiasts: (1) The magazines and bloggers you follow like us, they even wear our brand. (2) Try Lee Jeans and you will buy Lee Jeans.

Strategies

- Use introduction of new Curvy Fit, Easy Fit, and Modern Series collections to reintroduce the brand as style right and socially acceptable.
- Position the Lee Jeans story as a relevant and current part of today's fashion story.
- Leverage regular face time opportunities filled with authentic content and, when possible, fun-filled non-intimidating activity.

Tactics

Strategy 1 tactics: Use introduction of new Curvy Fit, Easy Fit, and Modern Series collections to reintroduce the brand as style right and socially acceptable.

- Continue meeting regularly with Lee's in-house product designers and trend experts to glean product and trend expertise, and stay abreast of enticing information to share with inquiring magazine editors.
- Keep established-relationship magazine editors abreast of the latest in design and style trends.
- Participate in a "Hot Looks for Fall" co-op satellite TV media tour hosted by acclaimed beauty blogger and journalist Gracie Gold, focus on new collections.
- Host March and September product reviews at Lee's New York showroom, highlighting the new collections and providing one-one-one opportunities for discussion.

Strategy 2 tactics: Position the Lee Jeans story as a relevant and current part of today's fashion story.

- Keep established-relationship magazine editors abreast of the latest in design and style trends.
- Participate in a "Hot Looks for Fall" co-op satellite TV media tour hosted by acclaimed beauty blogger and journalist Gracie Gold, focus on new collections.
- Provide a consistent flow of photography and product samples to editors.
- Host March and September product reviews at Lee's New York showroom, highlighting the new collections and providing one-one-one opportunities for discussion.

Strategy 3 tactics: Leverage regular face time and personal opportunities filled with authentic content and activity.

- Host two blogger trial events as "Blogger Style" parties, one in Minneapolis and one in Dallas, inviting influencer outfitting in Lee Jeans and positive future relationships with blogger attendees.
  - Host sites were in hip locations in each town.
  - In Minneapolis, Lee and Already Pretty (41,118 UMV) hosted a Girls' Night out with local female bloggers to highlight the new Curvy Fit and Easy Fit collections.
  - In Dallas, Lee, 7 on a Shoestring (37,707 UMV), and Days of a Domestic Dad (16,244 UMV) hosted a Date Night with local female and male bloggers to showcase the new Curvy Fit, Easy Fit, and Modern Series collections.
  - Lee's trend manager was the highlight of both events and gave each attendee his or her own one-on-one fit and style consultation, as well as fashion and trend tips to the larger group.
  - Provided a new pair of Lee jeans as a party favor to each guest.
- Attend the Dad 2.0 Summit, inviting the fitting of attendees in Lee Jeans and encouraging tweeted experiences.
  - Activated the Lee Denim Den as an active sponsor. The Den was host to friendly Lee brand ambassadors and encouraged Summit attendees who stopped by the Den to participate in a one-on-one fit session with the Lee product designer.
  - All Summit attendees who participated in a one-on-one fit session were given a new pair of Lee Modern Series jeans and informed they could share their story (a perfect opportunity for bloggers) by using the Lee-provided interactive photo station.
  - All fitted attendees were encouraged to use the hashtag #LeeModern-Dad for a chance to win a $250 Lee.com gift certificate.

- Recognize influential bloggers and editors for personal occasions and milestones to create touch points to keep the Lee brand top-of-mind.
  - Send birthday cards, recognition of personal accomplishments, quirky email communications such as "Happy Friday," and the like.

Timeline

- March to December 2014

Budget

- $130,000

Evaluation

In Process

- March and September product reviews and ensuing discussions and/or adjustments

Summative

To improve the perceptions of Lee Jeans in the online space, improvement demonstrated by amount and type of coverage, as well as source of coverage. Intent: host fun blogger events and outfit 20 influencers, attend Dad 2.0 Summit and outfit 200 attendees who Tweet their experiences.

- Two blogger style party events were successfully hosted during which 40 influencers were outfitted in Lee Jeans.
- Twenty-three new positive blogger relationships were established.
- Attendance at the Dad 2.0 Summit resulted in the outfitting of 250 attendees in Lee Jeans, from which 390 positive tweets were garnered.
  - The Dad 2.0 related 390 tweets resulted in more than 5 million social media impressions.
- The campaign efforts resulted in 237 quality, positive, and highly visual blog posts relevant to Lee's target market, totaling more than 3.6 million impressions.

To improve the perceptions of Lee Jeans within national and lifestyle magazines where favorable endorsements drive product purchase, improvement demonstrated by amount and type of coverage, as well as source of coverage. Intent: Secure at least 20 fashion placements in targeted national magazines.

- Secured 26 fashion placements in target national media outlets, including print and online, totaling more than 142 million impressions.
- Secured 21 interviews in *Hot Looks for Fall* co-op satellite TV media tour, totaling more than 12 million impressions.

Total positive Lee Jeans impressions for 2014: More than 162 millions.

B-9. Fight CRC One Million Strong Collection

Fight Colorectal Cancer (Fight CRC) introduced the "One Million Strong Collection" initiative as its 2016 annual One Million Strong awareness campaign. Launched in January 2016 and ending with an event on April 1, 2016, the 2016 One Million Strong Collection campaign ended by surpassing previously recorded awareness numbers.— Submitted by Director of Communication at Fight Colorectal Cancer

Background

- Fight CRC is a registered 501(c)(3) dedicated to the eradication of colon and rectal cancers.
- Colorectal cancer is a preventable disease and highly treatable if caught early; if caught late it can be a deadly disease.
- 1 in 20 individuals will get colorectal cancer in their lifetime.
- Though preventable and highly treatable in its early stages, public conversations about the disease and its prevention, as well as treatment options, have gradually taken place.
- 60% of deaths from colorectal cancer could be avoided with screening. If caught early (stage I) the survival rate is 90%.
- Research and anecdotal evidence demonstrates that a large portion of the US population is unscreened due to: a rationalized avoidance of the disease; lack of affordability of screening tests; no symptoms or family history; negative connotations of screening; no doctor recommendation to get screened; no personal connection to the disease; and low levels of healthy behavior.
- A May 2015 study from the US Centers for Disease Control and Prevention found only 25% of uninsured people and 60% of insured people were being screened for colon cancer as recommended.

- In 2010, Fight Colorectal Cancer joined the national effort to get the number of those properly screened to 80% by 2018.
- Colorectal cancer is the #2 leading cause of cancer deaths among men and women in the US combined, with more than 134,000 diagnosed each year and 50,000 succumbing to the disease.
- Colorectal cancer accounts for nearly 8% of cancer deaths in the US.
- Mission: Fight CRC envisions victory over colon and rectal cancers. We raise our voice to empower and activate a community of patients, fighters, and champions to push for better policies and to support research, education, and awareness for all those touched by this disease.
- Fight CRC is the leading, national patient advocacy group in colorectal cancer and an active participant in cancer research and advocacy on Capitol Hill.
- Fight CRC is widely known for its colorectal cancer awareness, advocacy, patient education, and research programs.
- Fight CRC is supported by many financial sponsors that look for meaningful ways to engage in campaigns to supplement their sponsorship dollars.
- Fight CRC partners and engages with other nonprofits, medical institutions, and members of Congress to collaborate and bring unity around the messaging and campaign.
- Fight CRC invites all people to "Join the Fight."
- Fight CRC wants to make the colorectal cancer conversation loud and clear.
- Fight CRC wants to ease unease about discussing the disease, its prevention, and treatment options.
- Fight CRC trains individuals to be involved in advocacy for change so they can change conversations about colorectal cancer and build a movement.
- Fight CRC envisions victory over colon and rectal cancers—the tagline of the organization is "get behind a cure."
- Fight CRC hosts an annual Call-on Congress in March each year.
  - Call-on Congress is a three-day event where colon and rectal cancer survivors, caregivers, and loved ones from all over the US unite to make their voices heard in Washington, D.C.
- Fight CRC unrolls an annual One Million Strong campaign with a new strategy for raising awareness each year.
- Fight CRC highlights the voice of colorectal cancer survivors, over 1 million of them, and celebrates their strength through the One Million Strong campaign.
- 2016 was the fourth year for the One Million Strong campaign.
- Fight CRC efforts culminate each year in the month of March, which is National Colorectal Cancer Awareness Month.

- Fight CRC's history of integrating the patient perspective into policy and medical research directed the organization to create a campaign to onboard survivors and families connected to the disease; its purpose was to open the dialogue about prevention and demand more action be taken to get to a cure.
  - Its commitment to an annual One Million Strong Campaign remained strong in 2016.
- As an interactive and mobile organization, Fight CRC was highly connected to thousands of survivors, families and caregivers, physicians and support staff, policy makers, celebrity endorsers, and the like.
  - End of March 2015 Fight CRC Facebook fans totaled 18,287; Twitter followers totaled 5,184; and Instagram followers totaled 1,726.
- The #StrongArmSelfie hashtag was introduced as part of the 2015 One Million Strong campaign and was a huge success netting more than 25,000 social media posts and reposts; its popularity was still a messaging opportunity.

Situation Analysis

Knowing that colorectal cancer survivors and their families are a key to changing policy, awareness levels, education levels, and the willingness to converse about colorectal cancer; Fight CRC positioned itself to re-energize its fans, supporters, and participants through an annual One Million Strong campaign. Because survivor stories are a key to every aspect of what Fight CRC does, and because the organization was highly connected to thousands of survivors, it knew it had an opportunity to collect their stories and use that power in its quest to make further inroads in conquering the disease. To incorporate the popularity of user-generated social media content into its campaign, Fight CRC created a way for users to contribute to the campaign in unique, meaningful, and creative ways.

Statement of the Opportunity

- To invite survivors, families, caretakers and fans to share their stories through creative expressions as part of a unified effort where the collection of their contributions would form a powerful message that Fight CRC could take the Hill, tell through existing partnerships, and facilitate through media coverage.

Goal

- To capture a collection of personal expressions and reflections from those who've been impacted by colorectal cancer and are willing to share their motivation for joining the fight.

Objectives

- To encourage all kinds of people, of all ages, to get involved and show why they're in the fight against colorectal cancer.
- To significantly surpass (by 20% or more) the end-of-March 2015 social media numbers: 18,287 Facebook fans, 5.187 Twitter followers, and 1,726 Instagram followers.
- To significantly surpass (by 20% or more) the end-of-March 2015 social media impressions/reach number: 57M.
- To significantly surpass (by 20% or more) the end-of-March 2015 website visit number: 57K
- To significantly surpass (by 20% or more) the end-of-March 2015 media placements number: 43M.
- To significantly surpass (by 20% or more) the end-of-March 2015 public service announcement (PSA) reach: 45.6M.
- To significantly surpass (by 20% or more) the end-of-March 20215 total awareness number: 176.6M.

Publics

Colorectal cancer community: Reached through email distribution, social media, website content, blogging, printed magazines, flyers, videos, etc. These people were already aware of Fight CRC and the deadly disease. In fact, most had already joined the fight by signing up to be an advocate with Fight CRC, using Fight CRC's patient resources, following Fight CRC on social media, or sharing their stories on the website. This was a primary group from which Fight CRC anticipated collecting stories. This was also the group with the people who, through personal relations, could encourage others to share their reasons to fight and contribute to the collection.

Sponsors and partners: Fight CRC had pre-One Million Strong Collection methods of communication established with this public. Their willingness to share the collection invitation or create their own way to add to the collection would boost Fight CRC's reach.

Celebrity endorsers: Celebrity status and endorsement is a key component of generating awareness in the saturated US message marketplace. Fight CRC could count on its positive relationships with key celebrities to extend the reach of the One Million Strong Collection invitation.

Media: Both a primary and an intervening public, the media was a powerful conduit that could carry the One Million Strong Collection invitation and elect to feature the all-important stories about colorectal cancer presence, danger, prevention, treatment, and policy.

Messages

Primary

Colorectal cancer community: Contribute to the One Million Strong Collection! Here's how: (1) CREATE! Come up with a way to share your story and express yourself. (If you're not super creative, post a #StrongArmSelfie!) (2) POST! Share a photo, video or link with us. Use the hashtag #OMScollection and tag us (@FightCRC) so we can find it. (3) VIEW! See the Collection at OMScollection.org.

Sponsors and partners: (1) Show us why YOU fight colorectal cancer by contributing to the One Million Strong Collection! (2) Share our flyer and information with your followers. (3) Post a #StrongArmSelfie to show your support!

Celebrity endorsers: (1) Flex a "STRONG ARM"! (2) Take a selfie. (3) Post a photo to Twitter or Instagram with the hashtag #StrongArmSelfie (4) Suggested message below—don't forget the hashtag! (5) Encourage your followers to help!

Media: (1) Tell the story of colorectal cancer survivors for March 2016—Colorectal Cancer Awareness Month. (2) Check out what celebrities and partners are doing to raise awareness.

Secondary

Colorectal cancer community: (1) Get involved with Fight CRC. (2) Sign up at FightCRC.org. (3) Attend our One Million Strong Showcase in Nashville or watch it via LIVESTREAM on YouTube to see highlights from the One Million Strong Collection and celebrate Colorectal Cancer Awareness Month.

Sponsors and partners and *Celebrity endorsers*: (1) We appreciate your support. (2) Get involved with Fight CRC in ways that make sense for your brand.

Media: (1) By telling stories about colorectal cancer you can save someone's life. (2) You owe it to your viewers/listeners/subscribers/readers to tell it to them.

Strategies

- Communicated the One Million Strong Collection significance to current followers.

- Capitalized on the momentum built during the last three One Million Strong campaigns; notably the social media success of #StrongArmSelfie, and kept it going.
- Found power in partnerships and celebrity endorsers.
- Tracked momentum and collected feature stories through the hashtag #OMSCollection through a dedicated online hub.

Tactics

Communicated the One Million Strong Collection significance to current followers.

- Chose 4 models (3 survivors /1 caregiver) who represented the demographics of CRC. Fight CRC created professional photos and videos with their stories to explain the campaign and put a "face" to the One Million Strong Collection.
- Previewed the campaign to a small group of dedicated volunteers (brand ambassadors) and asked them to be some of the first to contribute to the campaign once it launched in January 2016.
- Designed a flyer and social media graphics, as well as a video, dedicated to explaining how to submit to the One Million Strong collection and participate in the campaign.
- Designed OMSCollection.org as a dedicated online hub (and testimony to the significance of the call) and incorporated (1) hashtag feeding service that curated social media posts by users participating in the campaign, (2) videos and stories from models, (3) facts and stats about colorectal cancer, (4) links back to FightCRC.org so users could read blogs and see how to get involved, and (5) sponsor thank yous.
- Launched the campaign via email to full database in January 2016 with links to dedicated campaign website.
- Issued "Join the Fight / Contribute to the Collection" invitations, highlighting the dedicated website, through all social media avenues, including specially dedicated YouTube videos and graphics designed to drive traffic.
- Promised to feature submitted photos, stories, and videos so participants would gain the audience of the thousands of people watching Fight CRC and its partners for inspiration.
- Motivated submissions through the promise of branded t-shirts and other swag.
- Kept OMSCollection.org updated regularly with new and invigorating content.
- Reached out to select group of participants to write up full-length blog posts about their stories and why they fight.

- Launched the campaign during the NASDAQ bell ringing ceremony and used the photos and videos of the community as the PSA that ran throughout the month.
- Worked individually with community members to maximize their connections and opportunities to raise awareness
  - Connection to the Cleveland Cavaliers resulted in Fight CRC participation in Colorectal Cancer Awareness Night where the PSA played on the Jumbotron, Fight CRC logo and website displayed at the arena, volunteers staffed an awareness table on-site, and Fox Sports station interviewed local survivor and advocate.
- Connection to celebrities got them involved in social media and Nashville Showcase event.

Capitalized on the momentum built during the last three One Million Strong campaigns; notably the social media success of #StrongArmSelfie, and kept it going.

- Kept the popular "strong arm" pose.
- Replicated the 2015 hashtag technique/call with *#StrongArmSelfie.*
- Recruited support of sponsor whose $1 donation per post motivated users to participate in 2015.
- Created a dedicated day for posting #StrongArmSelfie photos that tied in with the same day that advocates were on the Hill during Call-on Congress, creating an easy way for members of Congress to engage in the campaign.
- Created ways to highlight the reasons for fighting at every event Fight CRC sponsored or planned to participate in throughout the year.
  - Showcased the One Million Strong Collection through guest speakers sharing testimonials and a video created by real people who submitted to the campaign during the One Million Strong Showcase.
  - Took a branded photo backdrop and flyers about the collection to every Fight CRC-sponsored event, encouraging posts with #OMSCollection and #StrongArmSelfie.
  - Trained people about how to host awareness events, share their stories, and get involved in advocacy.
  - Maximized a return to NASDAQ/Times Square through soundless video highlights with a CTA to view the collection for the NASDAQ screen.
  - Maximized the Nashville Showcase event through the participation of celebrities and high-profile partnering organizations all sharing their reasons for fighting cancer, and specifically colorectal cancer.
- Appealed through YouTube videos made for emotive sharing and presentation of the organization and ways to get involved.

- Invited media to participate in the story telling (pitched through news releases, email pitches, broadcast PSA, etc.).
- Encouraged past One Million Strong participants to personalize the campaign and find ways to express themselves as part of the 2016 One Million Strong Collection.
  - #31DaysofBlue, a hashtag started by a survivor in a prior year as part of One Million Strong, returned and became a way the advocate added to the collection.
  - A continued partnership between Fight CRC and the University of Central Missouri's Public Relations Program resulted in a video and awareness event on the campus as part of the collection.
  - A community in Puerto Rico that collected thousands of #StrongArmSelfie posts in 2015 made a video explaining how they did it as a way to contribute to the 2016 campaign; the video was played during the Nashville Showcase.
  - Coloring sheets were created and designed by volunteers so kids had an easy, fun way to get involved.

Found power in partnerships and celebrity endorsers.

- Made graphics and one-pagers with suggested language and links for current partners and sponsors; relied on them to share the collection invitation through their own channels of communication, especially their social media accounts.
- Asked partners, through email and face-to-face interaction, to work with their teams and find creative ways to add to the collection.
  - Partners engaged by showing support on social media by posting their own photos on #StrongArmSelfie day.
  - Partners sent presenters to speak during the Nashville Showcase.
  - Partners sent advocates to Call-on Congress to engage in advocacy.
- Sponsors found unique ways to engage in the campaign in addition to offering financial support.
  - Sponsors created volunteer activity by asking employees to write why they fight on a card tied around a blue awareness bracelet, given away during March for awareness.
  - Sponsors posted advocate guest posts about the campaign on their own websites
  - Sponsors attended the Showcase event and brought employees to learn more about the cause and find ways to raise awareness.
- Members of Congress posed with Fight CRC advocates for a #StrongArmSelfie photo on Hill Day.

- Engaged supporting celebrities shared their stories of why they fight to the collection; utilized their own social media accounts to notify followers and fans of their collection decisions and attended events whenever possible.
- Continued a strong partnership with Mayo Clinic for raising awareness during Colorectal Cancer Awareness Month.
  - For the 3rd year, teams collaborated to come up with a unique idea using social media.
  - Mayo Clinic created the #ScopeScope campaign—a live broadcast of a colonoscopy through Periscope (a live video app) as part of their contribution to the One Million Strong Collection.
  - Mayo Clinic posted and shared content about colorectal cancer all month and encouraged its followers (over 1 million on Twitter) to engage in Fight CRC's campaign.
  - Local, national, and industry media covered the live colonoscopy and shared the novelty of broadcasting such a procedure on a new social app.
  - Fight CRC played a short video with highlights from #ScopeScope in Times Square during the NASDAQ bell ringing ceremony

Track momentum and collect and share stories through the hashtags #OMSCollection / #StrongArmSelfie through a dedicated online hub.

- Replicated the 2015 hashtag technique/call with *#OMSCollection / #Strong ArmSelfie.*
- Designed OMSCollection as a dedicated online collection hub (and testimony to the significance of the call) and issued invitations highlighting a www.OMSCollection.org redirect to Fight CRC's host site.
- Used a hashtag feeding service that allowed for additional hashtags to be added and tracked as part of the campaign engagement.
- Fed in #ScopeScope posts to the #OMSCollection hashtag feed on the website.
- Added #31DaysofBlue and #StrongArmSelfie into the #OMSCollectionhashtag feed

Timeline (One Year)

- May 2015—Recruit sponsors to launch date.
- June 2015—Campaign planning to launch date.
- August 2015—Photo/video shoot and ambassador boot camp.
- October–December 2015—Campaign graphics and assets designed; Nashville event planning.

- December 2015—Soft launch flyer and video to ambassadors and dedicated volunteers.
- January 2016—Launch campaign via email, website, and social media to followers and partners; celebrity PSA distributed to stations requesting inclusion in lineup for March & beyond.
- March 2016—Campaign kickoff in Times Square for public audience—Colorectal Cancer Awareness Month; pitch media send.
- Mid-March—Call-on Congress in D.C.
- End of March/April 2—Culmination of campaign with Nashville Showcase.
- April/May—Evaluation and reporting.
- May/June 2016—Future campaign insights, value assessed, and sponsor recruitment.

Budget

- Less than $75,000.

Evaluation

Summative

To encourage all kinds of people, of all ages, to get involved and show why they're in the fight against colorectal cancer.

- A wide variety of notable personalities and organizations engaged with the campaign via social media including Mayo Clinic, NASDAQ, reality star from Real Housewives of Orange County Meghan King Edmonds, country music artist Craig Campbell, wrestling celebrity Big Gene Snitsky, Ozzy Osbourne, reality star from Ink Masters Clint Cummings, and actor Luke Perry. The top 10 social engagers with the campaign had a combined total of 2,883,866 followers.
- All kinds of amazing stories of "Why I Fight" were submitted and collected from veterans, active military, women, men, etc., featuring all variety of photos. A key takeaway was the use of humor by participants.
- The social and traditional media reach numbers indicated that people of all ages had the opportunity to get involved.

To significantly surpass (by 20% or more) the end-of-March 2015 social media numbers: 18,287 Facebook fans, 5.187 Twitter followers, and 1,726 Instagram followers.

- Objective reached. End-of-March 2016 social media numbers: 22,153 (or 21% increase) Facebook fans; 6,524 (or 26% increase) Twitter followers; and 3,725 (or 116% increase) Instagram followers.

To significantly surpass (by 20% or more) the end-of-March 2015 social media impressions/reach number: 57M.

- Objective reached. End-of-March 2016 social media impressions/reach number: 96.2M (69% increase).

To significantly surpass (by 20% or more) the end-of-March 2015 website visit number: 57K.

- Objective reached. End-of-March 2016 website visit number: 90K (58% increase).

To significantly surpass (by 20% or more) the end-of-March 2015 media placements number: 43M.

- Objective reached. End-of-March 2016 media placements number: 83.5M (94% increase).

To significantly surpass (by 20% or more) the end-of-March 2015 public service announcement (PSA) reach: 45.6M.

- Objective reached. End-of-March 2016 PSA reach number: 115.6M (250% increase).

To significantly surpass (by 20% or more) the end-of-March 2015 total awareness number: 176.6M.

- Objective reached. End-of-March 2016 total awareness number: 326.2M (85% increase).

B-10. Tips for Kids—Seventeen Years Later

Launched in 1999, Tips for Kids® was a finance and investment education program for middle school students made possible by American Century Investments, an internationally known asset management company headquartered in Kansas City, Missouri. American Century's community investments department developed the program as a signature community relations initiative. Tips for Kids was offered to any school in the country as a free public service program. Within one year of the launch date, schools in all 50 states and several other countries picked up the program. It won an acclaimed International Association of Business Communicators Gold Quill Award and significantly influenced Missouri's education curriculum standards.—Submitted by Randy Williams, ABC

Background

- Founded in 1958, American Century Investments is one of the largest asset management firms in the US.
- In 1999, American Century had employees in offices throughout the country with the majority in Kansas City, Missouri (headquarters location); Denver, Colorado; and Mountain View, California. The Denver office has since been consolidated with its Missouri operation.
- Having changed its name from Twentieth Century to American Century Investments in early 1997, the company was faced with an opportune time to redefine its community relations program.
- In 1999, American Century's Community Relations department's purpose was to foster mutually beneficial relationships and increase personal satisfaction within the community, American Century, and its employees.
  - A company commitment was to offer its expertise in a way that supported its communities.
- American Century research showed that a significant majority of people did not understand basic investment principles and money management. This was especially true of kids.
- The vast majority of schools throughout the country did not address financial education. In 1999, only thirteen states required an economics class, and only two states required a personal finance class for graduation from high school.
- American Century client feedback demonstrated that the majority of investors desired to help their children and grandchildren learn more about the importance of good money management.
- Middle school was a prime time to teach kids about life issues, including how to understand finance and manage money. These students would soon have their own income through part-time jobs. They typically had very little knowledge about how to handle their money. Research showed that a large majority of middle school children indicated that they worried about their future, and more than half were worried about not having enough money as they got older.
- Teachers had to teach certain subjects in their classrooms to meet curriculum standards set by the national and state education departments. Teacher workload predisposed them to shy away from any additional "add on" programs; however, they were interested in new approaches to teaching core subjects.
- Fewer than 20% of teachers reported feeling competent to teach personal finance topics.

- Investors were interested in supporting companies that supported the community. More than 50% of individuals indicated that they would rather buy products and services from companies that supported the community.
- American Century was headquartered in Kansas City in a state that, in 1999, did not require finance curriculum in its middle or high schools.
- American Century leadership was convinced that if students could learn simple money management techniques at a young age, it would help them be more successful with their life-long financial decisions.

Situation Analysis

As a newly renamed company, American Century faced both a challenge and an opportunity to redefine its dedication to the community. As a company long dedicated to community service and willing to lend its expertise in ways sure to benefit the community, American Century was in a position to continue that tradition with kids who had little to no knowledge about basic financial principles. Middle school children were of the age at which it was good to begin the money education process. Knowing the need to educate them, while recognizing the already overloaded plates of school teachers, American Century was positioned to meet the need to bring financial education to kids while not burdening the schools and their faculty.

Statement of the Opportunity

American Century had the opportunity to demonstrate its community commitment in a signature way and transform children's financial futures by providing easy-to-deliver financial education curriculum complementary to middle school curriculum already in place.

Goal

- To redefine the American Century community relations program, in keeping with the opportunity presented by its recent renaming (formerly Twentieth Century), while establishing a signature program benefitting the community.

Objectives

- To produce an all-inclusive program as a community service, free to schools using it.

- To generate media attention to assist in program launch awareness, a byproduct of which would help establish American Century as a good corporate citizen.
- To distribute a maximum of 500 kits to teachers in at least 10 states, with an emphasis on Missouri, Kansas, Colorado, and California (the states where major offices were located).
- To involve at least 12,500 middle school students in the program in year one.
- To conduct an initial evaluation, or beta test, of the program to gain additional insight from teachers before moving into production of more kits in the year 2000.

Publics

Middle school students: These were children aged 12 to 14 years old. This group wanted to learn about life issues and would soon start to have their own incomes through part-time jobs. They had very little knowledge about how to handle money. Most of the students worried about their future, and more than 50% worried about not having enough money when older. They were more interested in fun than in opportunities for serious studies. Their attention spans, as well as their frames of reference, were much shorter than those of the typical American Century target (investors).

Middle school teachers: They had to teach certain subjects in their classrooms to meet curriculum standards set by the national and state education departments. They did not want any additional add-on programs to consume more time and were interested in new approaches to teaching core subjects. Carefully prepared, easy-to-use, student-relevant, and comprehensive materials were preferred when introducing new subject matter.

American Century investors: Many investors had communicated their desire over the years to help their children and grandchildren learn about the importance of good money management. Almost all investors indicated they wished they had learned about finance much earlier in their own lives. In addition, market research showed 65% of individuals (including investors) would rather buy products and services from companies that supported the community.

Media: The media, both print and television, were an important intervening audience, especially for the launch of the program as a means through which teacher awareness would be generated. Print was of special importance because of its ability accommodate program details and be referred to time and again.

Messages

Primary

Middle school students: (1) You like money? You can like and learn it! (2) American Century has money fun ideas for you. (3) Grow up with enough money to do well.

Middle school teachers: (1) American Century can help you in meeting classroom needs and feel confident teaching kids about money. (2) American Century's education partner, The Learning Exchange, endorsed the financial curriculum for kids as easy to incorporate into core subjects and it's free to you. (3) We make money fun, interactive, and simple.

American Century investors: (1) We listened to you. American Century helps teachers help kids learn about money. (2) The Tips for Kids curriculum we designed is available to any teacher who requests it, and it complements core subjects like math, social studies, and language arts. (3) Kids nationwide, even in other countries, can learn from us.

Media: (1) We've got a program serving your community that your readers/viewers will want to know about. (2) Help kids and teachers find solid financial futures.

Strategies

- Make it accessible, interactive, easy-to-use, and as fun as possible.
- Partner with established programs.
- Support schools and already established core curriculum through stand-alone, easy-to-use messaging.

Tactics

Strategy 1 tactics: Make it accessible, interactive, easy-to-use, and as fun as possible.

- The curriculum was free to all requesting middle school teachers, even when demand exceeded supply.
- Supported national and state core curriculum standards in math, social studies, and language arts through students' interests in money.
- Developed a hands-on approach easily produced in classrooms, presented as a free kit to those teachers requesting it; the program was also supported with a designated website.
- Named the program Tips for Kids, which was fun and memorable.

Strategy 2 tactics: Partner with established programs.

- Partnered with The Learning Exchange, a well-known educational resource organization.
- Partnership and free curriculum opportunity was nationally and internationally attractive. It was communicated to the media via news releases sent prior to the July 1999 launch date, garnering widespread representation. It was featured in American Century's own Investor Perspective newsletter distributed to more than 2 million investors; many contacted the company about implementing Tips for Kids in their own districts.

Strategy 3 tactics: Support schools and already established core curriculum through standalone, easy-to-use messaging.

- The program was designed as a 10-week (semester) hands-on finance and investment curriculum with four modules: Money and Me (the history of money), Economic Encounters (consumer information and uses of money), Mastering Finance (financial planning and investing), and Business Building (developing and running a business).
- Produced the Tips for Kids kit featuring: a full instruction guide for teachers, posters to hang in the classroom addressing the four modules, an introductory video for classroom use, and certificates to be presented to students as they completed the different program modules.
- Kits were free to all requesting teachers; American Century underwrote production and mailing costs.

Timeline

1998–May 1999: Developed Tips for Kids curriculum, video, and website.

June 1999: Notified all American Century employees of the Tips for Kids initiative and planned launch.

July 1999: Tips for Kids formal launch took place in Colorado at a national education conference, accompanied by nationwide distribution of launch news release.

November 1999: Conducted evaluation, or beta test, to elicit teacher first impression feedback.

December 1999: Five hundred kits requested and mailed, with request for an additional 1,200.

April 2000: Additional 1,200 teacher-requested kits produced and mailed. Each kit cost nearly $65 to produce.

Evaluation

Summative

To produce an all-inclusive program as a community service free to schools using it.

- Accomplished with launch of program and introduction to schools taking place in July 1999.
- It was not long before Tips for Kids was recognized as American Century's signature community relations program; it was formally registered as an American Century servicemark.
- Tips for Kids earned international respect when it received the International Association of Business Communicator (IABC) Gold Quill award.
- Demand far exceeded expectations.

To generate media attention to assist in program launch awareness, a byproduct of which would help establish American Century as a good corporate citizen.

- Original release generated more than 60 articles nationwide over a four-month period. Syndicated columnists with the LA Times and Washington Post scheduled feature stories about Tips for Kids at the end of the school year.
- One national television news profile of Tips for Kids took place.
- Investor response was wholly positive, as noted through incoming phone calls and anecdotal evidence.
- More than 45 states were reached through the initial launch, exceeding the original hope to reach 10 states.

To distribute a maximum of 500 kits to teachers in at least 10 states, with an emphasis on Missouri, Kansas, Colorado, and California (the states where major offices were located.).

- More than 500 kits were requested and delivered by the end of September 1999. The estimated 500 did not last through the end of the year. A waiting list was developed and American Century promised to send kits to those schools on the backlog. An additional 1,200 kits were produced and mailed by April 2000.
- Exceeded objective—By the end of 1999, more than 1,800 kits had been requested, exceeding the original goal of 500 by 1,200.

To involve at least 12,500 middle school students in the program in year one.

- Exceeded objective—More than 33,000 students were introduced to the program in the first year.

To conduct an initial evaluation, or beta test, of the program to gain additional insight from teachers before moving into production of more kits in 2000.

- The evaluation of the program was completed on time, with the indication that the program (via the kits) was very well received by teachers and students. Only a few suggestions for change were noted.

Continuing Tips for Kids Impact

- In 2004, a second program was introduced as Tips for Life; this program served as a continuation of Tip for Kids and targeted high school education.
- In 2007, American Century was invited to work with Missouri's Department of Elementary and Secondary Education to change the state's graduation requirements for high school graduation to include a class in personal finance.
  - American Century's program was cited as an example of what should be taught in a personal finance class. The new requirement took effect with the 2010 high school graduating class.
- In 2010, American Century renamed the programs as part of their "Yes You Can" financial education initiatives.
- In 2014, only 17 states required finance curriculum and only five states required a stand-alone personal finance course for graduation.[1] Missouri is one of those five states.
- While the company deemed the program a success, in 2015, American Century scaled back the initiative to better align its community relations resources with programs tied to health and medical research. The move was inspired by the firm's unique ownership model. More than 40% of American Century is owned by the Stowers Institute for Medical Research.

Note

1. Council of Economic Education, 2014 Survey of the States http://www.councilforeconed.org/policy-and-advocacy/survey-of-the-states/

B-11. Dairy Queen's Fan Food Not Fast Food Campaign: Retrospective Case Analysis from the Outside

Dairy Queen® (DQ) approached consumers in a whole new way, successfully securing its future as a successful QSR brand supported by "fans," and not just customers. Backed by *nearly $1 million in annual research efforts designed to mine consumer insights, Dairy Queen launched an emotional connection campaign that successfully positioned it for positive annual sales growth (same-store and location expansion) as a hometown favorite for fans of all kinds.*—Case analysis authored by Tricia Hansen-Horn

As discussed in chapter one, the majority of case studies are historical linear documentations of what went on from hindsight clarity. Such is the case of this study, which is an excellent example of retrospective sense-making from outside an organization (similar to competitive analyses or academic case study research for educational purposes). Unlike the other cases in this book, this particular study was written without the direct participation of the featured organization, in this case Dairy Queen. It's an example of the analysis one might arrive at from studying an organization's success from secondary sources, which we do regularly for professional purposes.

Background

- Dairy Queen's roots date back to 1938, with its first "store" opening in 1940; its popularity tied to its famous soft-serve ice cream.[1–3]
- The year 2017 marked more than 75 years of Dairy Queen business operations.[1,4–6]
- Headquartered in Minneapolis, MN, Dairy Queen is a Berkshire Hathaway (NYSE: BRK.A and BRK.B) company. See Berkshire Hathaway Annual Report http://www.berkshirehathaway.com/subs/sublinks.html.[3,7,8]
- International Dairy Queen (IDQ), (NASDAQ: INDQA) which includes Dairy Queen, operates in the Quick Service Restaurant (QSR) market.[1,3,8]
- Dairy Queen has 35.8% of the "Ice Cream and Gelato Store Franchise" market share; it retains the largest market share of all US franchisers.[3]
- The company was acquired by Warren Buffett in 1998 for $580 million.[2,5,9]
- All but two Dairy Queen locations are locally owned and operated.[1,10]
- Historically, it's a brand with strong positive nostalgic consumer remembrances and perceptions. Emotional connectedness was and is a positive and strong brand attribute[1,4,9–13]
- Dairy Queen had a history as a consistent performing investment providing steady cash flow for investors.[5]
- In response to consumer demand, the brand began offering Dairy Queen cakes in 1981.[1]
- It acquired Orange Julius in 1987 as a means of adding natural, healthy options to its menu.[1,4,13]
- Dairy Queen's famous signature treat, the Blizzard® was introduced in 1985; more than 1 million were sold.[1] It still accounts for nearly 20% of Dairy Queen's business.[1,13]

- The brand debuted Grill & Chill® quick-service restaurants in 2001 as alternative to treat-only stores; the first one opened in Tennessee. In addition, Grill & Chill provided a route to better branding and food concept singular identity.[1,9]
- Dairy Queen is host to three lines: the long-popular soft-serve treat line and its recently re-introduced grill line, with Orange Julius a distant third. International DQ also owns Karmelcorn®.[1]
- Dairy Queen introduced its crispy chicken salad in 2001 as an alternative to its traditional menu items.[1]
- The Blizzard of the Month program began in 2003. In 2005, Dairy Queen introduced its Blizzard Fan Club.[1]
- Dairy Queen's first full year of national advertising took place in 2004.[1]
- The Grill Burger® was introduced via national television ads in 2005.[1]
- In 2006, Dairy Queen had an estimated 105 Grill & Chill locations and 1,600 Brazier stores.[9]
- In response to a growing QSR trend, Dairy Queen leveraged its drinks sales in 2009 by introducing its Happy Hour. Many of its stores recorded increases in traffic during relatively underutilized parts of the day. The traffic led to more food sales.[12,14]
- Prior to 2012, Dairy Queen was known for running treat specials each summer.[4]
- In 2012, Dairy Queen was still heavily associated by fans with ice cream treats and not non-ice cream QSR foods. This did not serve its food line profitability plans or its ability to let owners compete in large markets. A "treats" only store was poorly positioned in large markets host to many foods competitors.[2,4,5,9,11,12,15]
- Dairy Queen was well-known for community involvement, including Little League and other athletic team sponsorships.[1,4,9–11]
- Dairy Queen's history served and continues to serve it well as a hometown community restaurant at which to stop for celebratory treats. Dairy Queen was and is known as the "hometown" brand instead of a faceless conglomerate brand.[4,10]
- A 2012 Harris Poll EquiTrend® Study found Dairy Queen ranked by consumers as the number two top-rated quick service restaurant brand in light of brand equity, behind number one Subway, but ahead of direct competitors Wendy's, Five Guys, Chik-fil-A, McDonald's, and Burger King.[4,16]
  o The 2012 study was conducted online from January 31–February 20, and analyzed more than 38,500 consumer responses to key measures of brand health—including: (1) how well the public knows a brand, (2) how

positively the public thinks of the brand, and (3) the public's willingness to do business with or donate to a brand.

- 2008–2015 brought Dairy Queen seven years of consecutive stagnant or negative same-store transaction growth.[2,4]
- By 2013, Dairy Queen openly acknowledged the value of social media to its goals.[4,17]
- Internal assessments prior to 2013 indicated that franchisees needed reinvigorated reasons to renew their trust and faith in the company.[9,5]
- A long-standing partnership benefiting Children's Miracle Network Hospitals was established in 1984. #MiracleTreatDay was still highly popular in 2016.[1,18]
- In 2012, Dairy Queen was committed to spending $200,000 yearly in consumer research.[4]
- A new EVP of marketing joined Dairy Queen in 2012 with the challenge of driving the brand to annual sales growth, same-store transactions included.[2,4,5,9]
- Previous to 2012, many marketing decisions were largely driven by what the brand decision-makers knew or thought to be true and not in-depth consumer and market analyses.[4]
- In late 2012, Orange Julius drinks were made available in all stores as a way to build a healthier menu across all locations. The first ever Orange Julius national commercial kicked off.[4,19]
- Reported by Kantar Media Dairy Queen spent nearly $66.8 million on US measured media in 2012.[12]
- Dairy Queen operated in the US, Canada, Mexico and 17 other countries in 2013.[12]
- A Kansas City-based agency was retained in 2012 to revitalize Dairy Queen's brand image. Its research and strategic planning netted the introduction of the "Fan Food, Not Fast Food" brand initiative launched in 2013.[2,4,6,9–12,20]
- Market research showed that more than half of millennials (aged 18–34) were more likely to order a complete meal choice if dessert was included.[21]
- Market research showed that consumers aged 50 and older were projected to comprise more than 62% of fast food purchases of all fast-food drive-in restaurant business for years to come and, in fact, would outpace purchase increases from younger demographics.[22]
- Research also showed that today's boomers served as "enhanced grandparents," often attending their grandchildren's games, etc., and treating the children afterwards for family or fan celebrations.[22]

- Market research indicated that only if "food" replaced the historic "treats only" mentality among consumers could Dairy Queen owners successfully enter big city competition. Dairy Queen wanted to position itself for competitive growth in big city and international markets. It knew its Blazier to Grill & Chills conversion process needed to be simplified.[5,9,17]
- Established market trends demonstrated that packaged value meals resonated with lunch time consumers, especially those in Dairy Queen's target market share, including patrons of the $5 Box Lunch at Taco Bell, BK King Meals, and Subway's $5 foot longs.
- Pre-2013 television ads had centered on the Ri-DQ-lous campaign that invited consumers to participate in the brand's quirky and absurd ad humor. Dairy Queen acknowledged that this campaign was time-sensitive attempt that had successfully penetrated clutter, but it did not sell food nor build loyalty.[2,10,23]
- Dairy Queen found through research that its consumers were genuine fans of the brand and they wanted the organization to succeed.[10,11,17]
- Dairy Queen also knew that its fans visited an average of once a month, and if that average increased to twice a month business would dramatically increase. In addition, fans might be counted on to bring their friends.[10–12]
- Consumer research conducted in 2012 and 2013 highlighted the fact that today's consumers wanted more authenticity in their relationships with brands to which they were loyal, than they did historically.[4–6,10,13]
  - o The Dairy Queen brand was found to stand out relative to its competitors in the authenticity category.
  - o Dairy Queen consumers were found to actively support Dairy Queen because they saw it as a small, community-minded organization instead of a corporate giant like its competitors. This perception was found across age groups, occupations, and income.
  - o Research also established the fact that consumers gave the Dairy Queen brand low marks for affordability.
  - o Dairy Queen was also found to rank low in the available healthy food item category.
  - o Current loyal fans and prospective fans (millennials) were attracted to responsible brands that contributed to their communities. Dairy Queen's long partnership with Children's Miracle Network Hospitals was positively viewed by its consumers, as was its long-held hometown sponsor position.
- The Orange Julius League fan club was introduced in 2013.[1]
- Nearly half of frequent and occasional diners across all QSR categories were found to use their mobile phone to make a fast food choice.[16]

- Instagram's own research demonstrated that users spent more time per average visit to Instagram content, than during visits to social media competitor content. Dairy Queen launched an Instagram account in 2012.[22]
- In 2013 Dairy Queen's growing Facebook popularity was well-established with nearly 8 million followers. Twitter follower numbers came in a poor second, but still showed promise in 2013 at close to 6K. Launched in 2010, YouTube subscribers showed a steady increase with the first Blizzard commercial posted to Dairy Queen's YouTube channel in August 2013. And, finally, Dairy Queen's Tumblr account was launched in 2013 and provided fans the opportunity to engage and reengage fans in food content.[24]
- Dairy Queen's sales history demonstrated that ice cream purchases were weather-dependent. When temperatures dipped 6° lower than normal, regardless of the season or location, the company lost about 60 ice cream purchases per store per week. In addition, when temperatures climbed 6° higher than normal, ice cream transactions increased nearly 100 per store.[2,4,13]
- Dairy Queen's baked item menu expansion was introduced in 2015.[2]

Situation Analysis

Taking note of its pre-campaign flat same-stores sales, as well as its desire to be a strong competitor in the food market, Dairy Queen knew it needed to innovate its traditional marketing, advertising, and public relations approach. While penetrating promotional culture remained a priority, the brand also faced rising consumer demand for transparency and authenticity. Fortunately, Dairy Queen recognized that it already had a solid "fan" base in place; it just had not realized it yet. Those fans viewed the brand products with positive nostalgia and its locations as hometown gathering places that were preferred over faceless conglomerates' restaurants. Dairy Queen's long-established fan base and consumers' positive emotional connections were recognized as highly valuable to the brand's future success. A significant challenge was that positive fan emotions were heavily tied to perceptions of Dairy Queen as a treat only store. Millennials were found especially challenging as a target public, but research showed that Dairy Queen was positioned to successfully acquire a growing portion of the millennial lunch market, especially if it served lunches of value that included dessert. Finally, past and current perceptions of Dairy Queen as the hometown company, compared to its perceived large conglomerate competitors, suggested that Dairy Queen could leverage that hometown perception and invite current and prospective Dairy Queen consumers to consciously view themselves as "fans" of its brand's treats and foods.

Statement of the Opportunity

Dairy Queen had the opportunity to leverage its enviable position as a popularly known hometown restaurant, a place at which celebrations of family and community took place, while repositioning itself as a high quality QSR foods (as well as treats) provider for its "fans," many of whom were highly mobile and interested in value menus.[5]

Goal

To increase new- and same-store annual sales averages while positioning the brand for long-term domestic and global competitiveness and expansion in the QSR food and treat markets.

Big Idea .

Listen to Dairy Queen customer and franchisee feedback, formally recognize Dairy Queen consumers as fans, and attract future fans through appealing fan-based incentives and opportunities for participation in the brand communication process. The "Fan Food, Not Fast Food" tag was key to the big idea because it reminded fans that Dairy Queen offered food and treats.[12,13,20]

Objectives

1. To energize its well-established positive emotional regard and cast its consumers as conscious "fans" of its food and treat products, thereby encouraging increased visits and visits from fan friends.[4,5,9–13]
2. To position Dairy Queen as a quality food brand, while retaining its famous treats identity.[5,11,13]
3. To position the brand, by year end 2016, as the preferred option of the value-seeking lunch crowd.[4,5,6,10,13]
4. To generate increased annual sales, and current same-store sales by year end 2016.[2,5,6,9]
5. To grow the brand's social media fan base in significant ways beyond 2013 levels by year end 2016, moving Twitter followers from 60K to more than 400K, Facebook fans from (2013) 8 million to more than 10 million, Blizzard of the Month fans to more than 4 million, Julius League fan club members to more than 15K, YouTube subscribers to more than 7000, Instagram followers to more than 200K, and Tumblr subscribers to notable numbers.

6. To continue to position the brand for expansion into US large city and strategic international markets by year end 2016.[5,6,9,25]

Publics

Current fans: Many of the traditional generation X demographic who remember "celebrating when …" Grandparents taking their grandkids to celebrate, as well as all variety of "hometown" QSR restaurant enthusiasts. Highly loyal to Dairy Queen, they perceived it mostly as a treats store. Characterized by a willingness to interact with and/or endorse the Dairy Queen brand. Most, though not all, were social media and digital savvy.

Prospective and future fans: Interested in patronizing a hometown QSR environment. Interested in foods, desserts, drinks, and healthy options. Many characterized by social media and digital preferences. All generations populated this public, but value lunch seekers were signaled out as a significant segment crossing all demographic boundaries.

Value-seeking lunch crowd: Social media savvy and loyal, this group also traveled for weekly lunch deals away from work. Highly interested in value lunches that successfully competed with the Dairy Queen brand competitors. While a significant portion of this public was millennials, other groups were also included. This public was characterized by a desire for fast, quality, and value-added lunches with dessert that were easy to get.

Groups brought together through common participation or goals, such as organized athletic, service, civic, philanthropic, etc., groups: While easily part of other recognized publics in this campaign, this group held special interest as seekers of community sponsorship and celebrations as a means of continuing its "hometown" restaurant reputation.

Social media fans: A highly interactive and mobile group, many social media users also sought value lunches. In addition, their drive for transparency and interaction invited brand positioning through direct one-to-one connection. Their preferences provided the opportunity to more clearly build Dairy Queen's fan base, and even bypass traditional advertising at strategic opportunities as it rolled out new ideas and products. Largely part of the millennial demographic, social media fans were also comprised of teens, baby boomers, and the like. In addition, known for their short attention spans, demand for mobile optimized content, attraction to digital interaction, and desire for immediate responses this group presented Dairy Queen with opportunities and challenges. They wanted value, convenience, palate satisfaction, and ease of access.

Dairy Queen owners (primary intervening public): Because all Dairy Queen locations were locally owned and operated as franchises, owners were both a primary and intervening public. Post-2012, Dairy Queen needed to reenergize this public's trust of and faith in the company as capable of sustaining their long-term success. In addition, the brand also had to convince owners of the value inherent in any new initiatives that it wanted to offer fans. Consistency of brand promise and fan communication was at stake.

Messages

Primary

Current fans: (1) We value you, our fans. (2) You are part of the DQ brand. (3) We want you to participate with us. (4) We're more than just treats. We're quality food all year round, too.

Prospective and future fans: (1) We've got something for everyone. (2) Value meals and healthy menu options are plenty. (3) Don't believe us. Believe our fans. (4) Check out our quality foods and compare them to our competitors' options.

Value-seeking lunch crowd: (1) You spoke; we listened. (2) We make it easy to eat lunch with us. (3) Dessert is included.

Groups brought together through common participation or goals, such as organized athletic, service, civic, philanthropic, etc., groups: (1) We're still here committed to you. (2) We still support our hometowns.

Social media fans: (1) We've come to you. (2) Follow, like, or find us via your preferred social media channel; we're there! (3) We're mobile optimized and make communication easy. (4) Participate with us.

Dairy Queen owners (primary and intervening): (1) We've listened to you and have a plan to secure your DQ futures. (2) Fan Food, Not Fast Food is good for all of us.

Secondary

Current fans: (1) We listen to you. (2) We're committed to you. (3) We're your hometown QSR. (4) We meet you where you are at. (5) Don't believe us. Believe other fans. (6) We reward our fans.

Prospective and future fans: (1) You'll want to be our fan. (2) We reward our fans. (4) We listen to our fans.

Value-seeking lunch crowd: (1) Healthy choices can be made with us. (2) Compare our value lunches to those offered by our competitors. (3) Join our fan base.

Groups brought together through common participation or goals, such as organized athletic, service, civic, philanthropic, etc., groups: (1) Fans of teams, fans of ours. (2) We're still a fan of the little guy.

Social media fans: (1) Join our fan base. (2) We reward our fans. (3) You speak. We'll listen.

Dairy Queen owners (primary and intervening): (1) We can't do it without you. (2) You are our future.

Strategies

1. Changed the way Dairy Queen brought innovation to market to make it relevant to current customer demands and appetites.[1,2,4,9,11,13,14] (Supported objectives 1, 2, 5, 6)
2. Backed market decisions with in-depth data market analyses and projections.[4] (Supported objectives 1, 2, 5)
3. Reframed customers as "fans" who eat fan food (and treats), not "fast food." Built everything under the "Fan Food, Not Fast Food" message.[4,10,11,20] (Supported objectives 1, 2, 3, 4, 5, 6)
4. Positioned quality food options (healthy ones included) to appeal to Dairy Queen fans.[4,6,9,11,26] (Supported objectives 1, 2, 4, 6)
5. Appealed to value-driven fans and fan friends in innovative ways.[4] (Supported objectives 1, 2, 4, 6)
6. Highlighted food, as well as treats, in ways that invited new perspectives of enjoyment.[9,10] (Supported objectives 1, 2)
7. Complemented traditional efforts with digital approaches.[4,10] (Supported objectives 1, 2, 3, 4, 5, 6)
8. Highlighted Dairy Queen as a year-round hometown QSR, not just a warmer-weather-ice-cream destination.[2] (Supported objectives 1, 2, 3, 4, 5, 6)

Tactics

- Launched the "Fan Food, Not Fast Food" campaign via television, radio, print, and social media. Strategically featured fans speaking to fans, fans having fun, quality food items, and traditional sweets.[9–12,20]
- Committed to a 12-month advertising schedule.[5]
- Simplified the Blazier to Grill & Chill conversion process (reimaging and remodeling as well).[9,13]
- Debuted the $5 Buck Lunch, including a dessert (a sundae), that was available for purchase from 11 a.m. to 4 p.m. in 2013. This gave fans the quality

product they already knew for a value price; in addition, the included sundae could be upgraded to a small Blizzard for $1.[4,9,10,13,27] (Supported strategies 2, 5, 7, 8)

- Launched the dqcakes.com ecommerce site in 2014.[4,13] (Supported strategies 1, 7)
- Leveraged Orange Julius menu available at all locations to appeal to health-conscious and prospective fans, used humor when possible. Encouraged Julius League fan club participation.[4] (Supported strategies 1, 2, 6, 7)
- Introduced more value-added incentives such as year-long Blizzard promotions. Rewarded Blizzard Fan Club members. (Supported strategies 2, 3, 7, 8)
- Took better advantage of Orange Julius®—promotions poking fun at competitors' fake fruit products while highlighting the "real" fruit nature of Orange Julius products.[4] (Supported strategies 3, 4, 6)
- Began offering DQ Bakes turkey and grilled chicken wraps in 2015 as even healthier menu alternatives.[1,6] (Supported strategies 4, 8)
- A weather.com partnership was established to allow Dairy Queen to send out BOGO treat coupons to areas with temperatures 6 or more degrees above or below normal temperatures.[4] (Supported strategies 1, 2, 7)
- Created and implemented advertising spots highlighting fans enjoying Dairy Queen food, specifically 5 Buck Lunches with soft serve desserts included. This allowed fans to recruit fans while profiling the quality food available to them. Also posted ads to Dairy Queen YouTube channel.[4,10,11] (Supported strategies 1, 3, 5, 6, 7, 8)
- Creation and use of hashtag #LOVEmyDQ.[10] (Supported strategies 1, 7)
- Introduced "Fanniversary" in 2015 to commemorate its own anniversary. Continued Children's Miracle Network Hospitals partnership and gave away free soft serve cones while accepting CMNH donations from fans.[18] (Supported strategies 1, 3, 8)
- Created and implemented a new "brand anthem" through advertising spots.[10,12] (Supported strategies 1, 6, 8)
- Changed treat special offerings from summer only to all year long, including Blizzard of the Month, $5 Buck Lunches, and Happy Hour.[6]
    o Established marketing strategy guaranteeing that region-specific, BOGO Blizzard treat coupons were sent to Blizzard Fans when temperatures dipped 60 or more below normal.[4] (Supported strategies 2, 3, 5, 7, 8)
- In 2014, Dairy Queen began using geotargeting to send messages to consumers who had been at a McDonald's parking lot within the last five days, sending them a $5 Buck Lunch coupon.[4,13] (Supported strategies 1, 2, 7)

- Dairy Queen launched new Blizzard flavors via a #BlizzardBattle social media contest among fans beginning in September 2014. It featured a fan contest between #TeamApple or #TeamPumpkin.[13,15] (Supported strategies 1, 2, 6, 7)
- Regularly rewarded Blizzard Fan Club members through Blizzard of the Month/s. (Supported strategy 1)
- Invited fan feedback, contest participation, voting, etc., via all Dairy Queen social media channels.[16] (Supported strategies 1, 2, 3, 4, 5, 6, 7, 8)
- In 2016 Dairy Queen launched an Instagram campaign as a means of building Dairy Queen's Instagram presence and take advantage of the lack of dessert representation in the Instagram space.[16] (Supported strategies 1, 2, 6, 7)

Timeline

- 2012—December 2016
- 2012—Dairy Queen's EVP and market research allocation changes took place.
- 2013 (June)—Dairy Queen's "Fan Food, Not Fast Food" brand position balancing tradition and innovation launched.
- 2013—12-month advertising schedule launched.
- 2013—value meal launched.
- 2013—Concerted social media strategies undertaken and sustained.

Budget

- Initiative and goal appropriate.

Evaluation

In process

- Same-store sales increased by significant percentage points in the US, especially at Chill & Grill conversions.[2,6,9,13] Some domestic sales increased in 2014 by 7.5%.[2,5]
- Grill & Chill seemed to resonate well with fans, more so than Brazier.[5]
- Dairy Queen fans indicated through social media that they wanted the $5 Buck Lunch deal extended to all open hours at Grill & Chill stores. Dairy Queen listened and did so beginning in October 2016, #5BuckFreedom.[21]
- Dairy Queen grew its social media fan base exponentially from September 2013 to 2014. Facebook followers grew by more than 1 million to 9.2

million. Twitter followers increased by nearly 180K, from nearly 60,000 to 240,000.[4]

- Dairy Queen anticipated nearly 80,000 votes from its first #BlizzardBattle, but received more than 800,000 contest votes. Fan participation was an overwhelming success. In addition, the battle garnered attention from AdWeek, Nation's Restaurant News, Newsweek, People, and one local television station.[13,15]
- Between June 2013 and February 2015, the brand saw a 116% increase in social likes, an 80% increase in brand-related social comments, and a 77% increase boost in social shares.[4,13]
- By 2015, dqcakes.com accounted for more than 40% of cake orders.[4,13]
- Nearly 25% of consumers who were geotargeted and received $5 Buck Lunch coupons visited a Dairy Queen within two weeks of coupon receipt.[4]
- Since the June 2013 "Fan Food, Not Fast Food" launch, the brand was profitable 6 out of the last 7 quarters up through February 2015, with the unprofitable quarter explained as the result of extreme low weather temperatures across store locations.[4,13]
- International Dairy Queen (IDQ) ranked 16th among restaurant franchises in 2014, according to Franchise Times' numbers. DQ ranked 19th among restaurant franchisers, according to QSR Magazine rankings in its August 2014 Top 50 report.[5]
- Annual sales reached $4.1 billion in 2014.[5]
- In 2015, Grill & Chill restaurants comprised nearly one third of US stores and owners were operating successfully in big city markets like New York.[9,14,26]
- In 2015, some franchisees experienced double digit sales growth, largely on the food side.[5,6]
- Voluntarily introduced across time in various locations by Dairy Queen owners, in 2015 fans were found to really enjoy the Blizzard "Upside Down or Free," promise. In fact, they expected it across all locations, but owners still had the option to "opt out."[4,13,19]

Summative

- Dairy Queen's recent fan research showed that its $5 Buck deal was viewed as the best value consumers could find in the QSR category.[21]
- Balanced tradition and innovation, such as retained enthusiasm around the Blizzard treat favorite while increasing fan support through non-traditional channels such as social media interaction were achieved.[9,13]

- Dairy Queen fans were so engaged by 2017 that the brand was mentioned every 18 seconds on social media.[4]
- In March 2017, internet site numbers revealed the following: Dairy Queen Facebook followers totaled nearly 10.5 million, Twitter followers totaled more than 427K, its recent Instagram success was marked by more than 265K followers, YouTube subscribers totaled nearly 7.5K, Blizzard Fan Club members totaled more than 4.3 million and Julius League fans totaled 18K.
- Dairy Queen's social media fan base let it begin marketing products almost exclusively via social media and net sales responses that historically only occurred following large-scale national television advertising.[13]
- In spring 2015, with the support of its owners, Dairy Queen rolled out the guarantee of "Upside Down or Free" across all Dairy Queen locations. The website www.upsidedownorfree.com was dedicated to this commitment. The all store commitment brought consistency across the organization to a very popular brand promise.[4,28]
- Since 2010, Dairy Queen has been able to continue its US and international new store expansion, growing from 5,700 stores in 19 countries, including 652 locations outside the US and Canada to more than 6,700 at the end of 2017, including more than 1,400 stores in 27 countries outside the US and Canada.[3,9]
- The 2016 Instagram campaign reached more than 20 million people and drove ad recall among 25–24 year olds by 18 points, an 8-point increase in awareness of Dairy Queen's "Upside Down or Free" promotion, and facilitated a 3-point increase in purchase intent.[29]
- Dairy Queen announced in December 2016 that it had plans to develop 50 Grill & Chill locations in Korea over the next five years.[25]
- By year end 2016, franchises were characterized through internal research as trustful of the company, re-energized, and team-oriented.[5,9]
- Technomic named Dairy Queen the brand to beat in the limited service restaurant frozen dessert category. Dairy Queen owned nearly half of the frozen desserts industry in 2015, outselling its closest competitor by nearly $3 million.[30]

Notes

1. About Us. (n.d.). Retrieved March 31, 2017 from https://www.dairyqueen.com/us-en/Company/About-Us.

2. Patton, L. (November 5, 2015). Warren Buffett's ice cream chain looks to fix its winter problem. *Bloomberg News*. Retrieved February 15, 2017 from https://www.bloomberg.com/news/articles/2015-11-05/warren-buffett-s-ice-cream-chain-looks-to-fix-its-winter-problem.

3. Curran, J. (June 2016). *IBISWorld*. Industry Report OD5547: Ice cream & gelato store franchises in the US. Retrieved March 30, 2017 from http://clients1.ibisworld.com.cyrano.ucmo.edu:2048/reports/us/industry/default.aspx?entid=554.

4. Schiff, A. (February 6, 2015). Dairy Queen: "We don't have customers, we have fans." *Ad Exchanger*. Retrieved February 15, 2017 from https://adexchanger.com/advertiser/dairy-queen-we-dont-have-customers-we-have-fans.

5. Rebeck, G. (May 29, 2015). Dairy Queen is out to become the world's best-performing fast-food chain. *Minneapolis Post*. Retrieved February 14, 2017 from https://www.minnpost.com/twin-cities-business/2015/05/dairy-queen-out-become-world-s-best-performing-fast-food-chain.

6. Hughlett, M. (August 22, 2015). DQ bakes is Dairy Queen's largest-ever menu expansion: Soft serve purveyor hopes lineup of baked goods will broaden its appeal. *Star Tribune*. Retrieved February 14, 2017 from http://www.startribune.com/dq-bakes-is-dairy-queen-s-largest-ever-menu-expansion/322550051.

7. referenceUSA. (n.d.). International Dairy Queen. Retrieved March 30, 2017 from http://www.referenceusa.com.cyrano.ucmo.edu:2048/UsBusiness/Detail/Tagged/f9da751994b34d85b3355198a3612780?recordId=850741273.

8. LexisNexis Company Dossier. (n.d.). Snapshot: International Dairy Queen. Retrieved March 30, 2017 from http://www.lexisnexis.com.cyrano.ucmo.edu:2048/hottopics/lnacademic/?

9. Maze, J. (September 29, 2014). Dairy Queen's revival beyond ice cream. *Franchise Times*. Retrieved from http://www.franchisetimes.com/October-2014/Dairy-Queens-revival-beyond-ice-cream.

10. Brandau, M. (May 21, 2013). Dairy Queen to debut new ad campaign: Theme of advertisements is "Fan food, not fast food." *Nation's Restaurant News*. Retrieved February 15, 2016 from http://www.nrn.com/advertising/dairy-queen-debut-new-ad-campaign.

11. Gregory, J. (August 2013). From Fast Food to Fan Food: Dairy Queen's new ad campaign puts the spotlight on something other than ice cream. *QSR Magazine*. Retrieved February 15, 2017 from https://www.qsrmagazine.com/promotions/fast-food-fan-food.

12. Morrison, M. (May 21, 2013). Dairy Queen effort reaches beyond the blizzard to burgers and fries: Campaign aims to change behavior of fans who visit primarily for ice cream. *Advertising Age*. Retrieved February 15, 2017 from http://adage.com/article/news/dairy-queen-thinks-blizzard-campaign/241602.

13. O'Dell, P. (February 9, 2015). DQ's marketing to "fans," not "customers," pays off. *Chief Marketer*. Retrieved February 13, 2017 from http://www.chiefmarketer.com/ddqs-marketing-fans-customers-pays.

14. Dairy Queen boosts beverage sales. (November 1, 2009). Dairy Queen boosts beverage sales with Happy Hour drink deals. *QSRweb*. Retrieved February 15, 2017 from https://www.qsrweb.com/articles/dairy-queen-boosts-beverage-sales-with-happy-hour-drink-deals.

15. Collins, L. (November 5, 2014). Anatomy of an ad campaign: Dairy Queen's blizzard battle. *Kansas City Business Journal*. Retrieved February 15, 2017 from https://www.

bizjournals.com/kansascity/news/2014/11/05/anatomy-of-an-ad-campaign-dairy-queen-barkley.html.

16. 2013 Harris Poll EquiTrend®. (2013). Retrieved February 14, 2017 from http://www.theharrispoll.com/equitrend-rankings/2013/#2013-Quick-Service-Restaurant.

17. Building value with social media. (March 13, 2013). Building value with social media campaigns: Cinnabon, Dairy Queen share successful case studies. *Nation's Restaurant News.* Retrieved February 14, 2017 from http://www.nrn.com/archive/building-value-social-media-campaigns.

18. Dairy Queen celebrates $100 million in donations. (August 5, 2014). The Dairy Queen system celebrates $100 million in donations and a 30 year partnership with Children's Miracle Network Hospitals®. Retrieved February 16, 2017 from http://dairyqueen.com/us-en/News.

19. First ever Orange Julius national television. (April 29, 2013). First ever Orange Julius® national television commercial kicks off today. Retrieved February 16, 2017 from http://dairyqueen.com/us-en/News.

20. Fan food not fast food campaign kickoff. (May 23, 2013). The Dairy Queen system kicks off summer with new national campaign. Retrieved February 16, 2017 from http://dairyqueen.com/us-en/News.

21. DQ hits the magic price point. (March 29, 2013). DQ hits the magic price point with $5 buck lunch. *QRS Magazine.* Retrieved February 16, 2017 from https://www.qsrmagazine.com/news/dq-hits-magic-price-point-5-buck-lunch.

22. Frederick, C. (February, 8, 2017). QRS: Can baby boomers save the fast-food industry? *1851 Franchise.* Retrieved February 17, 2017 from http://1851franchise.com/details/10094/QSR-Can-Baby-Boomers-Save-the-Fast-Food-Industry.

23. National advertising campaign. (April 5, 2012). The Dairy Queen system rolls out national advertising campaign. Retrieved February 16, 2017 from http://dairyqueen.com/us-en/News.

24. Parks, J. & Parker, S. (June 3, 2013). QSR insights: 3 reasons why brands should join Tumblr. *QSR Insights.* Retrieved February 15, 2017 from http://www.qsrinsights.com/2013/06/3-reasons-why-qsr-brands-should-join-tumblr.

25. McAloon, C. (June 27, 2016). Technomic names Dairy Queen the brand to beat in the limited service restaurant frozen dessert category. *1851 Franchise.* Retrieved February 14, 2017 from http://dairyqueen.1851franchise.com/details/5048/Technomic-Names-Dairy-Queen-The-Brand-To-Beat-In-The-Limited-Service-Restaurant-Frozen-Dessert-Category.

26. Pace, G. (May 23, 2014). Eats beat: Dairy Queen to rule NYC. *New York Daily News.* Retrieved February 15, 2017 from http://www.nydailynews.com/life-style/eats/eats-beat-new-york-city-restaurant-news-sunday-25-article-1.1802028.

27. Value Meal Launch. (March 27, 2013). The Dairy Queen system launches value lunch. Retrieved February 16, 2017 from http://dairyqueen.com/us-en/News.

28. Upside down. (March 30, 2015). DQ brand invites America to get upside down and reach 20 million blizzard treat flips. Retrieved February 16, 2017 from http://dairyqueen.com/us-en/News.

29. Ord, R. (February 2, 2017). Restaurants creating crave on Instagram. *WebProNews*. Retrieved February 15, 2017 from http://www.webpronews.com/restaurants-creating-crave-instagram-2017-02.

30. Holman, J. & Chiglinsky, K. (December 20, 2016). Buffet's Dairy Queen to expand into Korea, open 50 stores. *Bloomberg Markets*. Retrieved February 15, 2017 from https://www.bloomberg.com/news/articles/2016-12-20/buffett-s-dairy-queen-to-expand-into-korea-open-50-locations.

Index

W

Z